BASIC BIBLE DOCTRINES

OF THE CHRISTIAN FAITH

HOMOSEXUALITY
The BIBLE and the CHRISTIAN

Edward D. Andrews

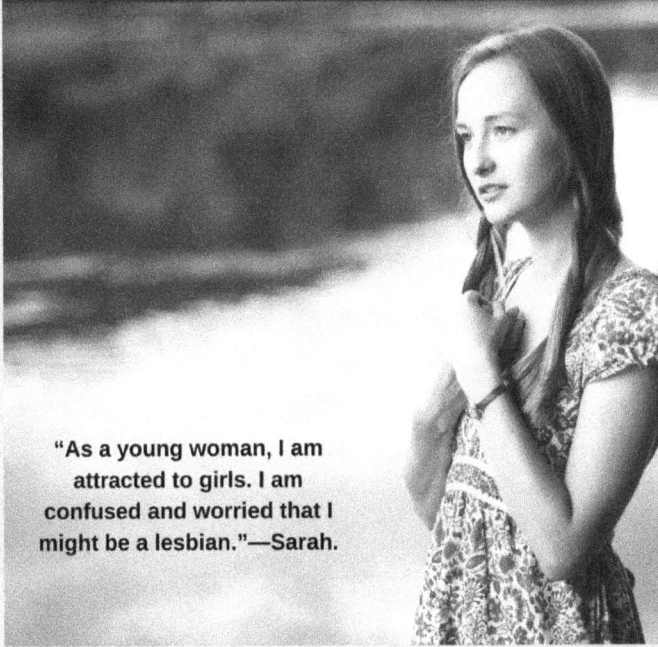

"As a young woman, I am attracted to girls. I am confused and worried that I might be a lesbian."—Sarah.

HOMOSEXUALITY
The BIBLE and the CHRISTIAN

Basic Bible Doctrines of the Christian Faith

Edward D. Andrews

Christian Publishing House

Cambridge, Ohio

Unless otherwise stated, scripture quotations are from *The Holy Bible, Updated American Standard Version (UASV)®*, copyright © 2016 by Christian Publishing House, Professional Conservative Christian Publishing of the Good News!

HOMOSEXUALITY The BIBLE and the CHRISTIAN Basic Bible Doctrines of the Christian Faith by Christian Publishing House

ISBN-13: 978-0692702345

ISBN-10: 0692702342

Table of Contents

PREFACE

Today there are many questions about homosexuality as it relates to the Bible and Christians. What does the Bible say about homosexuality? Does genetics, environment, or traumatic life experiences justify homosexuality? What is God's will for people with same-sex attractions? Does the Bible discriminate against people with same-sex attractions? Is it possible to abstain from homosexual acts? Should not Christians respect all people, regardless of their sexual orientation? Did not Jesus preach tolerance? If so, should not Christians take a permissive view of homosexuality? Does God approve of same-sex marriage? Does God disapprove of homosexuality? If so, how could God tell someone who is attracted to people of the same sex to shun homosexuality, is that not cruel? If one has same-sex attraction, is it possible to avoid homosexuality? How can I as a Christian explain the Bible's view of homosexuality? IT IS CRUCIAL that Christians always be prepared to reason from the Scriptures, explaining and proving what the Bible does and does not say about homosexuality, yet doing it with gentleness and respect. Andrews will answer these questions and far more.

Chapter 1 The Bible's Viewpoint of Homosexuality is the only chapter that will have to take on the graphic nature of the subject of homosexuality. It will not use foul language but will have to talk about these acts openly, as does the Word of God itself. The Scriptures do not dodge dealing with this subject, nor shall we in our efforts to give our read exactly what The Bible's Viewpoint of Homosexuality is.

CHAPTER 1 The Bible's Viewpoint of Homosexuality

The USA has the only large mainstream church ever to consecrate an openly gay bishop (Gene Robinson), the Episcopal Church in the United States of America. A vast majority voted in an openly gay pastor of the biggest Evangelical Lutheran Church in Saint Paul, MN (Bradley Schmeling), as the senior pastor. The Presbyterian Church (U.S.A.) is now allowing openly gay men and women in same-sex relationships to be ordained as clergy.

The issue is so divisive that it has split major denomination in half. Those who see somebody who is sexually involved with members of his or her own sex, as being just an alternative lifestyle, and acceptable as a church member or pastor, while the other side sees it as contrary to nature, and not acceptable for a church member, let alone a pastor, or bishop. Both sides use God's Word as a means of saying that their position is biblical. However, the law of noncontradiction helps us appreciate it is impossible for same-sex couples, who are actively in a sexual relationship to be both biblical and not biblical. In other words, someone is wrong in his or her interpretation of Scripture.

Some who support the right for church members, pastors, and bishops to be actively involved sexually with a person of the same sex, will argue,

I believe God made us all in His image; He did not make a mistake. We love whom we love, because God wants us to.

In making this comment, the supporters are thinking of the following text as their support,

Genesis 1:27 Updated American Standard Version (UASV)

[27] So God created man in his own image, in the image of God he created him; male and female he created them.

First, it should be noted that Genesis 1:27 is informing us of when Adam and Eve were perfect and had not yet rebelled, bringing sin (missing the mark of perfection into the world). God made Adam and Eve perfect but gave them free will that they could willfully choose to abuse and abuse they did. Once they were expelled from the Garden, inherited sin was passed on from generation to generation. Of course, the preflood generations all lived close to 1,000 years. To mention but a few of the preflood people and their lifespan, we read that all the days that Adam lived were 930 years, all the days of Seth were 912 years, all the days of Methuselah were 969 years. If we consider the progression after the flood, we will notice a dramatic drop in lifespans. Shem, who came through the flood, lived 600 years. (Gen 11:10, 11) Peleg lived 239 years. Abraham was born 352 years after the flood and died at the age of 175. Moses four generations later would live to 120 years of age.

After the flood, the lifespans of those who survived the flood to the other side, and postflood people, dropped drastically. This could be because the floodwaters that fell from the heavens had served as a shield in the heavens before their falling, protecting the people from the harmful radiation that would have increased without such protection. In addition, it must be remembered that preflood people were closer to perfect, and this is why they lived longer lives. A prayer of Moses, the man who penned the book of Genesis in the latter part of the sixteenth century B.C.E. under inspiration, spoke of a time, "As for the days of our years, within them are seventy years or if by strength eighty years, and their pride is trouble and disaster, for it passes quickly and we fly away." (Ps. 90:10, LEB) Today, science can actually do genetic screening, DNA analysis for medical purposes: the analysis of DNA samples of a group of people carried out in order to find out whether they carry the genes associated with specific **inherited diseases** or disorders. We have inherited diseases and mental disorders that can even skip generations, which affect us all because we are imperfect, unlike Adam and Eve. "... Sin came into the world through one man, and death through sin, and so death spread to all men because all sinned." – Romans 5:12.

What does the Bible say about Homosexuality? What does it say about same-sex marriage? What does it say about same-sex attraction? Is it a sin to be homosexually active? If it is a sin, then why does homosexuality exist? Is God just being unfair, or is it more complicated than that? Before going on, it might be good to qualify some terms. Many people dealing with same-sex attraction find the word homosexual offensive, because to them, it implies one who is sexually active with a person of the same sex. We must admit there are those who struggle with same-sex attraction but realize that the Bible condemns such activity, so they must constantly work to maintain control over themselves.

Baker *Encyclopedia of Psychology and Counseling* says "'Homosexuality' means 'same or like sexuality' and derives from the Greek word *homoitas* (likeness, similarity, or agreement). Sexuality is the God-given drive in every person toward wholeness and includes emotional, cognitive, psychological, and spiritual dimensions. This drive is expressed in adult human beings emotionally through intimate communications, physically through touching, and genitally through foreplay and the act of sexual intercourse. Sexuality and spirituality are interrelated in complex and multifaceted ways.

A homosexual orientation is to be distinguished from a homosexual act. A homosexual act is any sexual activity between two individuals of the same gender. A homosexual orientation describes an individual whose sexual drive is directed toward an individual of the same gender. Thus a homosexual orientation involves emotional attractions toward the same gender and may or may not involve homosexual acts. Most sociologists agree that the concept of homosexual orientation was not present in the culture of biblical times (Greenberg, 1988). Most evangelical psychologists believe that most individuals who own a homosexual orientation have not made an initial choice to direct their sexuality toward their own gender." (Benner and Hill 1985, 1999, 572)

Thus, out of respect for our brothers and sisters, who are struggling with same-sex attraction, and find the term homosexual repulsive when applied to those who struggle with same-sex attraction, we will just stick with the phrase same-sex attraction,

4

and qualify whether we are referring to sexually active or inactive. Before moving on, let us take a moment to consider how we came to be in this fallen imperfect condition.

Human Rebellion Excursion

It was God's intention that his first couple, Adam, and Eve, were to procreate, and cultivate the Garden of Eden until it covered the entire earth, filled with perfect humans worshipping him. – Genesis 1:28

If the first couple had not rebelled, they and their offspring could have lived forever. – Genesis 2:15-17

One of the angels in heaven (who became Satan), abused his free will (James 1:14-15), chose to rebel against God, and he used a lowly serpent to contribute to Adam and Eve abusing their free will, and disobeying God, believing they did not need him, and could walk on their own. – Genesis 3:1-6; Job 1-2.

God removed the rebellious Adam and Eve from the Garden of Eden (Gen 3:23-24) The first human couple had children, but they all grew old and eventually died (Gen. 3:19; Rom 5:12), just as the animals died. – Ecclesiastes 3:18-20

Genesis 6:5 (AT) tells us just before the flood of Noah, that "the wickedness of man on earth was great, and the whole bent of his thinking was never anything but evil." After the flood, God said of man, "the bent of man's mind may be evil from his very youth." (Gen 8:21, AT) Jeremiah 10:23 tells us "that it is not in man who walks to direct his steps." Jeremiah 17:9 says that "The heart is deceitful above all things, and desperately sick; who can understand it?" Yes, man was not designed to walk on his own. However, man was also not designed with absolute free will, but free will under the sovereignty of his Creator. Imperfect man is mentally bent toward wickedness, fleshly desires, to which Satan has set up this world, so it caters to the fallen flesh. "For all that is in the world, the desires of the flesh and the desires of the eyes and pride of life, is not from the Father but is from the world."—1 John 2:16.

Getting back to Genesis 1:27 that says, "God created man in his own image, in the image of God he created him; male and female he created them," meaning that man is born with a moral nature, which creates within him a conscience that reflects God's moral values. (Rom. 2:14-15) It acts as a moral law within us. However, it has an opponent as fallen man also possesses the "law of sin," 'missing the mark of perfection,' the natural desire toward wickedness. Listen to the internal battle of the apostle Paul. – Romans 6:12; 7:22-23.

Romans 7:21-23 Updated American Standard Version (UASV)

[21] I find then the law in me that when I want to do right, that evil is present in me. [22] For I delight in the law of God according to the inner man, [23] but I see a different law in my members, warring against the law of my mind [Paul's desire to obey God's law] and taking me captive in the law of sin [what wars against the law of his mind] which is in my members.

> Here Paul uses the law motif to illustrate from another angle the conflict he experiences. Two laws are mentioned: **the law of my mind** (his desire to obey God's law), and **the law of sin** (that which wars against the law of his mind). He states a principle by which these two laws conflict with one another: **when I want to do good, evil is right there with me**. All of us can identify with the apostle's succinct summary of the spiritual experience.

> Not only Paul, but all believers, have "left undone those things which we ought to have done." And as the Anglican confession rightly concludes ("there is no health in us"), Paul is about to explode with his own spiritual diagnosis.[1]

However, there is hope,

Romans 7:24-25 Updated American Standard Version (UASV)

[24] Wretched man that I am! Who will deliver me from this body of death? [25] Thanks be to God through Jesus Christ our Lord!

---

[1] (Boa and Kruidenier, Holman New Testament Commentary: Romans, Vol. 6 2000, 231)

So then, I myself serve the law of God with my mind, but with my flesh, I serve the law of sin.

One of the results of the gospel is that it delivers us from the condemnation of the law. "Of what use then is the Law? To lead us to Christ, the Truth—to waken in our minds a sense of what our deepest nature, the presence, namely, of God *in* us, requires of us—to let us know, in part by failure, that the purest efforts of will of which we are capable cannot lift us up even to the abstaining from wrong to our neighbor" (George MacDonald, in Lewis, p. 20).

The law did its perfect work in the apostle Paul, reviving his soul (Ps. 19:7a). It convicted him of his sin and showed him that the only deliverance for him was Jesus Christ. No wonder Paul could call the law a "tutor to lead us to Christ, that we may be justified by faith" (Gal. 3:24, NASB). That is exactly what the law did for him. Once delivered from the law, Paul was able to serve the ends of the law—righteousness—in the power of the Holy Spirit (Rom. 7:6).

Paul summarizes the entire chapter—the conflict of the believer that causes him or her to remain dependent upon the Spirit—in the final verse. When it is Paul the believer talking, he makes himself a **slave to God's law**. But when his sinful capacity speaks out, he is **a slave to the law of sin**. As mentioned in this chapter earlier, it is a shame that chapter divisions in our Bibles cause us to "stop" at certain points in the consideration of the text. While this is a logical point in the flow of Paul's thought for a pause, Romans 7 and 8 should be read together. Immediately, Paul moves from wretchedness to victory in declaring that the law of the Spirit of life in Christ Jesus has set him "free from the law of sin and death" (Rom. 8:2). The gospel is indeed good news, delivering the believer from death by law to life by grace through the Spirit.[2]

---

[2] IBID., 232

From the Old Person to the New Person

The apostle Paul wrote,

1 Corinthians 2:14 Updated American Standard Version (UASV)

[14] But the natural man does not accept the things of the Spirit of God, for they are foolishness to him, and he is not able to understand them, because they are examined spiritually.

This does not in and of itself mean, that the unbeliever cannot understand God's Word, as they can. Rather, some unbelievers see it as foolish; therefore, they reject it and refuse to apply it in their lives. What we are addressing is what Paul meant by natural man. This is one with no spiritual life, in that he follows the desires of his fallen flesh, setting aside God and his Word as mere foolishness. Paul informs us of hope that these unbelievers fail to find.

Ephesians 4:23 Updated American Standard Version (UASV)

[23] and to be renewed in the spirit of your minds,

We are **to be made new in the attitude of our minds**. How? You are what you think. You move in the direction of what you put into your mind and what you allow your mind to dwell on. So if you are not what you want to be, then you must begin to think differently. If you are to think differently, you must put into your mind that which you want to become. If you do, the Holy Spirit will use it to change you to become what you want to be. If you don't, you will never be what you want to be. It all depends on what you put into your mind. This is what it means to be made new in the attitude of your mind.[3]

Paul goes on to say,

Ephesians 4:24 Updated American Standard Version (UASV)

---

[3] (Anders, Holman New Testament Commentary: vol. 8, Galatians, Ephesians, Philippians, Colossians 1999)

24 and put on the new man, the one created according to the likeness of God in righteousness and loyalty of the truth.

We are **to put on the new self**. This means, we are to allow the new self to govern our activities. We are to begin living the lifestyle that corresponds to who we have become in Christ. This new holy self shows we are maturing, growing in unity with the body, and doing our part of the body's work.[4]

Colossians 3:9-10 Updated American Standard Version (UASV)

9 Do not lie to one another, seeing that you have put off the old man[5] with its practices **10** and have put on the new man[6] who is being renewed through accurate knowledge[7] according to the image of the one who created him,

Perverted passions, hot tempers, and sharp tongues are to be removed as part of the life-transformation process. These things, along with**[lying] to each other**, are not appropriate behavior for our new life in Christ. The remnants of the former lifestyle are to be discarded **since [we] have taken off [our] old self with its practices**. What is the **old self** (literally "old man") and the **new self** (literally "the new")? The "old man" refers to more than an individual condition ("sinful nature") and also has a corporate aspect. The corporate aspect of "the new" (man) is unmistakably seen in verse 11. What has been **put off** and what has been **put on?** Our former associations, the old humanity has been **put off**, and we now have a new association, the new community. As members of the new community, we are to conduct ourselves in ways which will enhance harmony in the community. Notice how the sins

---

[4] IBID.

[5] Or *old person*

[6] Or *new person*

[7] *Epignosis* is a strengthened or intensified form of *gnosis* (*epi*, meaning "additional"), meaning, "true," "real," "full," "complete" or "accurate," depending upon the context. Paul and Peter alone use *epignosis*.

mentioned in the previous verses disrupt community and damage human relationships.[8]

Romans 12:2 Updated American Standard Version (UASV)

[2] And do not be conformed to this world, but be transformed by the renewing of your mind, so that you may prove what the will of God is, that which is good and acceptable[9] and perfect.

In the beginning of a person's introduction to the good news, he will take in knowledge of the Scriptures (1 Tim. 2:3-4), which if his heart is receptive, he will begin to apply them in his life, taking off the old person and putting on the new person. (Eph. 4:22-24) Seeing how the Scriptures have begun to alter his life, he will start to have a genuine faith over the things that he has learned (Heb. 11:6), repenting of his sins. (Acts 17:30-31) He will turn around his life, and his sins will be blotted out. (Acts 3:19) At some point, he will go to the Father in prayer, telling him that he is dedicating his life to him, to carry out his will and purposes. (Matt. 16:24; 22:37) This regeneration is the Holy Spirit working in his life, giving him a new nature, placing him on the path to salvation. – 2 Corinthians 5:17. (Andrews 2013, 17)

Certainly, we may have thought this long excursion had us off in the weeds. However, it seemed important that the reader understands humanities fall into sin, and exactly what that means, so as to appreciate what is about to be said. Every physical, mental, and emotional issue that has fallen upon man is a direct result of our imperfection, something that God did not intend but has allowed to happen as an object lesson (See Chapter 8 – Why Has God Permitted Wickedness and Suffering). This means mental disorders like depression, bipolar, schizophrenia, anxiety disorder, obsessive-compulsive disorder, and so on are a result of inherited imperfection. This would also apply to persons who struggle with same-sex attraction.

---

[8] IBID., 330

[9] Or *well-pleasing*

Some argue that same-sex attraction is brought about through socialization. Somebody acquires a personality or traits through their background (nurture), impacted by family, friends, school, work, and so on. Others would argue that same sex attraction is brought about because one is genetically predisposed (nature).[10] We will take on the science of such an issue herein but not as a scientist.

Let me just say that it is likely a mixture of both. Let us take a young woman (true story),[11] who was in an abusive marriage, mentally, emotionally and physically. We will call her **Sandy**.[12] She had a very close friend (we will call **Cindy**), who also suffered from the ravages of an abusive husband. One night, after a very trying week, they find themselves alone, sitting on a couch, talking to each other as they watched a movie. Through tears and a broken heart, they unloaded as to just how bad it is. Soon, Sandy goes into an uncontrollable sob, so Cindy holds her in her arms, stroking her hair, comforting her with her soft voice. After a while, the sobbing stops, and Cindy brushes Sandy's tears away. Cindy then leans in and starts kissing Sandy, and Sandy does not pull away.

This begins a five-year same-sex relationship, until Sandy starts to feel wrong, and decides to return to her faith. In this true story, Sandy was not actually attracted to women; she did not have same-sex attraction (nurture). However, her childhood abuse, coupled with an extremely abusive husband, and a loving and comforting friend, led to her finding comfort in this relationship. Cindy on the other hand was and is a person that has same-sex attraction (nature). She entered the marriage with her husband because she was trying to avoid the stigma of being of the same-sex attraction. She went to the same Christian congregation as Sandy. Here could be a real-life case of one, who was socialized into the

---

[10] "A **genetic predisposition** (sometimes also called **genetic** susceptibility) is an increased likelihood of developing a particular disease based on a person's **genetic** makeup. A **genetic predisposition** results from specific **genetic** variations that are often inherited from a parent." – What does it mean to have a genetic predisposition to a ..., http://ghr.nlm.nih.gov/handbook/mutationsanddisorders/predisposition (accessed April 16, 2016).

[11] The account is true, but the names are changed.

[12] Names in this book have been changed.

11

same-sex relationship, and one that was genetically predisposed into a same-sex relationship.

This author would argue that the science is irrelevant to the Christian faith. Let us err on the side of those who say that, for some it is genetic, and they are predisposed toward same-sex attraction. If we concede this, it does nothing to remove the Bible's position on same-sex relationships. Remember, the Bible says that we are all mentally bent toward wickedness. What we should understand is that some lean toward different things in this mental bent and others lean heavily in other directions. By tentatively erring on this side of some being genetically predisposed, we can better help them, and better understand their struggles. Lastly, because we accept genetic predisposition, this does not exclude their gaining control over their body and mind, as well as they being able to take off the old person and put on the new person. Moreover, it does not exclude that many same-sex attraction cases are socialized.

What is the Bible's View of Homosexuality

What is said about homosexuality in the New Testament is grounded in what had already been said in the Old Testament. We have already discussed Genesis 1:26-27, which states that humans were made in the image of God. "The crowning point of creation, a living human, was made in God's image to rule creation. Our image . . . likeness. This speaks of the creation of Adam in terms that are uniquely personal. It establishes a personal relationship between God and man that does not exist with any other aspect of creation. It is the very thing that makes humanity different from every other created animal. It explains why the Bible places so much stress on God's hands-on creation of Adam. He fashioned this creature in a special way—to bear the stamp of His own likeness. It suggests that God was, in essence, the pattern for the personhood of man. The image of God is personhood, and personhood can function only in the context of relationships. Man's capacity for intimate, personal relationships needed fulfillment. Most important, man was designed to have a personal relationship with God. It is impossible to divorce this truth from the fact that man is an ethical creature. All true relationships have ethical ramifications. It is at this point that God's communicable attributes come into play. Man is a living being capable of embodying God's communicable attributes (cf. 9:6; Rom. 8:29; Col. 3:10; James 3:9). In his rational life, he was like God in that he could reason and had intellect, will, and emotion. In the moral sense, he was like God because he was good and sinless."[13]

Genesis 2:18-25 Updated American Standard Version (UASV)

[18] Then Jehovah God said, "It is not good for the man to be alone; I will make him a helper for him.[14] [19] And out of the ground Jehovah God formed every beast of the field, and every bird of the heavens; and brought them to the man to see what he would call them; and whatsoever the man called every living soul, that was its name. [20] And the man gave names to all cattle, and to the birds of the heavens, and to every beast of the field; but for man there was found no helper as a counterpart of him. [21] So Jehovah God caused a deep sleep to fall upon the man, and he slept; then he took one of his ribs and closed up the flesh at that place. [22] And the rib that Jehovah God had taken from the man he made into a woman and brought her to the man.

[23] Then the man said,

"This at last is bone of my bones
and flesh of my flesh;
she shall be called Woman,
because she was taken out of Man."

[24] Therefore a man shall leave his father and his mother and be joined to his wife, and they shall be as one flesh. [25] And the man and his wife were both naked and were not ashamed.

In Genesis 2:18–25 we find that there are physical differences between man and woman, yet God mat them compatible and complementary with one another. The man produces while the woman bears children, which is why we find Adam saying of Eve, "This at last is bone of my bones and flesh of my flesh," while God

---

[13] MacArthur, John (2005-05-09). *The MacArthur Bible Commentary* (Kindle Locations 1924-1933). Thomas Nelson. Kindle Edition.

[14] Lit., "as his opposite;" *counterpart or complement*, something that completes or perfects him

inspired Moses to say that "they [man and woman] shall be as one flesh." We find the foundation of how men and women were meant to be, a model, example, pattern, or standard as to their sexual relations. Therefore, God intended that marriage and sexual relations were/are to be between one man and one woman. Moreover, marriage and sexual relations between two persons of the same-sex would be contrary to God's personality, standards, ways, and will and purposes (sin) and contrary to nature.

Genesis 9:18-28 – If it is Ham that saw Noah's nakedness, why is Canaan the one getting cursed?

Genesis 9:18 Updated American Standard Version (UASV)

Prophecies about Descendants of Noah

[18] The sons of Noah who went forth from the ark were Shem, Ham, and Japheth. (Ham was the father of Canaan.) [19] These three were the sons of Noah, and from these the whole earth was scattered.[15]

[20] Noah began to be a man of the soil, and he planted a vineyard. [21] He drank of the wine and became drunk, and uncovered himself inside his tent. [22] And Ham, the father of Canaan, saw the nakedness of his father and told his two brothers outside. [23] Then Shem and Japheth took a garment, and laid it on both their shoulders, and walked backward and covered the nakedness of their father; and their faces were turned backward,[16] and they did not see their father's nakedness. [24] When Noah awoke from his wine,[17] he knew what his youngest son had done to him. [25] And he said,

"Cursed be Canaan;
a slave of slaves[18] shall he be to his brothers."

[26] He also said,

---

[15] I.e., *populated*

[16] I.e., *turned away*

[17] I.e., *drunkenness*

[18] Or *servant of servants*

"Blessed be Jehovah, the God of Shem;
and let Canaan be his slave.

27 "May God enlarge Japheth,
and let him dwell in the tents of Shem;
and let Canaan be his slave."

28 Noah lived three hundred and fifty years after the flood. 29 And all the days of Noah were nine hundred and fifty years, and he died.

Commenting on Genesis 9:24, which states that when Noah awoke from his wine he "got to know what his youngest son had done to him," a footnote in Rotherham's translation says, "Undoubtedly Canaan, and not Ham: Shem and Japheth, for their piety, are blessed; Canaan, for some unnamed baseness, is cursed; Ham, for his neglect, is neglected." Similarly, a Jewish publication, *The Pentateuch and Haftorahs*, suggests that the brief narrative "refers to some abominable deed in which Canaan seems to have been implicated." (Edited by J. H. Hertz, London, 1972, p. 34) In addition, after noting that the Hebrew word translated "son" in verse 24 may mean "grandson," this source states, "The reference is evidently to Canaan." The Soncino Chumash also points out that some believe Canaan "indulged a perverted lust upon [Noah]," and that the expression "youngest son" refers to Canaan, who was the youngest son of Ham. – Edited by A. Cohen, London, 1956, p. 47.

As is generally the case, context can clear the muddied waters, to see more clearly. We should mention here that there is no explicit evidence for the inference that we are about to suggest, so we are not being dogmatic about our understanding.

Genesis 9:18 Updated American Standard Version (UASV)

18 The sons of Noah who went forth from the ark were Shem, Ham, and Japheth. (Ham was the father of Canaan.)

One must ask why the account has an abrupt interruption here, with a parenthetical of introducing Canaan, before covering the drunkenness of Noah.

Genesis 9:22 Updated American Standard Version (UASV)

²² And Ham, the father of Canaan, saw the nakedness of his father and told his two brothers outside.

Here again, the account is pulling us back to Canaan. As the actions of Ham are being disclosed, the account goes out of its way to emphasize Canaan, saying "Ham, the father of Canaan." Both of these seem to imply that Canaan is an essential part of understanding the account.

We can accept that the expression "saw the nakedness of his father" as a means of expressing some kind of perversion or abuse on Noah by Canaan. If we turn to Leviticus, you will find that similar expressions are used in reference to sexual sins and incest. (Lev. 18:6-19; 20:17) Therefore, it is possible that Canaan committed some type of sexual abuse on the unconscious Noah, to which Ham had knowledge and did not take measures to prevent or discipline if it was after the fact. Worse still, he made this known to the brothers, which brought more embarrassment and shame on Noah.

Then, there is the matter of the curse itself. "Cursed be Canaan; a servant of servants shall he be to his brothers." (Gen. 9:25) There is no biblical evidence that Canaan was ever a servant to his uncles Shem or Japheth. However, we are dealing with Jehovah God, who possesses foreknowledge. Moreover, the curse is in the Word of God and thus shows that it was divinely inspired, and must therefore come true. We must keep in mind that God does not disfavor a person or people without a justifiable reason behind it. Is it possible that Canaan was already acting on some type of sinful leanings, such as same-sex attraction, and that Jehovah foresaw the outcome of that within the Canaanites, descendants of Canaan?

If we recall, Jehovah could read the heart-attitude of Cain, and had warned him of the results if he did not change his disposition. (Gen. 4:3-7) In addition, God was able to discern the level of wickedness that was to be in the preflood population. (Gen 6:5) Moreover, God was able to detect the genetic bent of the unborn Jacob and Esau, while they were still in the womb. – Genesis 25:23.

We see the justifiableness of God's curse on Canaan in the history of his descendants. They were so immoral that archaeologist that dug up their area was surprised that God had not destroyed them sooner. (Gen. 15:15-16) They too had a lust for the same sex. The Bible is right alongside secular history in exposing the sordid past of the Canaanites. The curse was fulfilled about eight centuries after Noah uttered the words when the Israelites conquered the land of Canaan. Later too, they would be subjected even further by the descendants of Japheth, by way of Medo-Persia, Greece, and Rome.

Leviticus 18:22 – Since "Christ is the end of the [Mosaic] law" (Rom. 10:4), does this include homosexuality?

Leviticus 18:22 Updated American Standard Version (UASV)

22 You shall not lie with a male as you lie down with a woman; it is an abomination.

The law against homosexuality is in the heart of the Mosaic Law, the book of Leviticus. This is the book of laws on the seriousness of sin and the importance of being holy. We know that the civil and ceremonial laws were done away with, as Jesus "canceled out the certificate of debt consisting of decrees against [the Israelites], which was hostile to [the Israelites]; and He has taken it out of the way, having nailed it to the cross." (Col. 2:13-14, NASB) Since the civil and ceremonial laws of the Old Testament were removed from the law of Christ[19] (Gal. 6:2), does this mean that they are not under any laws? No, as Jesus introduced "a new covenant," while 'making the first one obsolete,' based on his perfect human life. Christians are under this "new covenant" and are to be obedient to Christian laws. (Heb. 8:7-13; Lu 22:20) However, it must be remembered that many of the Christian Laws have been taken from the Mosaic Law. Christians are urged to "fulfill the law of Christ," as opposed to the civil and ceremonial

---

[19] "The **law of Christ**" (ὁ νόμος τοῦ Χριστοῦ) is a New Testament phrase found only in the Pauline Epistles at Galatians 6:2 and parenthetically (ἔννομος Χριστῷ "being under the **law** to **Christ**") at 1 Corinthians 9:21.

laws of the Hebrew Scriptures. (Gal. 6:2) Notice how Jesus took parts of the Mosaic Law and clarified the deeper sense of them.

"You Have Heard That It Was Said"

Matthew 5:17 Updated American Standard Version (UASV)

[17] Think not that I came to destroy the law or

Counsel on Anger

[21] "**You have heard that it was said** to the ancients, 'You shall not murder; and whoever murders will be liable to judgment.' [22] **But I say to you** that everyone who is angry with his brother will be liable to judgment; whoever says to his brother, 'You fool,'[20] will be brought before the Sanhedrin;[21] and whoever says, 'You fool!' will be liable to the fire of Gehenna.[22]

Counsel on Adultery

[27] "**You have heard that it was said**, 'You shall not commit adultery';[23] [28] **but I say to you** that everyone who looks at a woman with lust[24] for her has already committed adultery with her in his heart.

Counsel on Divorce

[31] "**It was said**, 'Whoever divorces his wife away, let him give her a certificate of divorce';[25] [32] **but I say to you** that everyone who divorces his wife, except on the ground of sexual immorality,

---

[20] Gr *Raca to*, an Aramaic term of contempt

[21] The Jewish supreme court, which held life and death over the people in ancient Jerusalem before 70 C.E.

[22] *geenna* 12x pr. *the valley of Hinnom*, south of Jerusalem, once celebrated for the horrid worship of Moloch, and afterwards polluted with every species of filth, as well as the carcasses of animals, and dead bodies of malefactors; to consume which, in order to avert the pestilence which such a mass of corruption would occasion, constant fires were kept burning–MCEDONTW

[23] Ex. 20:14; Deut. 5:17

[24] ἐπιθυμία [*Epithumia*] to strongly desire to have what belongs to someone else and/or to engage in an activity which is morally wrong–'to covet, to lust, evil desires, lust, desire.'– GELNTBSD

[25] Deut. 24:1

makes her commit adultery; and whoever marries a divorced woman commits adultery.

Counsel on Oaths

[33] "Again **you have heard that it was said** to those of old, 'You shall not swear falsely, but shall perform to the Lord what you have sworn.'[26] [34] **But I say to you**, Do not swear at all, either by heaven, for it is the throne of God, [35] or by the earth, for it is his footstool of his feet, or by Jerusalem, for it is the city of the great King. [36] Nor shall you make an oath by your head, for you cannot make one hair white or black. [37] But let your word 'yes' be 'yes,' and your 'no' be 'no'; anything more than this is from the evil one.

Counsel on Retaliation

[38] "**You have heard that it was said**, 'An eye for an eye, and a tooth for a tooth.'[27] [39] **But I say to you**, Do not resist the one who is evil; but whoever slaps you on your right cheek, turn the other to him also.

Counsel on Love of Enemies

[43] "**You have heard that it was said**, 'You shall love your neighbor[28] and hate your enemy.'[29] [44] **But I say to you**, love your enemies and pray for those who persecute you, [45] so that you may be sons of your Father who is in heaven

We notice that Jesus referred to parts of the Mosaic Law with the phrase "**You have heard that it was said.**" This was followed by a law or better yet the Pharisaical view[30] of that law, and then he closed with the phrase "**But I say to you.**" This was followed by a deeper understanding of the law, the moral value behind the law, the spirit behind the law. The deeper spirit behind the law will see continued anger as murder. The deeper spirit behind the law

---

[26] Lev. 19:12

[27] Ex. 21:24; Lev. 24:20

[28] Lev. 19:18

[29] A twisting of Deut. 23:3–6

[30] Pharisaical righteously obsessed with rules: acting with hypocrisy, self-righteousness, or obsessiveness with regard to the strict adherence to rules and formalities

will see continued lustful thinking as adultery. The deeper spirit behind the law will see divorcing over nothing as leading to adulterous remarriage. The deeper spirit behind the law will see tiresome-frivolous oaths to be pointless. The deeper spirit behind the law will see the wisdom of mildness over retaliation. The deeper spirit behind the law will see godly love that knows no bounds.

Finally, there are two important points to be made. First, Even though Christians are not under the Mosaic Law today, the divine principles behind them are still of great value to us because the spirit behind them will never change. Second, the moral laws of the Mosaic law were not done away with (nailed to the cross) because they are a part of God's character and are eternal. Just because the moral law, prohibiting homosexuality, is found in the book of Leviticus, where we also find many ceremonial laws, this does not mean that it too passed away.

If one argues that the moral law of homosexuality is to be removed because it is found in the book of Leviticus because much of the ceremonial and civil laws therein were abolished; they would have to argue against rape, incest, and bestiality as well. (Lev. 18:6-14, 22-23) In addition, we would have to abolish lying and theft (Lev. 19:11), oppressing your neighbor (Lev. 19:13), slandering your neighbor (19:16), hating your fellow man (Lev. 19:17), taking vengeance, nor bearing a grudge (Lev. 19:18), avoiding unjust balances (Lev. 19:36), sacrificing your children (Lev. 20:1-5), and committing adultery (Lev. 20:10). Moreover, Leviticus is quoted in the New Testament.

Leviticus	New Testament
Leviticus 19:2 Updated American Standard Version (UASV) 2 "Speak to all the congregation of the sons of Israel and say to them, 'You shall be holy, for I Jehovah your God am holy.	**1 Peter 1:16** Updated American Standard Version (UASV) 16 because it is written, "You shall be holy, for I am holy."

Leviticus 19:18 Updated American Standard Version (UASV)	**Matthew 22:39** Updated American Standard Version (UASV)
[18] You shall not take vengeance, nor bear any grudge against the sons of your people, but you shall love your neighbor as yourself; I am Jehovah.	[39] The second, like it, is this: 'You must love your neighbor as yourself.'
Leviticus 26:12 Updated American Standard Version (UASV)	**2 Corinthians 6:16** Updated American Standard Version (UASV)
[12] And I will also walk among you and be your God, and you shall be my people.	[16] And what agreement has the temple of God with idols? For we are the temple of the living God; just as God said, "I will dwell in them and I will walk among them, and I will be their God, and they shall be my people.

There can be no excuse that this moral law was only applicable to the Jewish people because it is applied to the Gentiles in Romans 1:26. Moreover, we just spoke of God condemning the Canaanites specifically for their homosexuality. (Gen. 18:1-3, 25) This moral law is specifically forbidden in the New Testament. – Romans 1:26-27; 1 Corinthians 6:9; 1 Timothy 1:10; and Jude 7.

The Bible and Sexuality [Excursion]

From the earliest times, God acknowledged the existence of and controlled the conduct of human sexuality. The sexual motivation comes from the inner nature of man, and it forms the drive to populate the earth (Gen. 1:28). Men and women can fulfill this mandate with the utmost fulfillment, provided they follow the teachings of the Bible on sexual conduct. Sarah even used the term pleasure to describe the sexual act (Gen. 18:12). God intended the physical union between man and woman to represent a holy intimacy, at times describing the very act as "knowing" the partner (Num. 31:17). Such knowledge assumes a deep personal connection between the husband and wife that extends far beyond the physical realm but includes the entire person.

God himself describes the sexual partners as forming "one flesh" (Gen. 2:24; Mark 10:7–8; Eph. 5:31). The man who engages a prostitute in intercourse becomes "one with her in body" (1 Cor. 6:16), a practice God commands us to "flee" lest we sin against our own bodies (1 Cor. 6:18). God intended the normal sexual function to include a commitment and love that went beyond sexual fulfillment.

The Old Testament required young women to remain virgins until marriage on penalty of death (Deut. 22:13–24). While God did not repeat the same restrictions for males, he implied it by prohibiting fornication (Exod. 22:16–17) and punishing it with varying penalties. Adultery was strictly forbidden, and this comprised one of the Ten Commandments (Exod. 20:14). God forbade any species of incest, physical unions between family members, although some people in the Bible ignored such warnings. Lot, seduced by his daughters into a drunken stupor, lost his powers of judgment and impregnated them (Gen. 19:30–38). Reuben slept with his father Jacob's concubine (Gen. 35:22), and Judah had relations with his daughter-in-law Tamar (Gen. 38).

Jesus and the apostles shed the clearest light of all on this delicate issue. Jesus redefined popular notions of sin by discovering its origins: it resides in the human heart. Consequently, a man commits adultery not only by engaging in unlawful intercourse with his neighbor's wife but by harboring such desires in his heart (Matt. 5:27–30).

Luke faithfully records the decrees of the early church that, among other things, prohibited sexual immorality (Acts 15:20). Paul constructed an elaborate theology of marriage, detailing both its positive privileges and strict parameters (1 Cor. 6:13–20; 7:1–40; Eph. 5:3–7; 1 Thess. 4:3).

Finally, the Bible forbids homosexuality of any sort (Lev. 18:22; 20:13; Rom. 1:26–27). The modern term sodomy derived its name from the failed attempts of the inhabitants of Sodom to rape the visiting angels (Gen. 19:4–11). The degree to which a society gives way to such practices is a good gauge to measure not only the nation's separation from God but also its prospects for long-term survival (see Lev. 18:24–25; cp. Gen. 15:16). The only island of sanity we find in a sea without sexual standards is the comprehensive biblical instruction on sexual behavior. On a positive and hopeful note, many whom God saved from pagan and hedonistic lifestyles have found peace, purpose, and fulfillment in Christ. God did a marvelous work in their lives and renewed them in the way they approach these matters. God leaves no one outside of the reach of his gracious provision in Christ, and many who once sought meaning in the empty relationships now find complete fulfillment in following the Bible's prescription for healthy and satisfying sexual behavior.[31]

Earlier, we read the Apostle Paul's words, "Do not be conformed to this world, but **be transformed by the renewal of your mind**, that by testing you may discern what is the will of God, what is good and acceptable and perfect." How can we renew our mind? The center of consciousness stores knowledge and can think, understand, and reason. Well, if it is the mindset of the world, which can get us askew, we must take in knowledge from another source, creating a different mindset. Paul made this very clear to the Ephesians, when he gave them instructions for Christian living, how to build a new life. Paul said, 'As a follower

---

[31] Anders, Max; Martin, Glen (2002-07-01). Holman Old Testament Commentary - Exodus, Leviticus, Numbers (pp. 227-229). B&H Publishing. Kindle Edition.

of the Lord, I order you to stop living like stupid, godless people. Their minds are in the dark, and they are stubborn and ignorant and have missed out on the life that comes from God. They no longer have any feelings about what is right, and they are so greedy that they do all kinds of indecent things.' (Eph. 4:17-19, CEV) Because of their callused hearts, the god of this world blinds these, so that the truth cannot get through.

Leviticus 18:22-24 – Is the Curse of Barrenness Behind God's Condemnation of Homosexuality?

Leviticus 18:22-24 Updated American Standard Version (UASV)

²² You shall not lie with a male as you lie down with a woman; it is an abomination. ²³ And you shall not lie with any animal and so make yourself unclean with it, neither shall any woman stand before an animal to lie with it:³² it is perversion.

²⁴ 'Do not defile yourselves by any of these things; for by all these the nations which I am casting out before you have become defiled.

Leviticus 20:13 Updated American Standard Version (UASV)

¹³ If a man lies down with a male as one lies down with a woman, both of them have committed a detestable thing; they shall surely be put to death. Their own blood is upon them.

The inability to conceive children is conveyed by the Hebrew words *aqar* ("barren," Gen. 11:30) and *galmud* ("barren," i.e. Isa 49:21; Job 15:34). Proverbs 30:16 gives its reader four examples of greed, "Sheol, and **the barren womb**, Earth that is never satisfied with water, And fire that never says, 'Enough.'" At each start of humanity, one perfect (Adam and Eve), one imperfect (Noah and family), God gave one specific command.

God had commanded both Adam and Eve as well as Noah and his family, "Be fruitful and multiply, and fill the earth" (Gen. 1:28; 9:7) In ancient times, a childless or barren womb, being

---

³² A woman must not offer herself to a male animal to have intercourse with it. (NLT); A woman shall not stand before an animal to copulate with it (LEB)

unable to conceive was viewed as a reproach, an illness, a punishment, one of the greatest calamities. "When Rachel saw that she bore Jacob no children, she became jealous of her sister [Leah]; and she said to Jacob, "Give me children, or else I die." (Gen. 30:1, NASB) Of course, God had the power of making a woman with natural barrenness able to conceive: Sarah (Gen. 11:30; 17:19; 21:1, 2), Rebekah (Gen. 25:21), Samson's mother (Judges 13:2, 3), Hannah (1 Sam. 1:10, 11; 2:5), a Shunammite woman (2 Ki 4:14-17), and Elizabeth (Lu 1:7, 36).

There are no Scriptures, which would indicate that homosexuality was sinful because of the inability to conceive. Moreover, "if homosexuals were punished because they were barren, then why were they put to death? The dead can't have any more children! Since it is against the desires of homosexuals, heterosexual marriage would have been a more appropriate punishment!"[33]

In addition, homosexuality was not just prohibited among the Jews, as all the nations (non-Jews) of the land of Canaan, who were being cast out, had become defiled with such homosexual practices. The Jewish people were not blessed based on their ability to have children but rather on their obedience to God.

Lastly, barrenness could not have been a divine curse; otherwise, singleness would have been sinful. However, both Jesus and the apostle Paul recommended singleness for those that could exercise self-control over themselves, so as to carry out their discipleship unhindered. – Matthew 19:11-12; 1 Corinthians 7:8.

Clearly, the whole of the Old Testament condemns and prohibits homosexuality. As we have just read in Leviticus 18:22 and 20:13, homosexual relations are condemned and prohibited. Some try to argue that these verses only refer to male homosexual relations, as though God would condemn and prohibit male homosexual relations but not female homosexual relations. The Bible uses the male gender about God and his Son, as well as to various angels and demons. The Bible is a book based on male gender because Adam was created first; he was to be the head of

---

[33] Thomas Howe; Norman L. Geisler. The Big Book of Bible Difficulties: Clear and Concise Answers from Genesis to Revelation

humanity. This is not to say that men are superior to women, but women are subordinate and in subjection to men. The Bible refers to the male gender, when the principle, rule or law is also applicable to women as well. The Creator of all things chose the setting, the language, and time in which his Word was to be introduced to man. In biblical times, speakers would address a mixed group of believers with the greeting "brothers." What have gender-inclusive translations (e.g., CEV, NLT, TEV, etc.) have been doing over the past seventy years?

The English Standard Version makes more boasts about the importance of literal translation and yet violates that philosophy in at least four ways: (1) Crossway Bibles hired Bill Mounce, a proponent of dynamic equivalent translation as its chief translator. (2) It uses *essentially* literal to qualify its level of literalness. (3) It abandons the literal rendering far too many times to count. (4) It has joined the gender-neutral or gender-inclusive translations. For example, a literal translation (ASV, RSV, NASB, and UASV) will always uses the word man for the Greek *anthropos*, even when the context suggests that both men and women are in view. However, the ESV and other gender-inclusive translations will render such as people or others.

What these gender-inclusive translators fail to understand is this: to deviate, in any way, from the pattern, or likeness of how God brought his Word into existence, merely opens the Bible up to a book that reflects the age and time of its readers. If we allow the Bible to be altered because the progressive woman's movement feels offended by masculine language, it will not be long before the Bible gives way to the homosexual communities being offended by God's Words in the book of Romans and Corinthians; so modern translations will then tame that language, so as to not cause offense. I am certain that we thought that we would never see the day of two men, or two women being married by priests, but that day has been upon us for some time now. In fact, the American government is debating whether to change the definition of marriage.

The point here is that Leviticus 18:22 and 20:13 may refer to **male** homosexual relations, but this is a reference to a male gender when the condemnation and prohibition are also applicable to women as well. It would be utterly ridiculous and willful ignorance to see it any other way. The act of homosexual relations in the Old Testament called for the capital punishment. Some may argue that Christ and the New Testament authors lightened the sentence and stigma for such offenses against God. However, this is just not the case. Jesus is just as clear, but we will quote Paul, who said, God would inflict "vengeance on those who do not know God and on those who do not obey the gospel of our Lord Jesus. They will suffer the punishment of eternal destruction." (2 Thess. 2:6-8) Some have tried to argue that Leviticus 18:22 and 20:13 is only speaking against cult prostitution. However, there is nothing within the context of these Scriptures, which refers to any kind cultic activity. Moreover, homosexual relations are condemned and prohibited in both the Hebrew Scripture and the Greek New Testament. To try to argue that only some particular type of homosexual relations is prohibited is just another attempt at diverting attention or misleading.

Why did God Destroy Sodom and Gomorrah? What Was the Sin of Sodom and Gomorrah?

Those in support of the LBGT[34] community argue that Sodom and Gomorrah was not destroyed because of homosexuality but rather it was the attempted homosexual rape. If this were the only verse in the Bible that spoke of homosexuality, one might be able to raise that argument. However, as we have already seen in the above, Genesis 9:18-28, where it was actually Canaan, who saw the nakedness of Noah (homosexual act on Noah), for which he was prophetically cursed. Again, we see the justifiableness of God's curse on Canaan in the history of his descendants. They were so immoral that archaeologist that dug up their area was surprised that God had not destroyed them sooner. (Gen. 15:15-16) They too had a lust for the same sex. The Bible is right alongside secular history in exposing the sordid past of the Canaanites. The curse was fulfilled about eight centuries after Noah uttered the words when the Israelites conquered the land of Canaan. The destruction of Sodom and Gomorrah was a precursor to the destruction that was to come at the hand of Joshua and the Israelite army. There is not

---

[34] LGBT or GLBT is an initialism that stands for lesbian, gay, bisexual, and transgender.

27

one biblical reference that would suggest that homosexuality is simply an alternative lifestyle but rather a gross sin, detestable, contrary to nature, "shameful lusts" "indecent," a "perversion," and "the degrading of their bodies."

Moreover, the sin of homosexual relations is found all throughout Scripture. Others from the LBGT community try to argue that the custom and culture of the common hospitality of the Ancient Near Eastern family at the time, a lack of hospitality and the ill treatment of strangers, was the reason for the destruction of Sodom and Gomorrah. According to the Ancient Near East, it was a host's obligation to protect the guests in his home, defending them even to the point of death if necessary. Lot was certainly prepared to do that. Liberal scholarship being used as a tool argues that it was a lack of hospitality and the ill treatment of strangers. The response is simple; Sodom and Gomorrah were destroyed for gross homosexual activity, which took place in a culture that greatly valued hospitality. Yes, the homosexual men of Sodom and Gomorrah were violating the social customs as they sought to rape two angels that they believed to be two men.[35]

Thus, if Isaiah the prophet in chapter one refers to Sodom and Gomorrah as a bad example of evildoing and depravity, to help Judah appreciate just how far they had fallen, this does not negate the evil and depraved homosexual attempted rape of two men by the men of Sodom and Gomorrah. When the prophet Jeremiah compares the prophets of Jerusalem to the evil and wickedness of Sodom and Gomorrah (Jer. 23:14), this does not support the social customs argument, as the destruction of those two cities can be used analogously for evil and wickedness. The prophet Ezekiel compares Jerusalem to Samaria and Sodom, saying that Jerusalem was following Samaria and Sodom's way of life and their wicked customs, and soon Jerusalem was more disgusting than they were. Again, we are talking about many disgusting things, of which homosexuality cannot be ruled out. Nevertheless, Ezekiel was specifically talking about a failure to help the poor and needy. Are we to believe that God destroyed Israel by Babylon because they just did not give enough to the needy? Hardly, Jerusalem was have perverted orgies under trees, worshipping false gods, offering their

---

[35] It was common for angels to materialize as men, never women.

sons in sacrifice to Molech, committing homosexual acts, and many other disgusting sinful things for centuries. The Old Testament prophets and the historical books list all of these things.

The argument is that it was the sin of being inhospitable, not homosexuality. Part of the LGBT argument is the fact that Lot implored that the males of the community 'not do this thing to these men, since they came under my roof for protection.' (Gen 19:8) They use this text to bolster their argument that it was a violation of the social norms of the day; the Ancient Near East had a custom that they would protect their guests, even a complete stranger with their own lives. They then use Ezekiel 16:49 to bolster that defense because Jerusalem is being compared to Sodom in order to Shame Jerusalem for her failure to "aid the poor and needy." Yes, the people of Sodom and Gomorrah were unhospitable, and verse 49 of Ezekiel chapter 16 mentions this as part of why they were judged adversely. However, the sin of Sodom and Gomorrah was selfishness, inhospitality, but also homosexuality. Verse 49 of Ezekiel chapter 16 is found within the context of 16:49-59, which shows the sin was their failure to aid the poor and needy (v 49), arrogance (v 50), and most of the text centers on engagement in detestable things, 'committed abominations before God.' (50-51) Abominations is the same word used at Leviticus 18:22, "You shall not lie with a male as one lies with a female; it is an abomination." Jesus half-brother Jude called the sin of 'Sodom and Gomorrah gross sexual immorality,' which is stated as "acted immorally and indulged in unnatural lust" in the Revised Standard Version (Jude 7).

Finally, the LGBT community and liberal scholars argue that the text of Genesis 19:5 does not even mention sexual acts. It reads, "They [men of Sodom and Gomorrah] called to Lot, 'Where are the men who came to you tonight? Bring them out to us, **that we may know them**.'" (Gen. 19:5, RSV) The Hebrew word for "know" *yada*, occurs 956 times in the Old Testament and had a wide range of meaning. Its primary meaning was 'to get to know.'[36] Moreover, they would argue that the vast number of uses

---

[36] William D. Mounce, *Mounce's Complete Expository Dictionary of Old & New Testament Words* (Grand Rapids, MI: Zondervan, 2006), 947.

Robert L. Thomas, *New American Standard Hebrew-Aramaic and Greek Dictionaries : Updated Edition* (Anaheim: Foundation Publications, Inc., 1998).

of *yada* In the Old Testament has nothing to do with sexual relations. However, the context determines the meaning because *yada* also has the meaning "to have sexual relations." The context of Sodom and Gomorrah, *yada*, clearly meant sexual relations. In Genesis, yada in almost every use between and man and a woman, it is referring to sexual relations. Moreover, in the same chapter at Genesis 19:18, Lot says to the men surrounding his house, "I have two daughters who **have not <u>known</u> man**," *yada* being a clear reference to the fact that his daughters had not had sexual relations with a man. Lastly, if the context was that all of the males of Sodom and Gomorrah were simply coming to Lot's house "to get to know," i.e., 'to get acquainted with' the two men, why was lot offering his two virgin daughters in their place to appease the men's sexual appetite? The reason is simple; the men of Sodom and Gomorrah were homosexuals, who were going to rape these two men, clearly an abomination.

However, the LGBT community and liberal scholars must try to isolate a few verses that seem to support their argument of why Sodom and Gomorrah were destroyed. Certainly, the people of Sodom and Gomorrah were guilty of more than homosexuality, and they can be used as an example for these other wicked behaviors as well. Even Jesus used the people of Sodom as an example of being inhospitable to strangers. However, this does not negate the fact that the inhospitableness was a community of homosexual men trying to rape two angels that they believed to be men at the time of the destruction. However, one problem exists for the liberal scholars, Jude, Jesus half-brother, writing under inspiration tells us exactly why Sodom and Gomorrah were destroyed. He wrote, "Just as Sodom and Gomorrah and the cities around them, since they in the same way as these indulged in gross sexual immorality and having gone after other flesh,[37] are exhibited as an example in undergoing the punishment of eternal fire." (Jude 7) On this, one liberal online group tries to justify Jude 7 this way,

---

R. Laird Harris, Gleason L. Archer Jr., and Bruce K. Waltke, eds., *Theological Wordbook of the Old Testament* (Chicago: Moody Press, 1999), 366.

[37] Gr *sarkos heteras*; Lit *went after different or other flesh*; i.e., pursued unnatural fleshly desires

A likely interpretation is that the author of Jude criticized the men of Sodom for wanting to engage in sexual activities with angels. Angels are described in the Bible as a species of created beings who were different from humans. The sin of the people of Sodom would be that of bestiality. Another possibility is that the "*other flesh*" refers to cannibalism, which was a practice associated with early Canaanite culture. However, there is no mention in Genesis 19 about actually eating the angels.[38]

The Greek word *sarkos heteras* literally *went after different or other flesh*. First, we should mention that Jude focuses not on the attempted homosexual rape but rather the men of Sodom were desiring to engage in sexual relations with other men, same-sex relations, which he states was deserving of God's judgment. Second, it does no good to argue that these were angels, suggesting that this is why it refers to *different* or *other flesh*. The angels had materialized as men, looking no different from any other man, so the men of Sodom knew no different. The *Greek-English Lexicon of the New Testament* gives the meaning of *sarkos heteras* as, "**ἀπέρχομαι ὀπίσω σαρκὸς ἑτέρας**: (an idiom, literally 'to go after strange flesh') to engage in unnatural sexual intercourse—'to have homosexual intercourse.' ὡς Σόδομα καὶ Γόμορρα ... ἀπελθοῦσαι ὀπίσω σαρκὸς ἑτέρας 'they committed homosexual intercourse ... like the people of Sodom and Gomorrah' Jd 7. Though in some societies homosexuality is extremely rare, there are always ways of talking about it, though frequently the expressions may seem to be quite vulgar."[39] Thomas R. Schreiner wrote,

> Was Jude saying that Sodom was like the angels in Gen 6:1–4 in the sense that they also wanted sexual relations with angels?[40] If so, the sin criticized was not necessarily homosexuality but the violation of the separation established between human beings and angels.

---

[38] What was the sin or sins of Sodom and Gomorrah?, http://www.religioustolerance.org/hombibg193.htm (accessed April 19, 2016).

[39] Johannes P. Louw and Eugene Albert Nida, *Greek-English Lexicon of the New Testament: Based on Semantic Domains* (New York: United Bible Societies, 1996), 771.

[40] For this view see Kelly, *Peter and Jude*, 258–59; Bauckham, *Jude, 2 Peter*, 54.

It is unlikely, however, that Jude made this specific point. The sin of Sodom was not precisely like the sin the angels committed. The most important evidence against the proposed interpretation is that the men in Sodom who had a sexual desire for the angels *did not know they were angels.*[41] Their sin consisted in their homosexual intentions and their brutal disregard for the rights of visitors to the city.[42] Furthermore, it would be strange to designate a desire for angels as a desire for "other flesh" (*sarkos heteras*). The term more naturally refers to a desire for those of the same sex; they desired flesh other than that of women. For various reasons some are attempting today to question the view that homosexuality receives an unqualified negative verdict in the Scriptures. Such attempts have been singularly unsuccessful. The biblical writers and the Jewish tradition unanimously condemned homosexuality as evil.[43] The reason Jude introduced the example of Sodom and Gomorrah is that their punishment functions as an "example" (*deigma*) of what God will do to the opponents in the future.[44]

The commentators who suggest the "*other flesh*" here is the sin of the males of Sodom and Gomorrah seeking to have sex with angels is just unfounded. Yes, it seems to transition well that Jude just spoke of the angels at the time of Noah, sinning by going after human flesh in an unnatural way; thus, Jude then mentions the men of Sodom going after angels. However, this just is not the case, as Genesis 19 is quite clear that the men of Sodom and Gomorrah were not aware these two were angels, they thought they were two men. Moreover, as Douglas J. Moo mentions, "Nor is 'flesh' a natural word to apply to angels." (Moo, 2 Peter, Jude,

---

[41] Rightly Moo, *2 Peter, Jude*, 242.

[42] Contra D. G. Horrell, *The Epistles of Peter and Jude*, EC (Peterborough: Epworth, 1998), 121.

[43] For further discussion of this point see T. R. Schreiner, *Romans*, BECNT (Grand Rapids: Baker, 1998), 93–97. See also Oecumenius in *James, 1–2 Peter, 1–3 John, Jude*, ACCS (Downers Grove: InterVarsity, 2000), 251. For a full treatment of the issue of homosexuality, see now R. A. J. Gagnon, *The Bible and Homosexual Practice: Texts and Hermeneutics* (Nashville: Abingdon, 2001).

[44] Thomas R. Schreiner, *1, 2 Peter, Jude*, vol. 37, The New American Commentary (Nashville: Broadman & Holman Publishers, 2003), 452–453.

242.) Rather, the "other flesh" for these **men** of Sodom and Gomorrah is the flesh of **men**, as far as they knew. The flesh is *other*, in that it is *other* than the flesh of a woman, whom God had joined together with man, making them one flesh. Paul wrote of others in his day, "The men abandoned the natural function of the woman and burned in their desire toward one another, men with men committing indecent acts and receiving in their own persons the due penalty of their error." – Romans 1:27, NASB.

Genesis 19:8 – Why was Lot not condemned for offering his daughters to the Sodomites?

Genesis 19:8 Updated American Standard Version (UASV)

[8] Now behold, I have two daughters who have not known[45] a man; please let me bring them out to you, and do to them as is good in your eyes;[46] only do nothing to these men, inasmuch as they have come under the shadow[47] of my roof."

In Chapter 19 of Genesis, we come to the event of where God sent two of his angels to visit Lot in Sodom. Showing the common hospitality of the Ancient Near Eastern family, Lot invited them to stay at his home. The evening certainly did not go as Lot had planned. The men of the city surrounded the house, for the purpose of sexually assaulting the visitors. They stood outside demanding the visitors be brought out.

Genesis 19:1-29 Updated American Standard Version (UASV)

[1] The two angels came to Sodom in the evening, and Lot was sitting in the gate of Sodom. When Lot saw them, he rose to meet them and bowed himself with his face to the earth [2] And he said, "Now behold, my lords, please turn aside into your servant's house, and spend the night, and wash your feet; then you may rise early and go on your way." They said however, "No, but we shall spend the night in the square." [3] But he pressed them strongly; so they turned aside to him and entered his house; and he made them a feast and baked unleavened bread, and they ate. [4] Before they

---

[45] Hebrew idiom for sexual intercourse (See Gen 4:1) I.e. had intercourse

[46] I.e., whatever you want

[47] I.e., under the shelter (protection) of my roof (house)

lay down, the men of the city, the men of Sodom, surrounded the house, both young and old, all the people from every quarter; [5] and they called to Lot and said to him, "Where are the men who came to you tonight? Bring them out to us that we may know[48] them." [6] But Lot went out to them at the doorway, and shut the door behind him, [7] and said, "Please, my brothers, do not act wickedly. [8] Now behold, I have two daughters who have not known[49] a man; please let me bring them out to you, and do to them as is good in your eyes;[50] only do nothing to these men, inasmuch as they have come under the shadow[51] of my roof." [9] But they said, "Stand aside." Furthermore, they said, "This one came in to sojourn,[52] and already he is acting like a judge; now we will treat you worse than them." So they pressed hard against the man Lot and came near to break the door. [10] But the men reached out their hands and brought Lot into the house with them, and shut the door. [11] They struck the men who were at the doorway of the house with blindness, both small and great, so that they wearied themselves trying to find the doorway.

Lot and His Family Urged to Leave

[12] Then the men said to Lot, "Whom else have you here? A son-in-law, and your sons, and your daughters, and whomever you have in the city, bring them out of the place; [13] for we are about to destroy this place, because their outcry has become so great before Jehovah that Jehovah has sent us to destroy it." [14] Lot went out and spoke to his sons-in-law, who were taking[53] his daughters, and said, "Up, get out of this place, for the Lord will destroy the city." But he appeared to his sons-in-law like a man who was jesting.

[15] When morning dawned, the angels urged Lot, saying, "Up, take your wife and your two daughters who are here, lest you be swept away in the punishment[54] of the city." [16] But he lingered. So

---

[48] Hebrew idiom for *sexual intercourse*

[49] Hebrew idiom for *sexual intercourse* (See Gen 4:1) I.e. had intercourse

[50] I.e., *whatever you want*

[51] I.e., *under the shelter* (protection) *of my roof* (house)

[52] I.e., *as an alien, a foreigner*

[53] I.e., *to marry*

[54] Or *iniquity*

the men seized his hand and the hand of his wife and the hands of his two daughters, for the compassion of Jehovah was upon him; and they brought him out and set him outside the city. [17] When they had brought them outside, one said, "Escape for your life! Do not look behind you, and do not stay anywhere in the valley; escape to the mountains, lest you be swept away." [18] But Lot said to them, "Oh no, my lords! [19] Now behold, your servant has found favor in your sight, and you have magnified your lovingkindness, which you have shown me by saving my life; but I cannot escape to the mountains, lest the disaster overtake me and I die; [20] now behold, this town is near enough to flee to, and it is small. Please, let me escape there (is it not a little one?) and my soul shall live.[55]" [21] He said to him, "Behold, I grant you this thing[56] also, not to overthrow the town of which you have spoken. [22] Hurry, escape there, for I cannot do anything until you arrive there." Therefore the name of the town was called Zoar.[57]

Sodom and Gomorrah Destroyed

[23] The sun had risen over the earth when Lot came to Zoar. [24] Then Jehovah rained on Sodom and Gomorrah brimstone and fire from Jehovah out of heaven, [25] and he overthrew those cities, and all the valley, and all the inhabitants of the cities, and what grew on the ground. [26] But his wife, from behind him, looked back, and she became a pillar of salt.

From Over Twenty Miles Abraham Sees the Destruction

[27] Now Abraham arose early in the morning and went to the place where he had stood before Jehovah; [28] and he looked down toward Sodom and Gomorrah, and toward all the land of the valley, and he saw, and behold, the smoke of the land ascended like the smoke of a furnace.

[29] Thus it came about, when God destroyed the cities of the valley, that God remembered Abraham, and sent Lot out of the midst of the overthrow, when he overthrew the cities in which Lot dwelt.

---

[55] I.e., *that my life may be saved*

[56] I.e., *request* or *favor*

[57] I.e., smallness

This event has certainly caused quite a bit of confusion, as all of us ask ourselves, 'how on earth can we reconcile the fact that Lot offered his two daughters up, to circumstances in which they would surely be raped, in place of two total strangers?' Lot seems to be a coward, trying to save himself. Even more confusing, is how God would inspire the apostle Peter to pen these words: "and if he rescued righteous Lot, greatly distressed by the sensual conduct of the wicked (for as that righteous man lived among them day after day, he was tormenting his righteous soul over their lawless deeds that he saw and heard)." (2 Peter 2:7-8) Did God approve of the behavior that appears so hideous to our modern-day minds?

We need to keep in mind that we are viewing the account through a modern-day mind, and this will cause us to misunderstand the account. In addition, we need to appreciate that, the Bible itself does not condone or condemn what actions Lot took that night. Moreover, it does not make us aware of what he may have been thinking and feeling, or what moved him to take the course he did. We are not operating blindly, though; we can infer some things from this account and other parts of the Bible. First, we know that Lot was no coward. There is no doubt that Lot found himself in what seemed like an impossible situation. We need to understand exactly what Lot meant by "for they have come under the shelter of my roof." We can understand that Lot would be moved to protect his visitors. However, just how far would he go? According to the Ancient Near East, it was a host's obligation to protect the guests in his home, defending them even to the point of death if necessary. Lot was certainly prepared to do that. In addition, Jewish historian Josephus reports that the Sodomites were "unjust towards men, and impious towards God . . . They hated strangers, and abused themselves with Sodomitical practices." This is evidence that Lot was not a coward, as he went *out* to talk with this unreasonable mob, shutting the door behind him.—Genesis 19:6.

However, there is more to what is meant by 'one coming under the shelter of one's roof.' This will help us understand a small facet of why Lot would offer his daughters up, in place of two strangers. The Bible critics assume the worst, but let us try to reason out other possibilities. We know that Lot was a "righteous man," by the inspired words of Peter, which is, in essence, God's view of Lot. A righteous man would be a man of faith. Lot was the nephew of Abraham, and was traveling with him and Sarah up unto this point. He was able to see Jehovah act in behalf of Sarah firsthand. The powerful Pharaoh of Egypt took Sarah because of her great beauty. Jehovah God acted in behalf of her and Abraham, before Pharaoh could violate Sarah. (Genesis 12:11-20) It is quite reasonable that he had faith that Jehovah would do the same for his daughters. In fact, is that not what happened? The angels of Jehovah stepped in and kept Lot and his daughters safe.

Another possibility was that Lot was trying to buy time. He knew the men were after the angels for homosexual purposes, and they would likely not find his daughters as an acceptable substitute. (Jude 7) In addition, these young women were engaged to two men in the city, and there is the possibility that this offer would cause a division among those men's households and the rest of the city. (Genesis 19:14) It is the old 'divide and conquer' approach.

Genesis 19:30-38 – Did God Condone the Incest of Lot with His Two Daughters?

Genesis 19:30-38 Updated American Standard Version (UASV)

Lot and His Daughters

30 Lot went up from Zoar, and stayed in the mountains, and his two daughters with him; for he was afraid to dwell in Zoar; and he dwelt in a cave, he and his two daughters. **31** And the firstborn said to the younger, "Our father is old, and there is not a man on earth to come in to us after the manner of all the earth. **32** Come, let us make our father drink wine, and we will lie with him, that we may preserve seed from our father."[58] **33** So they made their father drink wine that night, and the firstborn went in and lay with her father; and he did not know when she lay down or when she arose. **34** On the following day, the firstborn said to the younger, "Behold, I lay last night with my father; let us make him drink wine tonight also; then you go in and lie with him, that we may

---

[58] I.e., *preserve offspring from our father.*

preserve seed from our father."[59] [35] So they made their father drink wine that night also, and the younger arose and lay with him; and he did not know when she lay down or when she arose. [36] Thus both the daughters of Lot were with child by their father. [37] The firstborn bore a son, and called his name Moab; he is the father of the Moabites to this day. [38] And the younger, she also bore a son, and called his name Ben-ammi; he is the father of the sons of Ammon to this day.

We must take a moment and look at the historical setting while looking at the rest of God's Word. Lot lost his wife in the destruction of Sodom and Gomorrah, his daughters surviving. They fled to Zoar, but they soon felt unsafe and moved on to a cave. (Gen. 19:30) It is at this time the older daughter said to the younger: "Our father is old, and there is not a man on earth to come in to us after the manner of all the earth. Come, let us make our father drink wine, and we will lie with him, that we may preserve seed [offspring] from our father." – Genesis 19:31-32.

One indicator that Lot would have not supported incest is the fact they plotted to get him intoxicated, knowing if he were sober, he would have rejected such an idea. We must realize the mindset of the daughters, knowing that there was no way to continue the family line. Being in the land of Canaan, with no family, it meant the end of their family name. Thus, living among the Sodomites and their debased way of thinking had influenced them to the point that they so easily came up with such a scheme. Considering all of this, we must ask, 'what the value of adding this account?'

It certainly was not added for its sexual content, or to justify incest. The sons that would be born to the daughters, and therefore, related to Abraham, would become the Moabites and Ammonites (Gen. 11:27), who would have historical dealings with the Israelites centuries later. As you know, the Israelites are the sons of Israel (Jacob), Abraham's grandson. This helps us to understand later accounts, like why the Israelites never trespassed on the land of Moab and Ammon, when they were taking over the land east of the Jordan. – Deuteronomy 2:9, 18-19, 37.

---

[59] i.e., *preserve offspring from our father.*

What we have in Genesis, chapter 19 is the historical facts, for laying a foundation for events that would span about 3,000 years of Israelite history. Thus, there was no reason to include an approval or disapproval; it was simply an historical account. However, the Bible is not silent on drunkenness or incest. (Prov. 20:1; 23:20, 21, 29-35; 1 Cor. 6:9, 10; Lev. 18:6, 7, 29) The Bible critic will argue that the daughters lived hundreds of years before the Mosaic Law, so they were not under it. While this is true, Paul lets us know that God gave us an internal conscience that convicts us, or excuses us. This must have been the case with the daughters, why else get the father intoxicated? – Romans 2:14-15.

Why did God inspire Peter to call Lot a "righteous man"? This is certainly not because he condoned getting drunk, nor because he approved of the incest. However, we know that Lot is not perfect, and he was passed out during the incest. In addition, the Bible does not give us a historical picture of Lot as a drunkard. It is God, who is the reader of heart, who judged Lot as "righteous." Thus, we can surmise that most of his life were in walking with God. We could also see a very broken heart of a "righteous man" over the difficulty he found himself in, for the bad choices he made.

Instead of looking for contradictions, mistakes and evidence that the Bible is not inspired, the Lot account only reinforces our belief that the Bible is a book of truth. Jehovah God does not move his authors to cover up the mistakes of his prominent people, like that of secular history. Instead, he inspires the recounting of accurate and honest historical information, as background material, helping us, so we can better understand future events in his Word.

Jesus Never Spoke of Homosexuality

Liberal scholarship and the LGBT community also argue that the New Testament does not prohibit and condemn homosexuality to the extent that the Old Testament does. However, this is really not the case. The main chapters in the Old Testament that deal with homosexuality are the incident with Noah at Genesis 9:18-28; the destruction of Sodom and Gomorrah for their homosexual lifestyle among other things at Genesis 18:1-19:29; and the laws that prohibit and condemn homosexuality at Leviticus 18:22, 29;

20:13. The main chapters in the New Testament that deal with the issue of homosexuality are explicitly the lesbian and homosexual activities that are condemned at Romans 1:26-27. Then, there are the passive and active partners in consensual homosexual acts at 1 Corinthians 6:9. God condemning the practice homosexuality at 1 Timothy 1:10, and the condemnation and prohibition of homosexuality in New Testament times by referring to the historical example of Sodom and Gomorrah at Jude 7.

Liberal scholarship and the LGBT community also argue that Jesus never addressed the issue of homosexuality. This too is not entirely true. It would be better worded that Jesus did not explicitly mention homosexuality. However, by extension, he did explicitly rule out homosexuality, when he mentioned the Creation account that says marriage is between one man and one woman for life. (Matt. 19:3–12; Mark 10:2–12) Jesus did not have to address the subject of homosexuality head on because Jesus, his disciples, and his audience was Jewish, all being under the Mosaic Law until ransom sacrifice of Pentecost. Jesus did not accept polygamous marriage that was permitted during the Old Testament period.[60] Jesus did not accept divorce or homosexuality. Paul, on the other hand, had Gentiles in majority Jewish Christian congregations and congregations that were predominately Gentile. Therefore, Paul had to be more explicit in what he had to say. Below we will have an excursion into the historical setting that the apostles would have had to deal with, which Jesus did not have to consider when it came to his audience.

---

[60] God has never approved of polygamy. The first marriage in Eden was that of monogamy. Jesus Christ later restated that standard for his followers. (Gen. 2:18-24; Matthew 19:4-6) God exhorted the Israelites not to have multiple wives, especially after the disaster of Abraham and Jacob. (Gen. 16:1-4; 29:18–30:24; see Deut. 17:15, 17) God's foreknowledge allowed him to know the Israelites were going to be an obstinate people, so he did incorporate laws in the Old Testament. God endured it for a short time, while enforcing it rigorously to prevent abuses. (Ex. 21:10, 11; Deut. 21:15-17) The Son of God was used to reaffirm the marital standard set in Eden.

First Century Bible Background of Homosexuality

Clinton E. Arnold, 1 Corinthians 6:9

Paul uses specialized terminology here.[61] Roman law, in particular the *lex Scantinia* of the mid-second century B.C., legislated about homosexual behavior.[62] Such laws protected Roman citizens against homosexual acts. Corinth as a Roman colony would thus consider homosexual acts with fellow citizens as illegal, but not with noncitizens (i.e., non-Romans) and slaves.

Male prostitutes (6:9). This expression translates *malakoi*. The Greek word *malakos* transferred to the Latin *malacus*. It means in effect "a soft person" and took on the meaning of somebody effeminate. The fact that Latin has no indigenous word for such a person may suggest that a passive participant in a homosexual relationship was not condemned by Roman law so long as he was not a Roman citizen.

Homosexual offenders (6:9). This expression translates the Greek word *arsenokoitai*. This may be a word derived from the LXX [Septuagint] of Leviticus 18:22: "Do not lie with a man as one lies with a woman; that is detestable." The *malakos* (see previous comment) is probably the passive participant, whereas the *arsenokoitēs* is the active participant. Thus, both stand criticized by Paul within the Christian community. Note, however, that these are but two areas of life that Paul highlights, and the church has not always had the right balance.[63]

David E. Garland, 1 Corinthians 6:9

Pederasty [i.e., man who has sex with boy] was the most common male homosexual act in the ancient world (Schrage 1991:

---

[61] B. W. Winter, "Homosexual Terminology in 1 Corinthians 6:9: The Roman Context and the Greek Loan-word," in A. N. S. Lane (ed.), *Interpreting the Bible: Historical and Theological Studies in Honor of David F. Wright* (Leicester, U.K.: Apollos, 1997), 275–90 (ch. 14).

[62] This law was passed by the tribune Scantinius c. 146 b.c. See S. Lilja, *Homosexuality in Republican and Augustan Rome* (Helsinki: Societas Scientiarum Fennica, 1982), 112–21.

[63] Clinton E. Arnold, *Zondervan Illustrated Bible Backgrounds Commentary: Romans to Philemon.*, vol. 3 (Grand Rapids, MI: Zondervan, 2002), 132–133.

432). That is because sexual propriety was judged according to social values: "The ancients did not classify kinds of sexual desire or behaviour according to the sameness or difference of the sexes of the persons who engaged in a sexual act; rather, they evaluated sexual acts according to the degree to which such acts either violated or conformed to the norms of conduct deemed appropriate to individual sexual actors by reason of their gender, age, and social status" (Halperin, *OCD* 720; cf. Dover 1978: 277). A person's rank and status determined what was considered acceptable or unacceptable. On one side were free males; on the other side were women and slaves. A free male was free to choose women, men, or boys as sexual objects without the majority taking offense as long as he did not demean his status as a free male. A free male could not "indulge in passive acts of love like a woman or a slave" without incurring a stigma (Stegemann 1993: 164). But he could use boys, slaves, or persons of no account with impunity as long as he remained "on top." "Phallic insertion functioned as a marker of male precedence; it also expressed social domination and seniority... . Any sexual relation that involved the penetration of a social inferior (whether inferior in age, gender, or status) qualified as sexually normal for a male, irrespective of the penetrated person's anatomical sex, whereas to *be* sexually penetrated was always potentially shaming, especially for a free male of citizen status [e.g., Tacitus, *Annales* 11.36]" (Halperin, *OCD* 721). Homosexual acts between free males were regarded with contempt because one partner would have to take on the passive role (insertivity) suited only to women and slaves (Veyne 1987: 204). We see this cultural attitude manifested in Petronius's novel, *Satyricon* (91–100). Two close friends, Encolpius and Ascyltus, fight over the sexual favors of their slave boy, Giton; but they never engage in any homosexual act between themselves.

It should be noted also that "neither sexual desire nor sexual

OCD *Oxford Classical Dictionary*, edited by S. Hornblower and A. Spawforth, 3d ed. (Oxford: Oxford University Press, 1996)

OCD *Oxford Classical Dictionary*, edited by S. Hornblower and A. Spawforth, 3d ed. (Oxford: Oxford University Press, 1996)

pleasure represented an acceptable motive for a boy's compliance with the sexual demands of his lover" (Halperin, *OCD* 721). The younger partner was not to be motivated by, or express, passionate sexual desire for his senior lover, lest he compromise his own future status as a man. As a result, sexually receptive or effeminate males were ridiculed. Society would have considered same-sex sexual acts between two men of equal standing to be shameful. What some in modern society find acceptable—male same-sex eroticism between equals in a committed relationship— would have been condemned in ancient society. Dover (1978: 104) contends that penetration was not regarded as an expression of love but "as an aggressive act demonstrating the superiority of the active to the passive partner." J. Davidson (1997: 169–82) challenges this interpretation as anachronistic but imposes his own biases on the evidence and does not win the argument. Paul differed from his society's sexual mores in condemning all same-sex sexual acts.[64]

Below we will investigate Romans 1:26-27; 1 Corinthians 6:9; and 1 Timothy 1:10. We have already covered Jude 7 above, so, it will not be necessary to go over that material again. We will quote some top New Testament scholars extensively.

Ungodly People Inexcusable

Romans 1:24-32 Updated American Standard Version (UASV)

[24] Therefore God gave them over in the lusts of their hearts to impurity, so that their bodies would be dishonored among them. [25] For they exchanged the truth of God for the lie, and worshiped and served the creature rather than the Creator, who is blessed forever.[65] Amen.

OCD Oxford Classical Dictionary, edited by S. Hornblower and A. Spawforth, 3d ed. (Oxford: Oxford University Press, 1996)

[64] David E. Garland, *1 Corinthians*, Baker Exegetical Commentary on the New Testament (Grand Rapids, MI: Baker Academic, 2003), 217–218.

[65] Lit *into the ages*

²⁶ For this reason God gave them over to degrading passions; for their women exchanged natural relations⁶⁶ for those that are contrary to nature, ²⁷ and the men likewise gave up natural relations with women and were violently inflamed in their lust toward one another, males with males committing the shameless deed, and receiving in themselves the due penalty for their error.

²⁸ And just as they did not see fit to acknowledge God any longer, God gave them over to a depraved mind, to do those things which are not proper, ²⁹ being filled with all unrighteousness, wickedness, greed, evil; full of envy, murder, strife, deceit, malice; they are gossips, ³⁰ slanderers, haters of God, insolent, arrogant, boastful, inventors of evil, disobedient to parents, ³¹ without understanding, untrustworthy, unloving, unmerciful; ³² and although they know the ordinance of God, that those who practice such things are worthy of death, they not only do the same, but also give wholehearted approval to those who practice them.

Wordplays in this text communicate that human sin is rooted in a rejection of the glory of God (Klostermann 1933: 6; Jeremias 1954: 119; Hooker 1966–67: 182). Human beings failed to glorify God (οὐκ ἐδόξασαν, ouk edoxasan, v. 21) and exchanged his glory (ἤλλαξαν δόξαν, ēllaxan doxan, v. 23) for idolatry. Because people did not honor God by glorifying him, he gave their bodies over to be "dishonored" (ἀτιμάζεσθαι, atimazesthai, v. 24), and they had "dishonorable passions" (πάθη ἀτιμίας, pathē atimias, v. 26). The parallels in 1 Cor. 11:14–15, 15:43, and 2 Cor. 6:8 indicate that ἀτιμία (atimia, dishonor) is contrasted with δόξα (doxa, glory; cf. Hooker 1966–67: 182). The disgrace that has invaded human sexual relations is a consequence of rejecting God. The same connection is forged with another word linkage. Those who "exchanged" (ἤλλαξαν, ēllaxan, v. 23) God's glory and "exchanged" (μετήλλαξαν, metēllaxan, v. 25) his truth "exchanged" (μετήλλαξαν, v. 26) natural sexual relations for that which is unnatural. Once again, sexual immorality is evidently a consequence of human idolatry. Finally, those who did not see fit (οὐκ ἐδοκίμασαν, ouk edokimasan) to keep God in their knowledge have been handed over to an unfit mind (ἀδόκιμον

---

⁶⁶ Or *natural sexual relations*; Lit *natural use*

νοῦν, *adokimon noun*, v. 28). An unfit mind is the fruit of seeing God as unfit. Paul is not referring to Adam in these verses, but he is saying that human beings have gone the way of Adam, and that they have lost glory in trying to retain it.

Some interpreters have understood God's wrath as impersonal and described it in terms of cause and effect.[67] They appeal to the handing over (παρέδωκεν, vv. 24, 26, 28) to sin as evidence that God is not personally angry but merely allows sinners to experience the full consequences of sin. This interpretation betrays the influence of Deism[68] and an Enlightenment worldview rather than explaining Paul's worldview. The OT and Jewish view was that God was vitally and personally involved in his creation. In the OT the judgments inflicted on pagan nations and Israel are invariably the outworking of God's personal decisions. So too here, the handing over to sin is not to be construed impersonally. Three times (vv. 24, 26, 28) it is repeated that "God" (θεός, *theos*) handed over people to sin. To think of "laws" operating impersonally apart from God's personal superintendence reveals that many modern people think differently about his involvement with the created world than the ancient Jews did. The consequences that are inflicted because of sin are the result of God's personal decision. The wrath of God, then, is to be understood in personal terms. God's wrath is not, however, the arbitrary and capricious anger that was so characteristic of the Greek gods. It is his holy and righteous response to those who do not worship and esteem him as God.

Sexual sin is the first consequence of being handed over that Paul mentions (vv. 24, 26–27). Romans 1:24 speaks of being handed over "to uncleanness" (εἰς ἀκαθαρσίαν, *eis akatharsian*). Paul often uses ἀκαθαρσία (2 Cor. 12:21; Gal. 5:19; Eph. 5:3; Col. 3:5; 1 Thess. 4:7) to refer to sexual sin. Paul is perhaps simply describing sexual sin in general terms in verse 24, although his

---

[67] So C. Dodd 1932: 21–24; Hanson 1957: 69, 85; MacGregor 1960–61: 103–6; Byrne 1996: 68; Mounce (1995: 36) rightly critiques this view. Cf. Calvin (1960: 30), who incorrectly concludes that there is no emotion in God. This judgment implies that emotion is a sign of weakness.

[68] Andrews Note: Deism is belief in God based on reason rather than revelation and involving the view, which God has set the universe in motion but does not interfere with how it runs.

45

more specific words in verses 26–27 suggest that homosexual relations may be in his mind in verse 24 as well. Why does Paul focus on homosexual relations, especially since it receives little attention elsewhere in his writings (1 Cor. 6:9; 1 Tim. 1:10)? Probably because it functions as the best illustration of that which is unnatural in the sexual sphere. Idolatry is "unnatural" in the sense that it is contrary to God's intention for human beings. To worship corruptible animals and human beings instead of the incorruptible God is to turn the created order upside down.[69] In the sexual sphere the mirror image of this "unnatural" choice of idolatry is homosexuality (cf. Schlatter 1995: 43; Hays 1986: 191). Human beings were intended to have sexual relations with those of the opposite sex. Just as idolatry is a violation and perversion of what God intended, so too homosexual relations are contrary to what God planned when he created man and woman.

Although verse 26 is ambiguous regarding the precise sense in which women acted contrary to nature, verse 27 clarifies that what is unnatural is same-sex relations.[70] That homosexual relations are contrary to nature, in the sense that they violate what God intended, is communicated in saying that women abandoned "the natural use for that which is contrary to nature" (τὴν φυσικὴν χρῆσιν εἰς τὴν παρὰ φύσιν, tēn physikēn chrēsin eis tēn para physin, v. 26), and in saying that men "have left the natural use of women" (ἀφέντες τὴν φυσικὴν χρῆσιν τῆς θηλείας, aphentes tēn physikēn chrēsin tēs thēleias, v. 27). The word χρῆσις is often used of sexual relations in Greek writings (BAGD[71] 886), while the word

---

[69] After writing this sentence I came upon this observation from Chrysostom (*Homilies on Romans* 4 [on Rom. 1:26–27]), "But when God hath left one, then all things are turned upside down."

[70] Miller (1996) argues that verse 26 refers to unnatural heterosexual practices, not homosexuality. The close parallel with verse 27 renders this claim unlikely. Moreover, the restriction of the criticism to women in verse 26 would be strange since men and women together (according to Miller) were guilty of unnatural sexual behavior. Why would Paul indict only the women if men and women conspired to commit sexual sin? Miller's creative reading should be rejected because it suggests a much more difficult reading that would be less accessible to the Romans than the view that homosexuality is censured in both verses. Some commentators have attempted to explain why women are discussed before men, but no significance should be read from the order.

[71] BAGD A *Greek-English Lexicon of the New Testament and Other Early Christian Literature*, by W. Bauer, W. F. Arndt, F. W. Gingrich, and F. W. Danker, 2d ed. (Chicago: University of Chicago Press, 1979)

φύσις refers in this context to what God intended in creating men and women (Koester, *TDNT*[72] 9:273; Hays 1986: 196–99; cf. De Young 1988). The word φύσις does not invariably refer to the divine intention in Paul (cf. Rom. 2:14, 27; 11:21, 24 [3 times]; Gal. 2:15; 4:8; Eph. 2:3).[73] At least two pieces of evidence, however, indicate that an argument from the created order is constructed in Rom. 1:26–27. First, Paul selected the unusual words θῆλυς (*thēlys*, female) and ἄρσην (*arsēn*, male) rather than γύνη (*gynē*, woman) and ἀνήρ (*anēr*, man), respectively. In doing so, he drew on the creation account of Genesis, which uses the same words (Gen. 1:27 LXX [Septuagint]; cf. Matt. 19:4; Mark 10:6). These words emphasize the sexual distinctiveness of male and female (Moo 1991: 109), suggesting that sexual relations with the same sex violate the distinctions that God intended in the creation of man and woman. Second, the phrase "contrary to nature" (παρὰ φύσιν) is rooted in Stoic and Hellenistic Jewish traditions that saw homosexual relations as violations of the created order (see below). The latter point is borne out by verse 27, which specifies in three ways what constitutes the unnatural activity for men: (1) in forsaking sexual relations with women (ἀφέντες τὴν φυσικὴν χρῆσιν τῆς θηλείας); (2) in burning in desire for other men (ἐξεκαύθησαν ἐν τῇ ὀρέξει αὐτῶν εἰς ἀλλήλους, *exekauthēsan en tē orexei autōn eis allēlous*); and (3) in doing that which was shameful with other men (ἄρσενες ἐν ἄρσεσιν τὴν ἀσχημοσύνην κατεργαζόμενοι, *arsenes en arsesin tēn aschēmosynēn katergazomenoi*).[74] Verse 27 gives no indication that only specific kinds of homosexual activity are prohibited. Instead, homosexual

---

[72] *TDNT Theological Dictionary of the New Testament*, edited by G. Kittel and G. Friedrich; translated and edited by G. W. Bromiley, 10 vols. (Grand Rapids: Eerdmans, 1964–76)

[73] The use in 1 Cor. 11:14 is in the midst of a difficult passage. Paul's intention in this text is likely to preserve created distinctions between men and women as well (Fee 1987: 491–530; Schreiner 1991a: 137).

[74] D. Martin (1995: 339–49) argues that Paul indicts homosexuality not because it is contrary to nature but because in Paul's mind homosexual sexuality involves "inordinate desire," just as, say, gluttony is the inordinate desire for food. Martin understands Paul to say that desire for same-sex relations is not contrary to nature; it is proscribed because it is inordinate or beyond nature. Martin does not provide, however, a detailed argument supporting his view of "nature." I am still persuaded (as argued in the exegesis and exposition) that Paul appeals to the created order to justify his proscription. For Paul the very desire for homosexual relations is inordinate and beyond nature.

relations in general are indicted.

Modern controversy over homosexuality has led to a reevaluation of this text. Some scholars argue that Paul does not condemn all forms of homosexuality but only homosexual acts practiced by people who are "naturally" heterosexual (e.g., Boswell 1980: 109–12). According to this interpretation, to act contrary to nature involves engaging in sexual activity that is contrary to the personal nature or character of the individual. Thus, Paul should not be understood as implying that all homosexuality is contrary to what God intended from creation. He speaks only against homosexual acts that are practiced by those who are heterosexuals by nature.[75]

This interpretation should be rejected since there is no evidence that Paul understood the "nature" of human beings in the individualized and psychological sense that is familiar to us in the twentieth century. Instead, in accord with Stoic and Hellenistic Jewish tradition, Paul rejects homosexuality as contrary to the created order—homosexual activity is a violation of what God intended when he created men and women (Hays 1986: 192–94; Malick 1993: 335).[76] Paul's prohibition of all homosexual relations is also supported by the unanimous rejection of homosexuality in Jewish sources (see De Young 1990). For instance, Josephus (*Ag. Ap.* [Against Apion] 2.24 §199) declares that the marriage of a man and woman is "according to nature" (κατὰ φύσιν, *kata physin*), and proceeds to say that the OT law demands the death penalty for intercourse between males. Both Philo (*Spec Laws* [Laws On the Special Laws] 3.7 §38; cf. *Abr.* [On Abraham] 26 §§133–36) and Josephus (*Ag. Ap.* 2.37 §273) specifically criticize homosexual relations as παρὰ φύσιν. The author of the Testament of Naphtali (3.3–4) sees homosexuality as a departure "from the order of nature," and his appeal to creation in verse 3 reveals that he understands this in term of God's created intention.

---

[75] Countryman (1988: 110–17) argues that Paul does not classify homosexual acts as "sinful" but as impure and unclean. This interpretation has been decisively countered by T. Schmidt (1995: 64–85), whose entire discussion is extraordinarily useful.

[76] So also T. Schmidt 1995; Soards 1995. In surveying the evidence Scroggs demonstrates that in Judaism homosexuality is consistently rejected (1983: 66–84), while in the Greco-Roman world (1983: 17–65) there was significant acceptance of homosexuality.

Scroggs (1983: 109–18) attempts to minimize Paul's negative remarks on homosexuality in Rom. 1:26–27 by arguing that he is simply drawing on Hellenistic Jewish tradition, that probably only pederasty [i.e., man who has sex with boy] is being condemned, and that the focus of the section is theological rather than ethical. The first point reveals the weakness of Scroggs's case. There is no evidence that Paul reverses the unanimous Jewish conviction that homosexuality was sinful (e.g., Gen. 19:1–28; Lev. 18:22; 20:13; Deut. 23:17–18; Wis. 14:26; T. Levi 17.11;[77] Sib. Or. 3.596–600; see also the above citations of Josephus and Philo; and Boughton 1992).[78] Paul's negative comments on homosexuality, even if they are traditional, signal his acceptance of the tradition. The claim that only an abusive form of homosexuality is prohibited, such as pederasty, suffers from lack of evidence. The wording of Rom. 1:26–27 is not restricted to a specific kind of homosexuality but is a general proscription [i.e., banning or prohibition] of the activity. In fact, no mention is made of homosexual relations between men and boys but of "males with males" (ἄρσενες ἐν ἄρσεσιν, arsenes en arsesin, v. 27). Moreover, the idea that pederasty is in view is contradicted by the reference to the homosexual acts of women in verse 26 (Malick 1993: 339; Byrne 1996: 76), for pederasty, by definition, involves men and boys, and evidence is lacking that women engaged in sexual activity with girls. Finally, Scroggs artificially separates theology from ethics in Pauline thought, implying that the vices listed would not be part of Paul's ethical exhortations. But theology and ethics are closely wedded in all of Paul's letters. Any attempt to drive a wedge between them is unsatisfactory. The rejection of God theologically is concretely illustrated in evil that is promulgated by human beings.

Sheppard (1985) admits that Paul's rejection of homosexuality cannot be explained away but argues that loving homosexual relations can be accepted in the light of the canon as a whole and the recognition that our understanding of the Word of God advances as we gain more knowledge about homosexuality. To say that the whole of Scripture supports homosexuality is weak, since

---

[77] Levi Testament of Levi

[78] In fact, Scroggs himself (1983:66–84) demonstrates that the Jews of Paul's day were distinct from Greeks in that they consistently rejected homosexuality.

there is no canonical acceptance of homosexuality. Sheppard's argument depends ultimately not on the canon, but on his conviction that recent study and human experience validate homosexuality as a legitimate lifestyle. Furnish (1985: 79–80; so also M. Davies 1995) is more straightforward in saying that we can no longer accept Paul's view on homosexuality, for he was limited in his understanding of it.[79] For those who accept the Pauline proscription as authoritative (as I do), avoidance of homosexual relations is the path of happiness and holiness.

The last clause in verse 27 has engendered some controversy. What is the "penalty" (ἀντιμισθίαν, antimisthian) that people receive in themselves? The context suggests that the "penalty" is not something in addition to homosexuality. The penalty is rather being handed over to the sin of homosexuality itself. The words ἦν ἔδει τῆς πλάνης αὐτῶν (hēn edei tēs planēs autōn, which was necessary of their error) point in this direction. The πλάνη here is not an inadvertent mistake but the rejection of the true God for idols (Byrne 1996: 77). Thus people had to be (ἔδει) handed over to punishment precisely because they had scorned God's glory. Once again, the main theme of the text is driven home. The foundational sin of refusing to thank and glorify God leads to other sins.

The connection between rejecting God and human sin is forged again with the vice list appearing in verses 29–31. Vice lists are common in Paul (1 Cor. 5:10–11; 6:9–10; 2 Cor. 12:20; Gal. 5:19–21; Eph. 4:31; 5:3–5; Col. 3:5, 8; 1 Tim. 1:9–10; 6:4–5; 2 Tim. 3:2–4; Titus 3:3), and some of the vices are occasionally included because of problems in the church addressed. The list here, though, does not reflect ethical problems in the church in Rome. The list is a general and wide-ranging depiction of human sin. In introducing the vices Paul uses Stoic terminology (ποιεῖν τὰ μὴ καθήκοντα, poiein ta mē kathēkonta, to do things that are not fitting, v. 28). To conclude that Paul is charging every single Gentile of these specific sins (Räisänen 1983: 98) is unnecessary. Instead, he enunciates the principle that all Gentiles commit sin, in thought,

---

[79] For helpful surveys of the issue along with practical ministry suggestions see T. Schmidt 1995; J. Taylor 1995.

word, and deed (see Laato 1991: 113–15).

The vice list is organized into three main parts. First, the participle πεπληρωμένους (peplērōmenous, being filled) introduces four words that all conclude with -ια (-ia). These words are all general descriptions of human sin: ἀδικία (adikia, unrighteousness), πονηρία (ponēria, wickedness), πλεονεξία (pleonexia, covetousness), and κακία (kakia, wickedness or malice). Precise distinctions should not be drawn among the various words; they are used for effect to denote in a comprehensive way the wickedness of human beings. Second, five words modify μεστούς (mestous, full): φθόνου (phthonou, envy), φόνου (phonou, murder), ἔριδος (eridos, strife), δόλου (dolou, deceit), and κακοηθείας (kakoētheias, malice). Assonance is present in the first two words. It is unlikely that Paul is being so specific as to indicate that the last four sins listed stem from envy (Cranfield 1975: 130). Murder, strife, deceit, and ill will too often exist where envy is not present, and thus more conclusive evidence would be needed to establish such a connection. Finally, twelve words or phrases all in the accusative, appositional to αὐτούς (autous, them) in verse 28, conclude the list. The first two sins describe those who destroy others' reputations (ψιθυριστάς, psithyristas, gossips; καταλάλους, katalalous, slanderers), and once again we should not be overly specific in distinguishing these from one another. The next six expressions seem to be allied in terms of the shocking depth of evil. Θεοστυγεῖς (theostygeis, haters of God) could possibly be translated as "hated by God" (so Schlatter 1995: 44), but since the rest of the words in this list refer to human evil, the translation "haters of God" is preferable (Calvin 1960: 38). The words ὑβριστάς (hybristas, insolent), ὑπερηφάνους (hyperēphanous, arrogant), and ἀλαζόνας (alazonas, braggarts) are thematically related insofar as they point to the self-importance and rudeness of those who are convinced of their superiority. The next two vices are linked in that they are both two-word phrases: ἐφευρετὰς κακῶν (epheuretas kakōn, inventors of evil) and γονεῦσιν ἀπειθεῖς (goneusin apeitheis, disobedient to parents). Both signify the depth of evil. The former highlights their creativity in performing evil, while the latter reveals that sin ruptures relationships in the home. The list concludes with some rhetorical force by four terms that are joined together: ἀσυνέτους (asynetous, foolish), ἀσυνθέτους

51

(*asynthetous*, treacherous), ἀστόργους (*astorgous*, without natural affection), and ἀνελεήμονας (*aneleēmonas*, without mercy). All four words begin with ἀ-, and assonance connects the first two. The first three words all end with -ους, while the -ας ending on the last word is closely similar in sound. Dunn (1988a: 53) nicely catches the sense and partially reproduces the effect in translating the four terms "senseless, faithless, loveless, merciless," which I have adopted in my translation.

The depth and full weight of human sin is communicated with verse 32, which concludes this section. Flückiger (1954: 156–57) argues that verse 32 is not the conclusion of Paul's indictment of the Gentiles but is addressed to the Jews. This interpretation should be rejected since οἵτινες (*hoitines*, who) and the reference to the sins just described in the previous verses show a close connection between verse 32 and what precedes. The διό (*dio*, therefore) commencing 2:1 suggests that the chapter break between the two sections in our Bibles is appropriate.

The people in view are those who practice the evil described in the previous verses (αὐτὰ ποιοῦσιν, *auta poiousin*, they do them; οἱ τὰ τοιαῦτα πράσσοντες, *hoi ta toiauta prassontes*, those who practice such things). The things (αὐτά, τοιαῦτα) they practice probably include all the vices listed in 1:24–31. It is remarkable, despite their rejection of the true God and the darkening of their understanding (vv. 21–23), that they are still keenly aware of God's disapproval of their behavior. In fact, their awareness is even greater than this. They know "the ordinance of God" (τὸ δικαίωμα τοῦ θεοῦ, *to dikaiōma tou theou*), which is specified in the subsequent ὅτι (*hoti*, that) clause. God's ordinance is that those who indulge in such behavior are "worthy of death" (ἄξιοι θανάτου, *axioi thanatou*). It follows, then, that Gentiles, without specifically having the Mosaic law, are aware of the moral requirements contained in that law (cf. Thielman 1994a: 169; Wilckens 1978: 115). They not only know that God disapproves of their behavior but they also know that it deserves the punishment of death (cf. 6:23). Nonetheless, they continue to engage in such wicked behavior.

The depth of their evil is even greater. This is indicated by the οὐ μόνον ... ἀλλὰ καί (*ou monon ... alla kai*, not only ... but also) structure of the text. Not only do they continue to practice evil that they know deserves God's sentence of death, but they also "give commendation to those who practice these things" (συνευδοκοῦσιν τοῖς πράσσουσιν, *syneudokousin tois prassousin*). This verse manifests considerable diversity in the textual witnesses, presumably because many scribes (like many modern interpreters) questioned how encouraging others to practice evil was a graver evil than actually doing the evil (see the additional note on 1:32). But Cranfield (1975: 133–35) is right in arguing that the text is saying just what it appears to say. He notes correctly that the person who commits evil, even though his or her actions are inexcusable, can at least plead the mitigating circumstances of the passion of the moment. Those who encourage others to practice evil do so from a settled and impassioned conviction. Cranfield (1975: 135) says: "But there is also the fact that those who condone and applaud the vicious actions of others are actually making a deliberate contribution to the setting up of public opinion favourable to vice, and so to the corruption of an indefinite number of other people." The full extent of the rejection of God becomes evident in such an attitude. His judgment is known, yet people are encouraged to pursue evil anyway. Those who encourage others to pursue evil commit a greater evil in that they foment the spread of evil and are complicit in the destruction of others. The hatred of God is so entrenched that people are willing to risk future judgment in order to carry out their evil desires.[80] Once again, the text hints that the fundamental sin that informs all others is a refusal to delight in or submit to God's lordship. God's wrath is rightly inflicted on those who not only practice evil but find their greatest delight in it.[81]

1 Corinthians 6:9 Updated American Standard Version (UASV)

9 Or do you not know that the unrighteous will not inherit the kingdom of God? Do not be deceived; neither fornicators, nor

---

[80] Calvin (1960: 38) remarks, "A man who feels shame may still be healed; but when such a lack of shame has been acquired through the practice of sin, that vice, and not virtue, pleases us and has our approval, there is no more any hope of amendment."

[81] Thomas R. Schreiner, *Romans*, vol. 6, Baker Exegetical Commentary on the New Testament (Grand Rapids, MI: Baker Books, 1998), 92–100.

idolaters, nor adulterers, nor men of passive homosexual acts, nor men of active homosexual acts,[82]

1 Timothy 1:10 Updated American Standard Version (UASV)

[10] the sexually immoral ones, men who lie with men,[83] kidnappers, liars, perjurers, and whatever else is contrary to sound teaching,

---

1 Corinthians 6:9 and 1 Timothy 1:10

Paul also speaks against homosexuality in 1 Corinthians 6:9 and 1 Timothy 1:10. In both texts he used the term *arsenokoitai* [male partner in homosexual intercourse] to designate the sin of homosexuality. Paul's use of the term represents its first occurrence in Greek literature. David Wright is likely correct in suggesting that Paul derived the term from Leviticus 18:22 and 20:13.[84] When we look at both of these texts in the LXX, we can see the argument: *kai meta arsenos ou koimēthēse koitēn gynaikos bdelygma gar estin* (Lev. 18:22); *kai hos an koimēthē meta arsenos koitēn gynaikos bdelygma epoiēsan amphoteroi thanatousthōsan enochoi eisin* (Lev. 20:13). What Wright argues, and other scholars have followed him here, is that the Pauline term *arsenokoitai* [male partner in homosexual intercourse] is a Pauline innovation deriving from the phrase, *arsenos koitēn* in the two texts from Leviticus. The term refers, then, to those who bed other males. In other words, it is a vivid way of denoting same sex intercourse between males. The other word used to designate same sex relations in 1 Corinthians 6:9 is *malakoi*. This word refers to the passive partner sexually, an effeminate male who plays the role of a female.

Both 1 Corinthians 6:9 and 1 Timothy 1:10, also proscribe [ban or condemn] homosexuality in general. Dale Martin suggests that

---

[82] The two Greek terms refer to passive men partners and active men partners in consensual homosexual acts

[83] men who are sexually active with members of his own sex.

[84] David F. Wright, 'Homosexuals or Prostitutes? The Meaning of *Arsenokoitai* (1 Cor. 6:9 1 Tim. 1:10)', *Vigiliae Christianae* 38 (1984): 125–53. Dale B. Martin criticizes the interpretation supported by Wright in 'Arsenokoites and Malakos, Meaning and Consequences', in *Biblical Ethics and Homosexuality: Listening to Scripture*, ed. Robert L. Brawley (Louisville: Westminster John Knox, 1996), 119–23, In turn Gagnon defends Wright's view and exposes the weaknesses in Martin's interpretation (*Homosexual Practice*, 312–36).

the term *arsenokoitai* [male partner in homosexual intercourse] refers to those who exploit others sexually, but cannot be limited to same sex relations.[85] Such a broadening of the term, however, does not fit with either the background of the term in Leviticus 18:22 and 20:13 or the basic meaning of the word: bedding a male. Furthermore, the pairing of *arsenokoitai* with *malakoi* in 1 Corinthians 6:9 indicates that homosexual relations are in view. Paul could have used the more technical term *paiderastēs* (a pederast [man who has sex with boy]) if he had intended to restrict his comments to exploitative sex. Furthermore, if the only problem in view were sex that exploits others, there would be no need for Paul to mention the passive partner as well since he is the one being oppressed, and not the oppressor.

Robin Scroggs suggests another interpretation. He argues that the word *andrapodistais* (slave-dealers) in 1 Timothy 1:10 intimates that *arsenokoitai* refers to the slave dealers who sell boys and girls as slaves for brothel houses.[86] Scroggs's view is scarcely persuasive, it is hard to believe that kidnappers were exclusively involved in the sex-trade business. Moreover, the term for slave-dealers is lacking in the 1 Corinthians 6:9 context, and it can scarcely be imported there to explain the term *arsenokoitai*. Finally, there is no reason to think that the term slave-dealers casts any light on the meaning of *arsenokoitai* in the vice list in 1 Timothy 1:9–10. The sins listed represent particularly egregious violations of the ten commandments.

Alternative explanations are provided for *malakoi* as well. Scroggs thinks the reference is to effeminate callboys and prostitution.[87] In reply we can say that Paul's indictment would include such activities, but there is insufficient evidence to limit what Paul says here to male prostitution. Dale Martin argues that effeminacy broadly conceived is in view, so that the *malakoi* adorn themselves with soft and expensive clothes, consume gourmet foods, are pre-occupied with their hair-style, wear perfume, engage

---

[85] Martin, 'Arsenokoites and Malakos', 119–23

[86] Scroggs, *New Testament and Homosexuality*, 118–21.

[87] Scroggs, *New Testament and Homosexuality*, 106–109.

in heterosexual sex excessively, masturbate, are gluttons, lazy, and cowards, and also accept phallic penetration by another male.[88] Martin thinks such a view is misogynist and should not be endorsed in our day. The Pauline evidence, however, does not verify Martin's view. In 1 Corinthians 6:9 the word *malakoi* is paired with *arsenokoitai*, and the combination of the two terms indicates that same sex relations are in view, not heterosexual sex or effeminate behaviour in general. Paul, of course, in the very same verse says that those who live sexually immoral lives as heterosexuals will be excluded from the kingdom as well, but he does not have such a notion in mind when he uses the terms *arsenokoitai* and *malakoi*.

Sons and Daughters of Adam

As noted earlier, the biblical prohibition on homosexuality is questioned, because we allegedly have knowledge about homosexuality that was not available to biblical writers. For instance, it is sometimes said that homosexuality is genetic, and biblical writers were not cognizant of this truth. It is not my purpose here to delve into the question of the genetic character of homosexuality. The scientific evidence supporting such a conclusion, however, is not compelling. Most studies yield the rather common sense conclusion that homosexuality is the result of both nature and nurture, and cannot be wholly explained by genetic factors.[89]

However, I do want to look at the perspective of the Scriptures, relative to so-called genetic characteristics. Even if some sins could be traced to our genetics, it would not exempt us from responsibility for such sins. The Scriptures teach that all human beings are born into this world as sons and daughters of Adam, and hence they are by nature children of wrath (Eph. 2:3). They are dead in trespasses in sins (Eph. 2:1, 5), and have no inclination to seek God or to do what is good (Rom. 3:10–11). We come into the world as those who are spiritually dead (Rom. 5:12, 15), so

---

[88] Martin, '*Arsenokoites and Malakos*', 124–28.

[89] See, e.g., Stanton L. Jones & Mark A. Yarhouse, *Homosexuality: The Use of Scientific Research in the Church's Moral Debate* (Downers Grove: InterVarsity, 2000); Jeffrey Satinover, *Homosexuality and the Politics of Truth* (Grand Rapids: Baker, 1996); Schmidt. *Straight and Narrow?*, 131–59; Gagnon, *Homosexual Practice*, 396–432.

that death reigns over the whole human race (Rom. 5:17). Indeed, human beings are condemned by virtue of Adam's sin (Rom. 5:16, 18). Such a radical view of sin in which we inherit a sinful nature from Adam means that sinful predispositions are part of our personalities from our inception. Hence, even if it were discovered that we are genetically predisposed to certain sinful behaviours like alcoholism or homosexuality, such discoveries would not eliminate our responsibility for our actions, nor would it suggest that such actions are no longer sinful. The Scriptures teach that we are born as sinners in Adam, while at the same time they insist we should not sin and are responsible for the sin we commit. We enter into the world as slaves of sin (Rom. 6:6, 17), but we are still morally blameworthy for capitulating to the sin that serves as our master.

New Persons in Christ

When we think of a NT perspective on homosexuality, we must remember the proclamation of the gospel, the truth that those who are in Christ are new persons. In other words, we have substantial evidence that those who struggle with the sin of homosexuality can live a new life by God's grace. We are enabled to live new lives because of who we are in Christ. Those who put their trust in Christ are justified by faith (Rom. 5:1). They have peace with God and are reconciled to him through the cross of Christ (Rom. 5:1, 10). They are adopted as God's children (Rom. 8:14–17). They are redeemed and liberated from the power of sin, so that they may be zealous for good works (Tit. 2:14). They are now saved by grace through faith (Eph. 2:8). They have been born again through the Holy Spirit.[90] They are a new creation (Gal. 6:16; 2 Cor. 5:17). All people enter the world as sons and daughters of Adam and so are under the dominion of 'the old man'. But now, by virtue of union with Christ, they are clothed with the 'new man'.[91] They have put the old man off and have been endowed with the new man. Those who are in Christ are sanctified (1 Cor. 1:30; 6:11), so that they stand before God as those who are holy and clean in his sight. Their sins are truly forgiven, so that they do

---

[90] John 1:12, 3:3, 5, 8.

[91] Rom. 6:6; Col. 3:9–10; Eph. 2:15; cf. Eph. 4:24.

not live under the shackles of the past (Eph. 1:14; Col. 2:11–14).

The Continuing Struggle with Sin and the Promise of Moral Perfection

We face two dangers here. We may under-emphasize our newness in Christ, so that the redemption accomplished for us is negated or trivialized. On the other hand, we may fall prey to an over-realized eschatology that underestimates the continuing presence of sin in the lives of believers. The already, but not yet dimension of Christian teaching is immensely practical when it comes to understanding sanctification. First John 3:1–3 makes it clear that believers are not all that we will be. We will be conformed fully to the likeness of Jesus only when he returns. Hence, in the meantime, believers continue to struggle with sin. We stand in the right before God by virtue of the work of Christ, but we are not perfected. The emblem of the continuing presence of sin in our lives is our mortal body. The NT regularly teaches that we will experience moral perfection when our corruptible bodies become incorruptible, when this mortal puts on immortality.[92] In the meantime, we continue the struggle against sin as long as we are in our bodies until the day of resurrection (Phil. 3:20–21). The resurrection of our bodies testifies that the bodies are not inherently sinful, but as sons and daughters of Adam we are born into the world with sin reigning over us as whole persons (Rom 5:12–19).

The tension of Christian experience surfaces here. We are new creations in Christ and liberated from the power of sin, but at the same time, we await the fullness of our redemption. The newness of our redemption in Christ does not mean that we are completely free of sin. Rather, as believers we continue to battle against, and struggle with sin every day. First Peter 2:11 says, 'Beloved, I urge you as sojourners and exiles to abstain from the passions of the flesh, which wage war against your soul.' Notice that the passions and desires from the flesh are still powerful in all believers. They are so strong that they war against us.

We might think that we will not have any desires to do evil as

---

[92] Rom. 8:10–11, 23; 1 Cor. 15:52–54; Eph. 1:14.

believers in Jesus Christ, but as long as we are in the [imperfect] body, desires for sin, sometimes incredibly powerful desires, will be ours. Such desires do not mean that we are failures, or that we are not truly believers. They are a normal part of the Christian life before the day of resurrection. We ought not to think, therefore, that the newness we have in Christ means that believers will have no desire to return to a homosexual lifestyle. The newness we have in Christ does not mean that we are freed from old temptations. There is a progressive and even sometimes slow growth in holiness in our Christian lives. Indeed, we can sin dramatically as believers, even if we have been Christians for a long time. Even when we sin in such a way, there is no excuse for sinning [i.e., living in sin], and we are called to a deep sorrow and repentance for the evil in our lives.

This explains why we must fight the fight of faith afresh every day. Peter does not upbraid his readers for having desires to do wrong, but he does exhort them to abstain from these fleshly desires that war against our souls. In Romans 8:13, the apostle Paul says that believers are to put to death by the Spirit the desires of the body. Again, from this verse we see that Christians still face sin since they live in corruptible bodies, and the battle against sin is so fierce that the deeds of the body must be slain. They must be put to death. This fits with Colossians 3:5 where we are exhorted to put to death our members that are on earth. The metaphor of putting these desires and actions to death demonstrates that we are not talking about something easy and simple here.

The NT, of course, does not simply leave us with the message: 'Just say "no" '. It trumpets the grace of God in Jesus Christ that liberates us from the mastery and tyranny of sin. Those who have died and risen with Christ are no longer slaves to sin (Rom. 6). The power and dominion of sin has been broken decisively, so that we are now free from the tentacles of sin and are enabled to live in a way that pleases God. Romans 8:13 exhorts us to conquer sinful actions by the power of the Holy Spirit. We realize that we cannot triumph over sin in our own strength. We call on the Spirit to help us in our hour of need, and we realize that we will not be full of the Spirit (Eph. 5:18) unless the Word of Christ dwells in us richly (Col. 3:16). We remember the truth of the gospel that we are loved because Christ Jesus died for us. We are adopted, justified, reconciled, redeemed, and holy in Christ. The exhortation to live a new live comes from a Father who has loved us and delivered us from final condemnation. It is from a Father who promises to complete what he has started on the last day (Phil. 1:6). We have the promise that we will be fully, and finally sanctified (1 Thess. 5:23–24). Hence, we trust his promises to strengthen and free us from the allure of sin. We are not yet perfected, but we are changing by his Spirit. And we are changing because we have been changed and will be changed from one degree of glory to another, just as from the Lord who is the Spirit of freedom (2 Cor. 3:17–18).[93]

From what lies above, we can clearly see that there is absolutely no ambiguity in the Bible at all. God designed Adam and Eve, to procreate, and sex is to be between one man and one woman. (Gen. 1:27, 28; Lev 18:22; Pro 5:18-19) Fornication in Scripture is a reference to sexual sin by homosexual and heterosexual conduct. (Gal. 5:19-21)[94] We have certainly overturned many of the arguments given by the LGBT homosexual community in the above. God had warned of those, who would twist (distort) the meaning of the Scriptures. Since Jesus does not directly mention homosexuality but the apostle Paul does so explicitly many times in a condemnatory judgment kind of way, the only recourse for those that favor homosexuality is to undermine Paul's arguments, by twisting (distorting) the meaning of the text. The irony is that Peter said this very thing would happen. Peter wrote of Paul, "and regard the patience of our Lord as salvation; just as also **our beloved brother Paul**, according to the wisdom given him, wrote to you, as also **in all his letters**, speaking in them of these things, in which are **some things hard to understand**, which **the untaught and unstable distort**, as they do **also the rest of the Scriptures**, to **their own destruction**." (2 Pet. 3:15-16, NASB) We have followed the advice from Peter's first letter. "But in your hearts honor Christ the Lord as holy, **always being prepared to make a defense** to anyone who

[93] Thomas R. Schreiner, "A New Testament Perspective on Homosexuality," *Themelios* 31, no. 3 (2006): 70–75.

[94] Help is available for all who struggle with same sex attraction and those who struggle with intense opposite-sex attraction. http://www.aacc.net/

asks you for a reason for the hope that is in you; yet do it **with gentleness and respect**, having a good conscience, so that, when you are slandered, those who revile your good behavior in Christ may be put to shame." – 1 Peter 3:15-16, ESV.

The Bible's Viewpoint of Same-Sex Attraction

However, the Bible does not condone hating those who struggle with same-sex attraction, but we are to hate the sin. However, we are to make a stand against sin that is against the moral code of our Creator, and we are **not** to cave to public opinion. Our Christian lifestyle is reflective by the moral code within Scripture, and we have a right to our position, by the Creator himself. There is no reason that we should be ashamed of our viewpoint.

1 Peter 2:17 New Living Translation (NLT)

¹⁷ Respect everyone, and love your Christian brothers and sisters. Fear God, and respect the king.

Christians should not have an irrational hatred for those that struggle with same-sex attraction. We are to respect all people. Anyone who is spewing hatred, he is not truly acting Christlike. (Matt. 7:12) We are to reject same-sex relationships, the conduct, not the person. For those who are advocates for gay rights, this is their viewpoint, and we **respectfully** disagree, and **respectfully** articulate as to why. Nevertheless, we do not accept persons as being truly Christian, or members of a Christian congregation, who are living in any sin, which includes homosexuality. – Revelation 2:5; 1 Corinthians 5:5-13; 1 Timothy 1:19, 20; 3 John 9, 10.

If some make the argument that Jesus visited sinners and that he was tolerant of others, this is mixing some truth, but also misleading at the same time. Indeed, Jesus spent time with sinners, but he did not ever condone their sin, nor did he ever look favorably upon those who practiced sin, i.e., lived in sin. – Matthew 18:15-17.

Some may make the point I made in the above, but take it a step further. They may say, "I am born this way, it is not my fault, why should I be punished, or miss out on love, because of inheriting a genetic predisposition?"

We could respond that the Bible does not address the genetic predisposition of same-sex attraction, but then again it does not address the mental issues of bipolar either. It is not a science textbook, nor is it a mental health guide. Thus, we should not look for it to resolve the specifics. However, it does address certain thinking and certain actions. Therefore, the Bible might not explicitly address the genetic, but it does address same-sex acts.

Some have argued that addictive personalities are genetically predisposed (gambling, drugs, alcohol, intense opposite sex attraction, and pedophilia), as well as anger and rage are also viewed as genetic. Giving these ones the same benefit of the doubt as to the leanings being genetic, would we approve of a man that beats his wife, or another man that sexually abuses women, because they may be predisposed to those desires. Certainly not, we would send him to Christian counseling, and expect him to get control over his body and mind, by putting on the mind of Christ. Would we excuse a man who is genetically predisposed as a pedophile, who acts on his sexual desire for children? No, we would scream, lock him up and throw away the key. We would acknowledge that the wife beater and the pedophile struggle with these desires, and we would expect that they would not put themselves in an innocent appearing situations. Moreover, we would expect them through redemptive therapy by way of biblical counseling to get and maintain control over themselves.

What the Bible offers is reasonable, and it does not condone homophobic mindsets. The Bible expects those who have same-sex attraction to apply the same counsel, as those with intense opposite-sex attraction.

1 Corinthians 6:18 Updated American Standard Version (UASV)

[18] Flee from sexual immorality. Every other sin that a man commits is outside the body, but the sexually immoral person sins against his own body.[95]

---

[95] Paul began his conclusion to this section with an abrupt command: **Flee ... immorality**. It is likely that the apostle had in mind Joseph's example of fleeing Potiphar's wife (Gen. 39:12). Paul instructed the young pastor Timothy in a similar way (2 Tim. 2:22). Rather than moderate resistance to immorality, Paul insisted on radical separation.

There are hundreds of thousands, if not millions of men and women, who suffer from intense sexual attraction and addition. The Bible expects them to get control over their body, not give into temptation. The same is expected with those with same-sex attraction.

Deuteronomy 30:19 Updated American Standard Version (UASV)

¹⁹ I call heaven and earth to witness against you today, that I have set before you life and death, the blessing and the curse; and you must choose life so that you may live, you and your descendants,

Just as was true with the Israelites, we have the freedom to choose to serve the Creator with the hope of eternal life, or we ca choose to obey our fallen flesh and its desires, which will result in consequences.

Ephesians 4:19 Updated American Standard Version (UASV)

¹⁹ who being past feeling gave themselves up to shameless conduct, for the practice of every uncleanness with greediness.

The phrase "shameless conduct" can also be rendered "loose conduct," "sensuality," "licentiousness" "promiscuity" Greek, *aselgeia*. This phrase refers to acts of conduct that are serious sins. It reveals a shameless condescending arrogance; i.e., disregard or even disdain for authority, laws, and standards. This phrase does not refer to wrong conduct that is minor in nature. (Gal. 5:19; 2 Pet. 2:7) The *Greek-English Lexicon of the New Testament: Based on Semantic Domains* says *aselgeia* is "behavior completely lacking in moral restraint, usually with the implication of sexual

---

Paul's radical advice rested on the uniqueness of sexual sin. In contrast with **all other sins**, immorality is **against** one's **own body**. The meaning of these words is difficult to determine. Many sins, such as substance abuse, gluttony, and suicide, have detrimental effects on the body. Paul's words do not refer to disease and/or other damage caused by sin. Instead, his words are linked to the preceding discussion of 6:12–17. There Paul established that Christians' bodies are joined with Christ so that they become "members of Christ" (6:15) himself.

Sexual union with a prostitute violates one's body by bringing it into a wrongful "one flesh" union, and by flaunting the mystical union with Christ (6:15). It is in this sense that sexual immorality is a unique sin against the body. It violates the most significant fact about believers' physical existence: their bodies belong to Christ. – (Pratt Jr 2000, 101)

licentiousness—'licentious behavior, extreme immorality.' μὴ μετανοησάντων ἐπὶ τῇ ἀκαθαρσίᾳ καὶ πορνείᾳ καὶ ἀσελγείᾳ ᾗ ἔπραξαν 'they have not repented of the filthy things they have done, their immorality and licentious deeds' 2 Cor. 12:21. In some languages the equivalent of 'licentious behavior' would be 'to live like a dog' or 'to act like a goat' or 'to be a rooster,' in each instance pertaining to promiscuous sexual behavior.[96]

Ephesians 5:11-14 Updated American Standard Version (UASV)

¹¹ Do not participate in the unfruitful deeds of darkness, but instead even expose them ¹² for it is shameful even to speak of the things which are done by them in secret. ¹³ But all the things that are being reproved are exposed by the light, for everything that becomes visible is light.

¹⁴ For this reason it says,
"Awake, O sleeper,
  and arise from the dead,
and Christ will shine on you."

On this verse Max Anders in the *Holman New Testament Commentary* writes,

> Not only ought we not to do the same sins as those who are disobedient, but we should try to expose them. Paul may be referring to exposing the sins of church members, because the church is responsible to hold its members accountable for their lifestyles. If a Christian lives in flagrant, unrepentant sin, the church is to try to get them to turn from their sin (Matt. 18:15–20; Gal. 6:1).

> The context is dealing with the disobedient. This would indicate that the church should attempt to expose the sins of the non-Christian, which would be a full-time job if done very thoroughly. Society's major sins certainly need to be exposed.

> Sins are exposed by shining light into sin's darkness. An amazing thing happens. Darkness can no longer hide

---

[96] Johannes P. Louw and Eugene Albert Nida, *Greek-English Lexicon of the New Testament: Based on Semantic Domains* (New York: United Bible Societies, 1996), 770.

its nature and acts in secret. All is exposed to light. Light that **makes everything visible** brings an even more radical element. Literally, this reads, everything that is revealed is (or becomes) light. Light turns darkness into light. This is the church's mission. Whether the people in darkness are church members or society members, the goal is to transform them completely from darkness to light.

The poetic passage in verse 14 may be a quote from an ancient hymn based on Scripture. It is not a direct scriptural quotation. A person who was participating in the **deeds of darkness** is to wake up and **rise from the dead**, meaning to turn from those deeds. **Christ will shine on you** may mean that Christ is pleased with the person who turns from such deeds. He is light and the source of their light. His shining light exposes all their darkness and transforms them into light.[97]

Put to Death What Is Earthly in You

Colossians 3:5 Updated American Standard Version (UASV)

⁵ Therefore, Put to death therefore what is earthly in you: sexual immorality, impurity, passion, evil desire, and covetousness, which is idolatry.

One of the greatest mistakes of the Christian and religious leadership is, to be self-righteous in their dealings with those who have same-sex attraction, or those that have given into a homosexual lifestyle. The conduct of such ones is n more grievous that the spouse who commits adultery, or the churchgoer who commits fornication, or the churchgoer that finds himself or herself involved in the habit of masturbation or pornography. Sexual sin is sexual sin. There were Christians in the first century who had formerly led a life of homosexuality, who put on the new person as they worked toward becoming a Christian, getting control over themselves, and setting aside their former ways. — 1 Corinthians 6:9-11

---

[97] Max Anders, *Galatians-Colossians*, vol. 8, Holman New Testament Commentary (Nashville, TN: Broadman & Holman Publishers, 1999), 171.

Does God have the right to set the moral standards of humankind? Yes, he is the Creator of heaven and earth, as well as humans. He designed us to be free moral agents but under the umbrella of his sovereignty. We were never intended to have absolute freedom, the ability to set our own standards of right and wrong. Moreover, the natural desire is opposite sex attraction. The only reason that same-sex attraction exists at present is our fall into imperfection. It is a symptom of inherited imperfection. Once God has settled the issues raised by Satan and man's rebellion, we will no longer lean toward bad, but will lean toward good. The natural desire for Adam and Eve before the fall was toward good, and to think of or do bad would have been contrary to that nature. After the rebellion and imperfection entered the world, the further removed humans were from Adam and Eve, the more they were and are inclined toward their imperfections, leaning toward bad.

How do we benefit from fighting the desires of the flesh, and obeying God's moral standards, as set out in Scripture? While it may seem unfair now that one cannot act on, nor entertain same-sex attraction, even though it may seem natural to him or her, this is a temporary situation. A time is coming when those, who have sided with God and have remained loyal, will receive eternal life. Can you imagine living for hundreds of millions of years, and looking back on that mere 70-80 years of imperfect desires?—John 3:16

God's View Homosexuality

While the liberal religious leaders of the day have watered down the Bible, this does not remove the clear statements from scripture. God created Adam and Eve, man and woman, with the desire, the sexual attraction of man toward woman and woman toward man. God is deeply saddened over the rebellion of Adam and Eve, and the subsequent fall into a sinful, depraved world. However, he is correcting the issues that were raised. God condemns all sin; that is all that is anything not in harmony with his personality, standards, ways, will, and purpose.[98]

---

[98] (See Job 2:10; Psa. 39:1; Lev. 20:20; 2 Cor. 12:21; Pro 21:4; Rom. 3:9-18; 2 Pet. 2:12-15; Heb. 3:12, 13, 18, 19)

What if you find yourself having feelings of same-sex attraction, does this necessarily mean that you are a homosexual, in the sense that you are not attracted, nor ever will be attracted to the same sex, and that you will fall away into having a sexual relationship with a person of the same sex. No. We do not fully understand our imperfections, and it could be a period of time that you feel this way. However, there is no sense in deceiving ourselves; some will only ever have a same-sex attraction in this imperfect age that we live in, and they are obligated to have control over themselves, just as the same as any other with inappropriate sexual desires. If one seeks out excellent, competent Christian counseling, can they put on the new person and take off the old person, to the point that they find themselves attracted to the opposite sex? Yes, some will be able to, but a few will have to live with and maintain control over their same-sex attraction until God brings this imperfect system of things to an end.

Just as some mental health professionals, believe that same-sex attraction is genetic, and others that it is social, they also believe the same thing about addictive personalities. They also believe the same thing about adults that are sexually attracted to children. We have already agreed in the above that it is likely that it is both. You have a child who grows up in a household where he is sexually abused, and once he is older, the doctors diagnose him as having sexual attractions toward very young children. Now, just because this one has genetic leanings in the direction of young children, and he was socialized in this direction, there is no rational person who would make the argument, "this is who he is, God made him this way, he should be allowed to continue having sexual relations with children." Just because he was born with this leaning and was raised in such an environment that only perpetuated his desires, rational society would expect him to seek professional help. They would expect that he overcome his leanings, and if not, possibly acquire coping skills to maintain control. If he acts out, he would be arrested and locked away. While society has legalized or, at least, ignored the laws against homosexuality, God has not, and he expects that one get help to overcome, or gain control of the unnatural desires.

Aside from getting professional help from a Christian counselor, what can you do to gain control over your unnatural desires? You can pray to God, really going at him with the issues, opening your heart to him.

Psalm 139:23-24 Updated American Standard Version (UASV)

23 Search me, O God, and know my heart;
  Examine me, and know my anxious[99] thoughts;
24 And see whether there is in me any painful way,[100]
  And lead me in the everlasting way

Proverbs 23:7 says, "For as he thinks in his heart, so is he." If we are to get control over our irrational thinking, we do well to fill our mind with good thoughts. (Phil 4:8) This means that we need to be in God's Words daily. The Bible has the power to mold our mind. (Heb. 4:12) Scripture can have a powerful effect on our thinking if we study it in the appropriate way.

Another measure that needs to be taken is the fleeing from anything that will generate wrong desires, which lead to wrong actions. This means keeping our eyes and ears away from pornography and homosexual advocates. (Col. 3:5) We need to understand that the Bible's moral values are not respected in today's world.

Parents, teachers, coaches and the like influenced the youth of the 1950s and 1960s. Most young people today are very much influenced by hip-hop, rap, and heavy metal music, as well reality television, celebrities, movies, video games, and the internet, especially social media. Parents are now allowing their children to receive life-altering opinions, beliefs, and worldviews from the likes of Snooki, a cast member of the MTV reality show *Jersey Shore*. Kim Kardashian and her family rose to prominence with their reality television series, *Keeping Up with the Kardashians*.

The ABC Family Channel (owned by Disney) comes across as a channel that you would want you children watching. However, most of the shows are nothing more than dysfunctional families, promotions of homosexuality as an alternative lifestyle, and young actors and actresses that are playing underage teens in high school,

---

99 Or *disquieting*

100 Or *hurtful way*

running around killing, causing havoc, and having sexual intercourse with multiple characters on the show. In August 2006, an all-new slogan and visual style premiered on ABC Family: A New Kind of Family. The channel shows such programming as Pretty Little Liars, Twisted, The Fosters, Melissa & Joey, Switched at Birth, The Lying Game, Bunheads and Baby Daddy.

The world has added new words to their vocabulary, like "sexting," which is the act of sending sexually explicit messages and/or photographs, primarily between cell phones. The term was first popularized in 2007. Then, there is "F-Bomb," which we are not going to define fully other than to say that the dictionary considers it "a lighthearted and printable euphemism" for something far more offensive. If all of the above is unfamiliar to us as parents, and we have a teen or preteen child, we may want to Google the information.

Regardless of the degree of the relationship, these relationships often influence the thinking of a young life. It is important that we do not allow the wrong persons to change our children or us. The truth is our thoughts, and our actions are a direct result of bad associations, be it the bad friends, music, celebrities, video games, or social media. The same holds true of good relationships, like our parents, teachers, coaches, and good friends. Paul warned, "For there are many **rebellious men**, **empty talkers,** and **deceivers**," from whom we should watch out! – Titus 1:10.

In the end, with help from God's Word, the Christian congregation, the pastor, family, and Christian counseling, you have a reasonable expectation that you will not act on the same-sex desires. Moreover, there is the possibility that you may be one of the few that begins to alter oneself to the point that the desires are no more. If not, self-control will be the way of things until God brings this wicked age to an end. The final warning offered herein is this. Do not allow charismatic religious rhetoric to suggest that you can be healed by laying on of hands. This will only leave you vulnerable, as you will then let down your guard, and not seek the help that you need. What they espouse is just not how it works and is unbiblical.

Review Questions

- What human condition do we have because of the human rebellion of Adam and Eve? Explain the extent.

- How does one go from the Old Person to the New Person?

- What is the Bible's View of Homosexuality?

- Genesis 9:18-28 – If it is Ham that saw Noah's nakedness, why is Canaan the one getting cursed?

- Leviticus 18:22 – Since "Christ is the end of the [Mosaic] law" (Rom. 10:4), does this include homosexuality? Explain

- What is the Bible view of sexuality?

- Leviticus 18:22-24 – Is the curse of barrenness behind God's condemnation of homosexuality?

- Why did God destroy Sodom and Gomorrah? What was the sin of Sodom and Gomorrah?

- The Greek word *sarkos heteras* of Jude 7 literally *went after different, or other flesh* means what?

- Genesis 19:8 – Why was Lot not condemned for offering his daughters to the Sodomites?

- Genesis 19:30-38 – Did God condone the incest of Lot with his two daughters?

- Why did Jesus not need to speak specifically about Homosexuality?

- Explain the first century Bible background of homosexuality.

- Why are ungodly people inexcusable? Explain Romans 1:24-32.

- What is the Bible's viewpoint of same-sex Attraction?

- Why and how do we 'put to death what is earthly in us'?

- Does God have the right to set the moral standards of humankind?

- What is God's view of homosexuality?

- How are we to evangelize the LGBT homosexual community?

- How are we to help those struggling with same-sex attraction?

CHAPTER 2 Explaining the Bible's View of Homosexuality

'If I was lying on my deathbed and I had kept this secret and never ever did anything about it, I would be lying there saying, "You just blew your entire life. You never dealt with yourself," and I don't want that to happen,' Bruce Jenner said in her Vanity Fair interview, who is now known as "Caitlyn Jenner."

Miley Cyrus came out as a pansexual (i.e., a sexuality that expresses itself in many different forms), saying, 'I am literally open to every single thing that is consenting and doesn't involve an animal and everyone is of age,' she told Paper magazine. 'Everything that's legal, I'm down with. Yo, I'm down with any adult — anyone over the age of 18 who is down to love me. I don't relate to being boy or girl, and I don't have to have my partner relate to boy or girl.'

There is actually a coming out day, 11 October. On this day, an article in Gay Star News, **22 celebrities who came out and changed the world in 2015**, *Roger Rock*, a retired British rail worker comments, "Congratulations to all of you - well done I wish I'd come out a lot earlier than 54 it will 20 years next year - never looked back!" Paula Key, from Toronto, Ontario, who studied at the University of Toronto, commented on the same above article. "So happy to blog these lesbians on ... There is such a need for gays/lesbians in homophobic countries to learn about their history. Just over 200, 212 visitors - the need is there."[101]

The Advocate is an American LGBT-interest magazine, printed bi-monthly, ran an article, 53 People Who Came Out This Year, referring to 2015. They write, "We're always glad when anyone comes out, although it's particularly noteworthy when well-known people do. They provide role models for young LGBT people and drive home the message that we are everywhere, while usually enhancing their own lives in the process — living openly and honestly is good for the soul. We're looking back at some famous

---

[101] 22 celebrities who came out and made 2015 the best year ..., http://www.gaystarnews.com/article/25-celebrities-who-made-2015-the-best-year-ev (accessed April 23, 2016).

folks who've come out as lesbian, gay, bisexual, transgender, pansexual, or fluid this year. Of course, you don't have to be famous for your coming-out to make an impact. When people know someone who is LGBT, they're far more likely to support our rights. 'Every person who speaks up changes more hearts and minds, and creates new advocates for equality,' notes the Human Rights Campaign."[102]

Pew Research Center[103]

Acceptance of homosexuality is rising across the broad spectrum of American Christianity, including among members of churches that strongly oppose homosexual relationships as sinful, according to an extensive Pew Research Center survey of U.S. religious beliefs and practices.

Amid a changing religious landscape that has seen a declining percentage of Americans who identify as Christian, a majority of U.S. Christians (54%) now say that homosexuality should be accepted, rather than discouraged, by society. While this is still considerably lower than the shares of religiously unaffiliated people (83%) and members of non-Christian faiths (76%) who say the same, the Christian figure has increased by 10 percentage points since we conducted a similar study in 2007. It reflects a growing acceptance of homosexuality among all Americans – from 50% to 62% – during the same period.

Among Christians, this trend is driven partly by younger church members, who are generally more accepting of homosexuality than their elder counterparts. For example, roughly half (51%) of evangelical Protestants in the Millennial generation (born between 1981 and 1996) say homosexuality should be

---

[102] 53 People Who Came Out This Year | Advocate.com, http://www.advocate.com/people/2015/12/23/53-people-who-came-out-year (accessed April 23, 2016).

[103] The Pew Research Center is a nonpartisan American think tank which is based in Washington, D.C. It provides information on social issues, public opinion, and demographic trends shaping the United States and the world. It also conducts public opinion polling, demographic research, media content analysis, and other empirical social science research. Pew Research Center does not take explicit policy positions, and is a subsidiary of The Pew Charitable Trusts. – Pew Research Center - Wikipedia, the free encyclopedia, https://en.wikipedia.org/wiki/Pew_Research_Center (accessed April 23, 2016).

accepted by society, compared with a third of evangelical Baby Boomers and a fifth of evangelicals in the Silent generation. Generational differences with similar patterns also are evident among Catholics, mainline Protestants and members of the historically black Protestant tradition.

At the same time, however, a larger segment of older adults in some Christian traditions have become accepting of homosexuality in recent years, helping to drive the broader trend. For instance, 32% of evangelical Protestant Baby Boomers now say homosexuality should be accepted, up from 25% in 2007.

Regardless of age, seven-in-ten Catholics – whose church teaches that homosexual behavior is "intrinsically disordered" – say that homosexuality should be accepted by society, a 12-percentage-point increase since 2007. Similar jumps have occurred among mainline Protestants (from 56% to 66%), Orthodox Christians (from 48% to 62%) and members of the historically black Protestant tradition (from 39% to 51%).

Most Mormons and evangelical Protestants still say homosexuality should be discouraged by society – in line with the teachings of many of their churches – but 36% of both groups say it should be accepted. Among Mormons, there was a 12-point increase (from 24% to 36%) in acceptance since 2007, and among evangelicals there was a 10-point rise (from 26% to 36%). Jehovah's Witnesses remain perhaps the most opposed of any U.S religious tradition toward homosexuality, with just 16% saying it should be accepted by society.

The trend of growing acceptance is evident across many specific Protestant denominations, including some conservative denominations with official teachings that remain strongly opposed to same-sex marriage. For example, among members of the Lutheran Church-Missouri Synod, the share saying homosexuality should be accepted by society grew by 12 points (from 44% to 56%) between 2007 and 2014. And although Pentecostals who identify with the Assemblies of God remain largely opposed to homosexuality, 26% now say it should be accepted by society, up from 16% in 2007.

Among members of the Southern Baptist Convention – an

evangelical church and the nation's largest Protestant denomination – the share saying homosexuality should be accepted increased 7 points, from 23% to 30%.

Members of several mainline churches – some of which have officially embraced same-sex marriage – have become even more accepting of homosexuality in recent years. For instance, 73% of members of the Evangelical Lutheran Church in America now say it should be accepted by society, up from 56% in 2007. Members of the United Methodist Church, the Episcopal Church, the Presbyterian Church (U.S.A.) and the United Church of Christ also have become more accepting toward homosexuality.[104]

Members of many Protestant denominations now more accepting of homosexuality

% saying homosexuality should be accepted by society

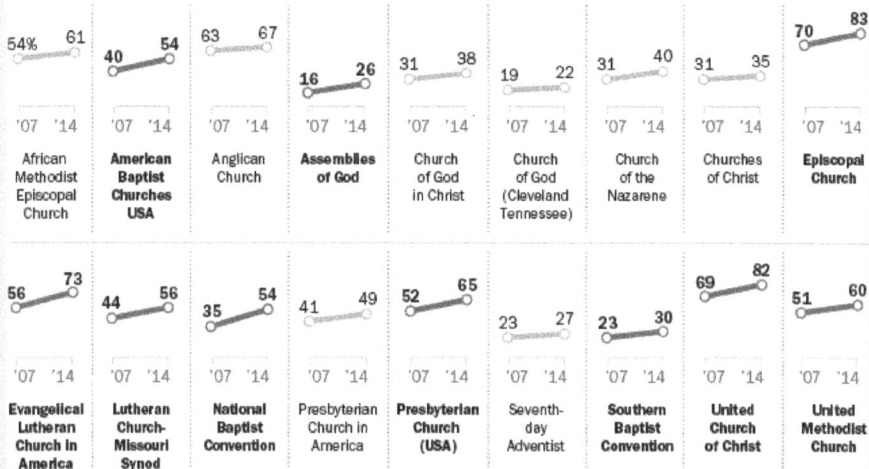

'07 '14	'07 '14	'07 '14	'07 '14	'07 '14	'07 '14	'07 '14	'07 '14	'07 '14
54% 61	40 54	63 67	16 26	31 38	19 22	31 40	31 35	70 83
African Methodist Episcopal Church	American Baptist Churches USA	Anglican Church	Assemblies of God	Church of God in Christ	Church of God (Cleveland Tennessee)	Church of the Nazarene	Churches of Christ	Episcopal Church

'07 '14	'07 '14	'07 '14	'07 '14	'07 '14	'07 '14	'07 '14	'07 '14	'07 '14
56 73	44 56	35 54	41 49	52 65	23 27	23 30	69 82	51 60
Evangelical Lutheran Church in America	Lutheran Church-Missouri Synod	National Baptist Convention	Presbyterian Church in America	Presbyterian Church (USA)	Seventh-day Adventist	Southern Baptist Convention	United Church of Christ	United Methodist Church

Source: 2014 Religious Landscape Study, conducted June 4-Sept. 30, 2014. Statistically significant change shown in bold.
PEW RESEARCH CENTER

TheRichest.com claims to be "the world's leading source of shocking and intriguing content surrounding celebrities, money, global events, society, pop culture, sports and much more." They write, "The year was 2003, Britney shocked the world when she and Madonna went into a kiss with full on mouth-to-mouth. After

[104] More U.S. Christians OK with ... - Pew Research Center, http://www.pewresearch.org/fact-tank/2015/12/18/most-u-s-christian-groups-grow-m (accessed April 23, 2016).

the fact, Spears announced that she had never kissed a female before and never would again. In an interview with CNN, the pop star stated, 'I didn't know it was going to be that long and everything.' Evidently, she and Madonna discussed the possibility during rehearsals, but did not have a solid plan. When asked if she would 'do it again,' she decided that she would not, but maybe if it was Madonna again."[105]

The world is going liberal-progressive right before our eyes. The above, while once shocking is a regular occurrence. There are more websites than can be counted that run articles about homosexuals and homosexuality. The comments on these innumerable sites are into the millions likely. If one takes a stand as a Christian, saying homosexuality is a sin, they are labeled a homophobe, a bigot, prejudiced and judgmental. Many are afraid to defend the Word of God and their faith.

We have to understand that just as this generation is rapidly growing to accept homosexuality as an alternative lifestyle, the same is true of many Christian beliefs. However, God's Word is true and the values, morals, and ethics therein are always the same and do not change because of public opinion.

Ephesians 4:14 Updated American Standard Version (UASV)

[14] So that we may no longer be children, tossed to and fro by the waves and carried about by every wind of teaching, by the trickery of men, by craftiness with regard to the scheming of deceit;

On this verse, Max Anders writes, "The Ephesian church, as most of the churches Paul wrote, faced teachers with opposing viewpoints. They divided the church body into factions, each opposing the others. Their presence required the type of spiritual maturity and church unity Paul had described. Without such unity the church would act like a group of babies, each crying out because of his own pains and needs, each inconsistently saying one thing and then another, each at the mercy of cunning, deceitful

---

[105] 10 Shocking Same Sex Celebrity Kisses - TheRichest, http://www.therichest.com/rich-list/most-shocking/10-shocking-same-sex-celebrity (accessed April 23, 2016).

teachers. To avoid infantile behavior, the church must mature into unity of the faith and of knowledge of Christ.[106]

When it comes to Satan's world, which Jesus said we were to be no part of (John 15:19; 17:14-16), and Paul said that while we must live in the world, we need not fully use it. (1 Cor. 7:31) What did Paul mean? "To handle matters of this life properly, Christians must remember that these things are not permanent. On the one hand, believers live in this world with its pleasure, pain, and responsibilities. On the other hand, they belong to the next world that will replace this life forever. This is why Paul described his own life in paradoxical terms: dying but living, beaten but not killed, sorrowful but rejoicing, poor but making others rich, having nothing but owning everything (2 Cor. 6:9–10).[107]

On the subject of homosexuality, true Christians adhere to the Bible's view. What is the Bible's view of homosexuality? If we are going to obey to the Bible and not water down the Word of God, how are we to evangelize those who see us as a homophobe, a bigot, prejudiced and judgmental?

What is the Bible's View of Homosexuality?

We have covered this extensively in chapter 1, so we will only offer the gist if it here. We were created in the image of God, and we were designed male and female, to have sexual relations between one man and one woman, only within the marriage arrangement. Men are not to have sexual relations with a male, as with a woman, nor are women to have sexual relations with a woman as with a man; it is an abomination. (Gen. 1:27-28; Lev. 18:22; Pro 5:18-19) The Bible condemns fornication (Gr. *Porneia*, sexual immorality), which applies to both homosexual and forbidden heterosexual conduct." (Gal. 5:19-21) Sexual immorality unlawful sexual intercourse, which includes adultery, prostitution, sexual relations between unmarried individuals, homosexuality, and bestiality.

---

[106] Max Anders, *Galatians-Colossians*, vol. 8, Holman New Testament Commentary (Nashville, TN: Broadman & Holman Publishers, 1999), 153.

[107] Richard L. Pratt Jr, *I & II Corinthians*, vol. 7, Holman New Testament Commentary (Nashville, TN: Broadman & Holman Publishers, 2000), 121–122.

How Should Christians View Homosexuality?

We do not hate homosexuals. Nevertheless, we cannot approve of same-sex relationships of any kind. We can empathize with those who struggle with same-sex attractions, as many heterosexuals struggle with inappropriate sexual attractions to persons of the opposite sex that they ought not. We proudly but not arrogantly live by the moral code found within the Bible. This is our lifestyle choice just as some have made homosexuality their lifestyle choice. We will not hate those who are free to make choices at odds with ours, even if many evidence hatred of us, viewing us as a homophobe, a bigot, prejudiced and judgmental. We will not be ashamed of what we have a right to, a biblical worldview. – Joshua 24:15; Psalm 119:46.

Are Christians to Respect Everyone?

"Unquestionably, the Bible says: "Honor **all people**, love the brotherhood, fear God, honor the king." or, "**Respect everyone**, love other believers, honor God, and respect the Emperor." (1 Pet 2:17, NASB and GNT) However, we have a problem with the word homophobic, as it is defined as "showing an irrational hatred, **disapproval**, or fear of homosexuality, gay and lesbian people, or their culture." (Bold mine) If anyone asks us if we are homophobic, we will have to qualify it. Why? If we just say that we are not homophobic, they might believe we **do not** disapprove of it.

Are you homophobic? Respond, "I do not have any hatred of homosexuals, or fear of homosexuality, gay and lesbian people, or their culture. However, I do not approve of same-sex relations of any kind, except friendships."

Is the Christian Stance Not Encouraging Prejudice Against Homosexuals?

Certainly not, Christians reject homosexual relations, not the people themselves. If any Christian does otherwise, he or she is not being obedient to God's Word. True Christians cannot be faulted for radical Christian groups like the Westboro Baptist Church, who are nothing more than hate mongers. If we look at the link to their homepage (http://www.godhatesfags.com/), we can see that they are not true Christians. They and a handful of other groups like them are but a few thousand at most out of 200 countries with more than 2.18 billion Christians. Of course, not all of these 5.18 billion make up genuine Christianity. Certainly, there are those within the LBGT community, who would say that there others, who are radical and hate Christians merely because they are Christians. We as Christians cannot fault the whole for the select few. We are not to be prejudice toward the LBGT community and hope that they will not be prejudice toward us. We both can respect each other as persons and agree to disagree on certain matters.

Did Jesus Teach Tolerance?

First, let us define "tolerance." Like any word, it has different meanings in different contexts. It can mean, (1) acceptance of different views, (2) putting up with somebody or something irritating or otherwise unpleasant, (3) ability to endure hardship, and (4) the loss of effect that a drug can have. Our meaning is number (1), which can be better defined as, "the acceptance of the differing views of other people, e.g. in religious or political matters, and fairness toward the people who hold these different views."

Second, let us take a brief look at Jesus. While Christians certainly seek to imitate him to the best of their ability, it is impossible to do so fully, as we are imperfect, while he was a perfect man, as well as divine, the Son of God. In addition, he is the judge of whether someone receives eternal life or eternal destruction. (Matt. 25:31-46; 2 Thess. 1:8) Therefore, Jesus can judge a person as to life or death, for he can read hearts and minds. Humans are not to judge in this sense, nor do they have those abilities.

Third, Jesus did not have tolerance, accepting different views, as he clearly stated, "My food is to do the will of him [the Father] who sent me and to accomplish his work." (John 4:34) He also said, "Truly, truly, I say to you; the Son can do nothing of his own accord, but only what he sees the Father doing. For whatever the Father does, that the Son does likewise ... I can do nothing on my own. As I hear, I judge, and my judgment is just, because I seek not my own will but the will of him who sent me." (John 5:19, 30, ESV) Jesus' will would be the same as the Father's will and vice versa. They are one, in full agreement, and there are no divisions between them, as they are united in the same mind and the same judgment. Christians seek to be one as they are one. – John 10:30.

We can understand the values, the character, the moral code of the Father and the Son because of Scriptural revelation. Jesus would not accept any view that was not in harmony with his and the Father's personality, standards, ways, and will. (Lev. 20:20; Num. 9:13; Job 2:10; Ps 39:1; 2 Cor. 12:21; Jam. 4:17) Christians with a biblical worldview would be in agreement, united in the same mind and with the same purpose. Therefore, no, Jesus would not tolerate homosexuality, and nor would Christians. Any congregation that would allow a homosexual to become a member of that congregation, let alone a pastor or bishop, would be contrary to the above and the rest of Scriptures. They would be false teachers, leading people astray. They are 'untaught and unstable as they distort Paul's teachings, as they also do the rest of the Scriptures, to their own destruction.' (2 Pet. 3:16) Just because Christians do not tolerate, or accept different views that are in conflict with Scripture (e.g., homosexuality), this does not mean that they are to disrespect such ones.

Is Not Homosexuality Genetically Predisposed?

The Bible does not directly disclose that same-sex attraction is genetic. However, it could be inferred from God's curse of Canaan, (the forefather of the Canaanites), the grandson of Noah, who, it appears, sexually assaulted Noah when he was unconscious from alcohol. It can be inferred that we inherit leanings and dispositions. Certainly, we inherit sin, i.e., imperfection. (Rom. 5:12) In addition, the Bible does say that some of our imperfect traits are deeply ingrained. (2 Cor. 10:4-5) Therefore, if homosexuality is predisposed to some, this does not equate that "God made me this way." It only means it is imperfection passed on like any other. Thus, the fault lies with Satan and Adam.

Many accept that anger can have a genetic root. If this is true and at present there is no reason to doubt it, are we to accept men beating their wives, or wives beating their children because they may have been genetically predisposed to anger? Science argues that pedophilia is a genetic predisposition, so, are we to claim that pedophiles are acceptable? Some claim that alcoholism is genetic, so, are we to accept alcoholics as a part of the norm? Some from the LGBT community are offended when pedophiles are brought into the conversation because those sexual acts are an abomination, disgusting, revolting and rightly, they do not want to be associated with such ones. However, God feels the same way about homosexuality. We would expect that those with anger issues, those suffering from alcoholism, and those preferring child-sex (pedophile) would get control over themselves and avoid such unsavory activity. God's Word expects the same from those who have same-sex attraction.

Is It Not Cruel to Tell Those with Same-Sex Attraction to Control Themselves?

We would not accept a pedophile just because he or she has a child-sex attraction. Yes, God gave us sexual impulses, desires that are natural. However, sin, i.e., imperfection came into the world through Adam, and death through sin, imperfection, and so death spread to all men because all sinned, i.e., are imperfect. (Rom 5:1) We expect people that have impulses for things we find revolting not to act on them but tend to rationalize when our impulses are pointed out. Christian 'Therefore consider the members of their earthly body as dead to immorality, impurity, passion, evil desire, and greed, which amounts to idolatry.' – Colossians 3:5.

The LGBT community, as well as all others, lives by some ethical code, which means that there are things that they view as deplorable. They would agree that stealing is terrible and unacceptable. The Bible and thus Christians with a biblical worldview, have a moral code, which prohibits certain behaviors, as well as certain types of sexual conduct, e.g., homosexuality. (1 Cor. 6:9-10) The Bible is not unreasonable, nor is it encouraging its readers to be prejudice. The Bible expects those with same-sex attraction to do the same as those with an opposite-sex attraction, namely, "Flee from sexual immorality!" (1 Cor. 6:18) The Greek word *porneia* (sexual immorality) which again includes unlawful sexual intercourse, namely, adultery, prostitution, sex between unmarried individuals, homosexuality, and bestiality. Many do not realize that there are millions of *heterosexuals*, who are trying to get control over their sexually immoral leanings as well. If a person with same-sex attraction wants to conform to the Word of God, they can live happily without fulfilling their sexual urges. If their desire to please God is greater, this can be the case. Remember, it is only temporary.

If we want to please God, we should shun experimenting with conduct that the Bible describes as sexually immoral. (Eph. 4:19; 5:11) It has been socialized over the last few decades for boys to see lesbians as sexually appealing but gay men as unappealing. Almost all movies, TV, and music today promote girls kissing girls. The last few years, they have started promoting guys kissing guys. One cultural difference should make the point. In the 1980's a teen boy kissing a girl was the thing; however, today, teens as young as thirteen see oral sex and kissing a person of the same sex as being no different from what older teens did only for decades ago. The entertainment industry his indoctrinated our young ones, so that they do not consider oral sex to be wrong, but rather no different from kissing. If we feed our minds on such things, it will only enhance the leanings we may already have. The Bible offers us eternal life and it is an attainable goal for any of us if we choose not to act on any wrong desires.

Review Questions

- What is the Bible's view of homosexuality?

- How should Christians view homosexuality?

- Are Christians to respect everyone? Explain.

- Is the Christian stance not encouraging prejudice against homosexuals? Explain.

- Did Jesus teach tolerance? Explain.

- Is not homosexuality genetically predisposed? Explain.

- Is it not cruel to tell those with same-sex attraction to control themselves? Explain.

CHAPTER 3 Avoiding Homosexuality and Controlling Same-Sex Attraction?

"I remember that once when I slept with a girlfriend, I had a strong desire to kiss her, and that I did so. I could not help being terribly inquisitive over her body, for she had always kept it hidden from me. . . . I go into ecstasies every time I see the naked figure of a woman. . . . It strikes me as so wonderful and exquisite that I have difficulty in stopping the tears rolling down my cheeks. If only I had a girlfriend. – Anne Frank[108]

How many gay people are there in the United States? "The Williams Institute at the UCLA School of Law, a sexual orientation law and public policy think tank, estimates that 9 million (about 3.8%) of Americans identify as gay, lesbian, bisexual or transgender (2011). The institute also found that bisexuals make up 1.8% of the population while 1.7% is gay or lesbian. The number of LGBT persons in the U.S. is subjective. Studies pointing to the statistics are estimates at best. The most widely accepted statistic is that 1 in every 10 individuals is LGBT; however some research estimates 1 in 20."[109] With the internet conversation being flooded with articles on homosexuality, with it being inundated on discussion sites, one might think the statistic would be much higher. Homosexuality is talked about more openly today than it was several decades ago. One would have to be a very brave soul to say that they disapprove of such a lifestyle. The person would be labeled a homophobe, that he or she was prejudiced and judgmental. The scathing comments would be so overwhelming; it might be tempting to remain silent about one's position on this hot-button topic.

Yong Christians are afraid to take a stand for biblical truths. In addition, it has also created a permissive attitude that has popularized experimentation with same-sex relationships. Many young girls claim to be lesbian, bisexual, or bi-curious. Other young

---

[108] She is one of the most discussed Jewish victims of the Holocaust. Her diary, The Diary of a Young Girl, which documents her life in hiding.

[109] Gay Population Statistics, http://gaylife.about.com/od/comingout/a/population.htm (accessed April 24, 2016).

girls have propositioned female Christian girls as young as twelve. These are serious pressure moments because to reject such propositions can get one labeled a homophobe, a religious zealot. The new mentality of today is that homosexuality is just an alternative lifestyle. We have young ones who are attracted to the same-sex, who may be afraid to express their feelings to a pastor, who is not equipped to have such a conversation. They may feel that they are a homosexual and thus condemned for their feelings, which they have tried to shake but just will not go away.

What Causes Homosexuality

We will talk more about whether we have a genetic predisposition in chapter 4 Homosexuality – Genes or learned? For now, we must address some things that some of the LGBT community tries to deny. Over time, the things that we feed our mind on, these will play a role in same-sex attraction. Some men start watching porn that is between a man and a woman. Of course, after time, it is like drugs, he needs something more hardcore. Therefore, he moves on to lesbian porn. Then, he advances to shemale on shemale porn. A shemale is a transvestite, a passive male homosexual. Shemale is a term used in sex work to describe trans women with male genitalia and augmented female breasts from breast augmentation and/or use of hormones. In this, he convinces himself that he gets to watch what appear to be two women. After some time, the male genitalia now arouses him, and so he is building himself up to same-sex attraction.

Another factor that contributes to homosexuality is abuse as a child. When a young child is forced or coerced into having sex with a parent or relative of the same sex, it lays the groundwork for same-sex attraction. Then, we couple this with the experiences that the young one goes through in grade school, junior high, and high school. Then, there is the sensitivity of some young boys, who lack a father, so they are seeking to bond with other males. One of the problems that the church faces is, they do not address homosexuality, or when they do, it is a charismatic sermon, which hits heavily on the abhorrent factor. So much so, that anyone struggling with same-sex attraction will only withdraw into himself or herself. Eventually, they will act on those desires. Then, there is the mistaken stereotype that homosexuals are sexual deviants, or worse still, sexual predators. Therefore, those struggling with same-sex attraction feel like they are perverts, suffering great shame and excessive guilt, which means it is unlikely they will come forward seeking help. The goal of the church counsel is not to make someone straight but rather to help the person mature in Christ, to put on the new person, to have the mind of Christ. Some are trading their unmet needs in same-sex feeling that they can get filled in their relationship with Christ.

God's View of Homosexuality

We have covered this extensively in chapter 1, as well as chapter 2, so we will only offer the gist if it here again. We were created in the image of God, and we were designed male and female, to have sexual relations between one man and one woman, only within the marriage arrangement. Men are not to have sexual relations with a male, as with a woman, nor are women to have sexual relations with a woman as with a man; it is an abomination. (Gen. 1:27-28; Lev. 18:22; Pro 5:18-19) The Bible condemns fornication (Gr. *Porneia*, sexual immorality), which applies to both homosexual and forbidden heterosexual conduct." (Gal. 5:19-21) Sexual immorality unlawful sexual intercourse, which includes adultery, prostitution, sexual relations between unmarried individuals, homosexuality, and bestiality.

What about those who argue that God's Word was written some 2,000 – 3,500 ago, making it out of date? The reason they make such an argument is that their desires are greater than their knowledge of God's Word. They do not believe that it is fully inerrant and inspired, but rather believe it is the word of man. They do not wish to face their desires, so they see anyone accepting the Bible as inspired and fully inerrant, as foolish. It teaches something different from what they want to believe and is at odds with their same-sex attraction. We do not want to be closed-minded in our thinking.

The biblical truth is, if one has same-sex attraction but does not act on those sexual leanings, this does not make them a homosexual. If you are young, and your passions are strong, easily sexually aroused, coupled with social pressure, the same-sex attraction may be something that passes with time. Until this time has passed, you must refrain from homosexual practices of any sort. How?

Prayer: King David prayed, "Search me, O God, and know my heart! Try me and know my thoughts! And see if there be any grievous way in me, and lead me in the way everlasting!" (Ps 139:23-24, ESV) God by his Word can strengthen us, helping us to control our thoughts, as well as our desires. The apostle Paul encouraged us to, "do not be anxious about anything, but in everything by prayer and supplication with thanksgiving let your requests be made known to God. 7 And the peace of God, which surpasses all understanding, will guard your hearts and your minds in Christ Jesus." (Phil. 4:6-7, ESV) Yes, if we can know that "the supreme power belongs to God, not to us." – 2 Corinthians 4:7.

Replace Bad Self-talk with Upbuilding Self-Talk: A daily Bible reading schedule is paramount. The apostle Paul said, "Finally, brothers, whatever is true, whatever is honorable, whatever is just, whatever is pure, whatever is lovely, whatever is commendable, if there is any excellence, if there is anything worthy of praise, **think about these things**." (Phil 4:8, ESV) Paul also told us that "the word of God is living and active, sharper than any two-edged sword, piercing to the division of soul and of spirit, of joints and of marrow, and discerning the thoughts and intentions of the heart." (Heb. 4:12, ESV)

The Pornography Trap: This will be dealt with more extensively in the chapter on Pornography. Nevertheless, it is best to read the basics here and then reread it yet again in chapter 5.

Pornography can fuel a same-sex attraction that may not even be established as genetic. If we are a young girl looking at images of naked women, or even sensually dressed women, with lustful intent in our heart, how is this helping us to get control over ourselves? When God sees us looking at such material, is He not going to be devastatingly hurt, feel betrayed, and feel as though we have abandoned him? The information below is based on helping heterosexual couples but has been adapted to those struggling with same-sex attraction as well. This is not misinterpreting the Scriptures or twisting the Scriptures but rather taking the principles for heterosexuals and applying them to those who struggle with same-sex attraction.

Damage to Us Spiritually

Colossians 3:5 Updated American Standard Version (UASV)

⁵ Therefore, Put to death therefore what is earthly in you: sexual immorality, impurity, passion, evil desire, and covetousness, which is idolatry.

In telling believers to **put to death** certain behaviors, Paul is calling for complete extermination, not careful regulation. What must go? Paul gives us an "outside in" perspective. He starts with external actions and then moves to the internal drives which cause the conduct. In his "vice lists" Paul mentions three categories of behavior: (1) perverted passions, (2) hot tempers, (3) sharp tongues.

> First on the list is **sexual immorality** (*porneia*), a broad, general term for all kinds of illicit sexual behavior. God created sex to be enjoyed by one woman and one man in the confines of marriage. Any sexual activity that does not fit that definition is not to be part of a believer's life. The perverted passion list continues with mention of **impurity**. This reminds us that immorality is "unclean" or dirty and incompatible with the purity of our Savior. Believers are not to be slaves of their **lust** or **evil desires**.[110]

Matthew 5:27-28 Updated American Standard Version (UASV)

²⁷ "You have heard that it was said, 'You shall not commit adultery';[111] ²⁸ but I say to you that everyone who looks at a

---

[110] Max Anders, vol. 8, Kendell H. Easley, vol. 12, Galatians, Ephesians, Philippians, Colossians, Holman New Testament Commentary, 329 (Nashville, TN: Broadman & Holman Publishers, 1998).

[111] Ex. 20:14; Deut. 5:17

woman with lust[112] for her has already committed adultery with her in his heart.

Again, this verse is mean for heterosexual relationships; however, what was meant can be useful in controlling same-sex desires, so it will be adapted below.

In verse 28 of Matthew chapter 5, you will notice the phrase "**lustful intent**," keying in on the word "intent." This is not a woman walking along who catches sight of a beautiful woman and has an indecent thought, which she then dismisses. It is not even a woman in the same situation that has an indecent thought, who goes on to entertain and cultivate that thought. No, this is a woman that is staring, gazing at a woman with the intent of lusting, and is looking at the woman, with the intention of peaking her interest and desire, to get her to lust.

Verse 25 of chapter 26 in Proverbs warns the son against just that, do not get "lustful intent" in your heart because of her beauty. The same is true of a man not getting "lustful intent" in his heart because of the beauty of another man. Yes, even when the evil man is seeking to flame such desires. Aside from the fact that it violates God's Law, for mere moments of immediate gratification at a very inexpensive price, you are risking your eternal life.

When we view pornography, let alone take up the time to get addicted, we are out for self-gratification, and we are, in no way, reflecting the Christian quality of love. The apostle Paul wrote,

1 Thessalonians 4:3-7 Updated American Standard Version (UASV)

³ For this is the will of God, your sanctification; that is, that you abstain from sexual immorality;[113] ⁴ that each of you know how to possess his own vessel[114] in sanctification and honor, ⁵ not in lustful passion, just as also the Gentiles who do not know

---

[112] ἐπιθυμία [Epithumia] to strongly desire to have what belongs to someone else and/or to engage in an activity which is morally wrong–'to covet, to lust, evil desires, lust, desire.'– Johannes P. Louw and Eugene Albert Nida, *Greek-English Lexicon of the New Testament: Based on Semantic Domains* (New York: United Bible Societies, 1996).

[113] Gr porneia, *fornication*

[114] I.e. body

God; 6 that no man transgress and wrong his brother in the matter because the Lord is an avenger in all these things, just as we also told you before and solemnly warned you. 7 For God has not called us for impurity, but in sanctification.

Pornography especially takes selfish or unfair advantage of women and children, and young men, who are likely in abusive situations, for the personal gain of self-gratification. Simply objectifying them for your gratification is demeaning them. If you are using their images, you are also supporting whatever company exploits them, taking advantage of their circumstances. Just taking advantage of images, makes you indifferent, at worst a hater of women and a sexual deviant, toward the very people group that the Mosaic Law and Jesus Christ tried to protect.

Breaking the Habit

Some early Christians, before finding Christ, they were 'unrighteous, sexually immoral, adulterers, men who practice homosexuality, and drunkards' However, they "were washed, you were sanctified, you were justified in the name of the Lord Jesus Christ and by the Spirit of our God." – 1 Corinthians 6:9-11.

Psalm 55:22 Updated American Standard Version (UASV)

22 Cast your burden on the Lord,
    and he will sustain you;
he will never permit
    the righteous to be shaken.

This begs the question, how do we throw our burdens on Jehovah (i.e., the Father), and how does he sustain us. How it is that he will not permit the righteous to be moved? In addition, if we are looking at porn, are we not unrighteous? Let us get ever closer to the answer.

1 Corinthians 10:13 Updated American Standard Version (UASV)

13 No temptation has overtaken you but such as is common to man; and God is faithful, who will not allow you to be tempted beyond what you are able, but with the temptation will provide the way of escape also, so that you will be able to endure it.

Many Christians, even very mature ones, as well as those leading congregations, have succumbed to pornography. Therefore, you should not feel alone in your battle to get control over your vessel.

Hebrews 4:12 Updated American Standard Version (UASV)

¹² For the word of God is living and active and sharper than any two-edged sword, and piercing as far as the division of soul and spirit, of both joints and marrow, and able to judge the thoughts and intentions of the heart.

This verse contains four statements about God's Word. First, it is **living.** God is a **living** God (Heb. 3:12). His message is dynamic and productive. It causes things to happen. It drives home warnings to the disobedient and promises to the believer. Second, God's Word is **active,** an emphasis virtually identical in meaning with the term **living.** God's Word is not something you passively hear and then ignore. It actively works in our lives, changes us, and sends us into action for God.

Third, God's Word penetrates the **soul and spirit.** To the Hebrew people, the body was a unity. We should not think of dividing the soul from the spirit. God's message is capable of penetrating the impenetrable. It can divide what is indivisible. Fourth, God's message is discerning. **It judges the thoughts and attitudes of the heart.** It passes judgment on our feelings and our thoughts. What we regard as secret and hidden, God brought out for inspection by the discerning power of his Word.[115]

Proverbs 2:1-6 Updated American Standard Version (UASV)

¹ My son, if you receive my words
   and treasure up my commandments with you,
² making your ear attentive to wisdom
   and inclining your heart to discernment;[116]
³ For if you cry for discernment[117]

---

[115] Thomas A. Lea, vol. 10, *Hebrews & James*, Holman New Testament Commentary, 72 (Nashville: Broadman & Holman Publishers, 1999).

[116] The Hebrew word rendered here as "discernment" (*tevunah*) is related to the word *binah*, translated "understanding." Both appear at Proverbs 2:3.

[117] See 2.2 ftn.

and raise your voice for understanding,
⁴ if you seek it like silver
    and search for it as for hidden treasures,
⁵ then you will understand the fear of Jehovah
    and find the knowledge of God.
⁶ For Jehovah gives wisdom;
    from his mouth come knowledge and understanding;

Now, let us return to our questions, and provide answers. How do we throw our burdens on God?

We do so, by going to him fervently in prayer, asking him for help with the problem that we are trying to overcome. Our adding this in our prayers repeatedly shows him our deep concern.

How does he sustain us?

God sustains us by the Word of God, which contains the very knowledge of God, as explained in Hebrews 4:12 above. Thus, we need to discover the Bible verses that are applicable, and we then need to know what the author meant by the words that he used, as should have been understood by his original readers. In other words, we need to discover the original meaning. Then, we need to find the pattern of meaning that would apply to us. This is called working on behalf of our prayers. However, we are not done yet. We must be obedient to the Word of God. If we obey 50 percent, we will get 50 percent results. If we apply it 100 percent into our lives, we will get 100 percent results.

1 John 5:2 Updated American Standard Version (UASV)

² By this we know that we love the children of God, when we love God and do his commandments.

2 John 1:6 Updated American Standard Version (UASV)

⁶ And this is love, that we walk according to his commandments. This is the commandment, just as you have heard from the beginning, that you should walk in it.

What is love? It plays itself out in the real world in obedience. The essence of love is that we keep God's commandments. This glorifies God, is best for others, and is best for us. Everything God asks of us is intended to give something good to us or keep us from harm. First John presented the same emphasis on love and the same link between love and obedience. (Walls and Anders 1996, 237)

How it is that he will not permit the righteous to be moved?

God said he would never 'permit the righteous to be moved.' What is meant by 'move'?" It means to stumble or fall down spiritually or get into a practice of sin that you seem to be in. In other words, God will help you to become stable, steadfast, or unmovable, not giving into sin. **If we are looking at porn, are we not unrighteous?**

No, this is not the case. We are all sinners, and God hates sin. However, he hates the **unrepentant** practice of sin. The unrighteous person is the one who lives in sin unrepentantly. If you are reading this, and you have been praying, trying to find a way to get control over yourself; then, you are not unrepentant. God makes allowance for our inherited sin from Adam, which means he understands our human weaknesses.

Thus, the steps are (1) Go to god fervently in prayer, (2) act in harmony with that prayer, by (3) research what the Bible offers toward recovery, (4) apply what you learn, and (5) get your stride again if you stumble, or get up when you fall down.

How often do you come across pornography?

- Never
- Sometimes,
- Rarely
- Daily,
- Weekly

Where do you come across pornography?

- Television,
- Stores,
- Internet,
- Cell phone,

- Email,
- Work,
- School,
- Other

Do you see a pattern of how these encounters come about, and how you deal with them?

Is there a pattern to your encounters?

Do you find yourself depressed or angry, so you look at pornography, because of the feeling that override the depression, even though you know, even worse depression is on the horizon for failing to be faithful? Do you receive email attachments from friends that contain pornography?

The good thing about the internet is that its filters are far better than ten years ago, In order to get a popup, or end up with wrong pages; you need to be very specific in your search. For example, if you Google "race cars," there will be links and images the movement that you get a few letters in. However, if you Google the word "porn," it will do nothing until you hit enter. The same is true with email, like Yahoo and Gmail. The ads in the margins are only reflective of sites that you have been visiting.

How do you react the moment that your eyes see pornography?

- You turn away immediately so that you could barely describe what you saw
- You look at it for a moment before turning away, and could better explain what you saw
- You continue to look until your desires lead you to search for more

The foremost thing that will help you to overcome the habit of viewing pornography is to appreciate the seriousness of it, as well as what your actions mean to you, to God, to your spouse, to your family, and to the victims in the images. You have to get to the point where you "hate evil." – Psalm 97:10.

Remove yourself from whatever results in the viewing of pornography. After one has had success for a time, they begin to become over confident and think they are strong enough to deal with temptation. This is such a mistaken notion.

Proverbs 22:3 Updated American Standard Version (UASV)

³ The prudent sees danger and hides himself,
but the simple go on and suffer for it.

Be determined that you will not let your eyes fall upon pornography, and if they do unintentionally, you will immediately turn away. When surfing the internet, this is especially important. Each time when we encounter someone that stimulates us sexually, it just continues to feed our desires. Each person is tempted when he is lured and enticed by his own desire.

Job 31:1 Updated American Standard Version (UASV)

¹ I have made a solemn promise
never to look with lust at a woman [or man].

Depending on your circumstances, you can apply the following as best you can.

- You only get on the internet when another is in the room

- You will place the computer in a public space

- You will leave your office door open

- You will immediate close out or delete anything inappropriate

- You will find a sponsor that can talk with you when you are feeling weak, stressed, or have stumbled

The Self-Abuse of Masturbation: This subject will be dealt with extensively in Chapter 6. The Bible condemns quite clearly such sexual sins as fornication, adultery, homosexuality, and bestiality; masturbation is not mentioned. (Genesis 39:7-9; Leviticus 18:20, 22-23; 1 Corinthians 6:9-10) Another factor to consider is that the language of the New Testament, Koine Greek, contained several words to describe the practice masturbation in the Greek-speaking world, but they are not used in the New Testament.

While the opinion of most physicians is that masturbation is harmless physically, it seems that the human conscience rejects it, as most are not as comfortable talking about masturbation as they are about another bodily function, like washing your hands. If you doubt me, the next time you are at a restaurant, and the women excuse themselves to freshen up, when they return, ask them if they masturbated. If it is as natural, you will not have any reservations about asking, and they will not have any embarrassed or angry looks on their face. This may sound extreme, but it makes the point.

Adam and Eve were created in the image of God and were a reflection of his qualities and attributes. Even after the fall, in our state of imperfection, all humans still maintain a good measure of that image. We all have a moral nature, which produces the faculty of conscience. This moral nature and associated conscience are seen in that most countries have laws that are based on the Bible's moral values, do not kill, do not steal, and do not commit adultery, and so on. Why is it that most people feel guilty, ashamed, dirty, embarrassed, or abnormal when discussing masturbation? It is the conscience that God gave us.

Put to Death Evil Desire

Colossians 3:5 Updated American Standard Version (UASV)

⁵ Therefore, Put to death therefore what is earthly in you: sexual immorality, impurity, passion, *evil desire*, and covetousness, which is idolatry.

> The ... two words belong together. "Lust" (*epithymia*) and "passions" (*pathos*) or "evil desires," as translated in the NIV, generally refer to strong desires gone bad. Although the word can, on occasion, be used of an honorable desire (1 Tim 3:1), the normal use is negative. It refers most often to the misdirected fulfillment of bodily appetites, usually sexual appetites. A passion is uncontrolled and habitual lust. When lust goes unchecked, a passion for what is forbidden arises. Habits are formed

which feed each other. Lust encourages passion, and passion produces more perverted lust.[118]

"Deaden, therefore, your body members," urges the Bible, "as respects . . . **sexual appetite**." (Col. 3:5) This "sexual appetite" is not the new sexual sensations that most youths feel during puberty, of which there is no need to be ashamed. "Sexual appetite" exists when these feelings are intensified so that one loses control. Such sexual appetite has led to gross sexual immorality, as described by Paul at Romans 1:26-27.

However, does not masturbation "put to death" these "evil desires"? Hardly, in order to masturbate, one must feed his mind on evil desires, as well as pornographic images. Like any addiction, it takes stronger content to achieve the same gratification. If you drink one beer a day, soon you will have to move on to two, to get the same feeling. If you look at pornographic images, soon they will have to be viler, to achieve the same results. Eventually, you will need the real thing because the imagination is not achieving the same outcome. The world is full of opportunity, where you will find yourself aroused in a wrong moment or an inconvenient time, and you will commit fornication if single, or adultery if married.

Your Thoughts Will Lead You Astray

Moreover, you're using women or men objectively in your imagination will carry over into the real world. Masturbation means that you need to view and think of women as a tool, as a means to an end, as opposed to sensitive human beings. In addition, you will start to see your own body as an object as well; a means to self-gratification. Self-abuse is self-centered. The person loses sight of love and moves toward sexual pleasures. Our Creator intended man and woman to find their sexual satisfactions within the marriage bed, between one man and one woman, and within expressions of love.

---

[118] Richard R. Melick, Jr, vol. 32, Philippians, Colossians, Philemon, The New American Commentary, 291 (Nashville: Broadman & Holman Publishers, 1993).

How does God view our human weaknesses?

Psalm 86:5 Updated American Standard Version (UASV)

⁵ For you, O Jehovah, are good, and ready to forgive,
and abundant in lovingkindness to all who call upon you.

When we slip up and fall short, succumbing to masturbation, we certainly feel guilty, which is appropriate. However, we do not want to beat ourselves down to where anxiety and stress cause future failures.

1 John 3:20 Updated American Standard Version (UASV)

²⁰ in whatever our heart condemns us; for God is greater than our heart and knows all things.

We may find ourselves falling short on masturbation many times, as it has a stronger hold on us than we may have realized. This results in our feeling guilty, ashamed, dirty, embarrassed, or abnormal. We do not feel worthy of God's Love. We need not think that God is no longer forgiving us, as this is exactly what Satan would like. The fact that you feel as distraught as you do means that God still loves you, and you have not committed the unforgivable sin. Simply be steadfast in the process of overcoming this habit, and continue fervently to go to God in prayer, begging him for forgiveness and cleansing and help. However, we as imperfect humans can be accredited a righteous standing before God, being accepted back into the family of God. **He makes allowances** for our imperfection.

Below is how he views a repentant sinner,

Psalm 103:8-14 Updated American Standard Version (UASV)

⁸ Jehovah is compassionate and gracious,
slow to anger and abounding in lovingkindness.
⁹ He will not always find fault,
nor will he keep his anger forever.
¹⁰ He does not deal with us according to our sins,
nor repaid us according to our iniquities.
¹¹ For as high as the heavens are above the earth,
So great is his lovingkindness toward those who fear him.
¹² As far as the east is from the west,

so far does he remove our transgressions from us.
¹³ As a father has compassion on his children,
   so Jehovah has compassion on those who fear him.
¹⁴ For he himself knows our formation;
   he remembers that we are dust.

Isaiah 38:17 Updated American Standard Version (UASV)

¹⁷ Look, it was for my welfare
   that I had great bitterness;
but in love you have delivered my soul
   from the pit of destruction,
for you have cast all my sins
   behind your back.

Micah 7:18-19 Updated American Standard Version (UASV)

¹⁸ Who is a God like you, pardoning iniquity
   and passing over transgression
   for the remnant of his inheritance?
He does not retain his anger forever,
   because he delights in lovingkindness.
¹⁹ He will again have compassion on us;
   he will tread our iniquities underfoot.
You will cast all our sins
   into the depths of the sea.

You will notice in Psalm 103:12, that God removes the sins of the repentant one as far as the east is from the west. The picture being painted is, to the human mind that is the farthest you can remove something as there is no greater distance. In Isaiah 38, we are given another visual, God throwing our sins behind his back, meaning he can no longer see them, as they are out of sight, thus out of mind. In Micah, our last example, we see that God hurls all of the sins of a repentant person into the depths of the sea. In the setting of the ancient person, this meant that retrieving them was literally impossible. In other words, God has removed them, never to be retrieved or brought to mind ever again. This was the viewpoint that he had before Jesus ever even offered himself as a ransom sacrifice.

However, just because God is so forgiving, this will never justify sinning unrepentantly, as his patience will wear out, or the evil age of Satan will end when we least expect it. He hopes that you will continue to work toward setting aside the habit of masturbation, as it is an unclean habit.

Destructive Self-Talk

It is not the troubles of this would that actually cause us to feel bad. It is what we tell ourselves that contributes to how we feel. Self-talk is what we tell ourselves in our thoughts. In fact, it is the words we tell ourselves about people, self, experiences, life in general, God, the future, the past, the present; it is specifically all the words we say to ourselves all the time. Destructive self-talk, even subconsciously, can be very harmful to our mood: mood slumps, our self-worth plummeting, our body feeling sluggish, our will to accomplish even the tiniest of things is not to be realized and our actions defeat us.

Intense negative thinking will always lead to our feeling blue, painful emotions or even a depressive state. Our thoughts based on a good mood will be entirely different from those based on our being upset. Negative thoughts that flood our mind are the actual contributors of our self-defeating emotions. These very thoughts are what keep us sluggish and contribute to our feeling worthless. Therefore, this thinking is the key to our relief.

Every time we feel down about something, attempt to locate the corresponding negative thought we had to this feeling down. Because it is these thoughts that have created our feelings of low self-worth, by learning to offset them and replace them with rational thoughts we can actually change our mood. Remember the thoughts that move through our mind, with no effort, is the easiest course to follow because we have developed a way of thinking, a pattern of thinking. It is so subconscious that they even go unnoticed because we are not searching for them.

The centerpiece of it all is the mind. Our moods, behaviors and body responses result from the way we view things. It is a proven fact that we cannot experience any event in any way, shape, or form unless we have processed it with our mind first. No event can depress us; it is your perception of that event that will. If we are only sad over an event, our thoughts will be rational; but if you are depressed or anxious over an event, our thinking will be bent and irrational, distorted and simply wrong.

It may be difficult for each of us to wrap our mind around the concept that we are responsible for our thinking that leads to most depressive episodes, but we are excellent at telling ourselves outright lies and half-truths, repeatedly throughout each day. In fact, some of us are so good at it that it has become our reality and led to depression and anxiety. Look at the statements below.

(1) **Self-degrading**: I am gay, or I will never control my desires because I am a pervert. Everything I try seems to fail. Even when I do all I can to get control over myself; I just **end up failing because I am a failure.**

(2) **Situation degrading**: Life is the same every day; I do not even know why I bother getting up! Life just kicks me in the face every day it stinks!

(3) **Future degrading**: I am never going to make it in life; I do not know why I even try. It is a waste of time! I will never find happiness like everyone else. Hope, what is that!

We must appreciate that our thinking can deceive all of us, contributing to our belief that the negative mood, which has been created, because of our thoughts, is reality, when it is not. If we have established a negative way of thinking, an irrational way of thinking, our mind will naturally accept it as truth. Within a moment, we can alter our mood, and it is not even likely we notice it taking place. These negative feelings feel as though they are the real thing, which only reinforces to the deceptive thinking.

Talk Therapy for Depression

Talking with a trained therapist is one of the best treatments. Some people choose to be in therapy for several months to work on a few key issues. Other people find it helpful to continue in therapy for years, gradually working through larger problems. The choice is up to you and your therapist. Here are some common types of treatment:

- **Cognitive behavioral therapy**[119] helps you see how behaviors and the way you think about things plays a role in your depression. Your therapist will help you change some of these unhealthy patterns.

- **Interpersonal therapy** focuses on your relationships with other people and how they affect you. Your therapist will also help you pinpoint and change unhealthy habits.

- **Problem-solving therapy** focuses on the specific problems you face and helps you find solutions.[120]

We know by now, having come this far in this publication, most of our minor to moderate mental distresses can be overcome by changing the way we think. We also know that the way we think has taken some time to become our pattern of thinking, and

---

[119] **Cognitive behavioral therapy (CBT)** is a form of psychotherapy. It was originally designed to treat depression, but is now used for a number of mental disorders. It works to solve current problems and change unhelpful thinking and **behavior**.

A Biblical Approach to Cognitive-Behavior Therapy. After pointing out several limitations and criticisms of secular cognitive-behavior therapy, Tan (1987) provided the following guidelines for conducting a Christian, biblical approach to cognitive-behavior therapy that is more broad-based. One guideline is to emphasize the primacy of agape love and the need to develop a warm, genuine, and empathic relationship with the client that is collaborative. Therapists must deal more adequately with the past, especially unresolved developmental issues or childhood experiences, with the judicious use of inner healing prayer or healing of memories where appropriate (see Tan & Ortberg, 1995). They must also pay special attention to the meaning of spiritual, experiential, and mystical aspects of faith and life and not overemphasize the rationalistic dimension. The possibility of demonic involvement in some cases should also be seriously considered. Therapists can use biblical truth and not relativistic, empirically oriented values in conducting cognitive restructuring and behavioral change interventions to modify problem thinking and behaviors. They can also emphasize the Holy Spirit's ministry in producing inner healing and cognitive, behavioral, and emotional change. Prayer and the Scriptures as God's Word will be crucial in this process.

It is useful to pay more attention to larger contextual factors such as familial, societal, religious, and cultural influences and use community and church resources more. Therapists may use only those techniques that are consistent with biblical truth, morality, and ethics and not simplistically use whatever techniques work. They can reaffirm biblical perspectives on suffering, including the possibility of the "blessings of mental anguish" or the "dark night of the soul," with the ultimate goal of therapy being holiness or Christlikeness (Rom. 8:29) and not necessarily temporal happiness. They can utilize rigorous outcome research methodology before making definitive conclusions about the superiority (not just the general effectiveness) of cognitive-behavior therapy, whether Christian or secular. – (Benner and Hill 1985, 1999, 217)

[120] Treatments for Depression - WebMD, http://www.webmd.com/depression/symptoms-depressed-anxiety-12/treating-depressio (accessed April 02, 2016).

is deeply ingrained by now. However, if we are persistent about challenging our thinking every time we have an irrational thought, we can unhinge our irrationally, deep-seated ways of thinking.

At first, we will have to be alert to our thoughts, because most of it is subconscious, and will go unnoticed otherwise. We could carry a small pocket tablet with us, to record the times of the day, or how many times in the day, we catch ourselves feeding ourselves irrational thoughts, and how successful we were in overcoming them. If we fail to take this exercise seriously, it will be like a person with diabetes, who refuses his shots, which inevitably leads to major health issues, even death. The same applies to our mental distress, if we lack trust in the process, it will not be long before we have a major depressive shipwreck and act on our same-sex desires. Below we are going to borrow a powerful section from Matt Moore's blog.[121]

10 Empowering Truths For The Same-Sex Attracted Christian

1) You are not an anomaly. You may have grown up in a culture that taught you homosexuality was the grossest and strangest of sins, but if you're going to believe the Bible, you've got to toss that mentality aside. Your desires are jacked up, yes – but so are everyone else's. Every person's sexuality is perverted by sin. Don't be fooled for a second into thinking you are more sinful than your "straight" friend who is tempted to fornicate, commit adultery, or watch pornography. All are inclined to sin sexually because all have been born with a corrupt nature (Romans 5: 12-21).

2) It's not because you "lack faith" that this struggle remains. There is hellish doctrine floating around in some Christian circles that teaches people their struggle with same-sex attraction exists because their faith doesn't. This teaching is unbiblical and spiritually toxic. You are not still attracted to the same sex because you've yet to believe "big" enough. You suffer

---

[121] 10 Empowering Truths For The Same-Sex Attracted Christian, http://www.moorematt.org/10-empowering-truths-for-the-same-sex-attracted-christi (accessed April 25, 2016).

this temptation for the same reason all Christians suffer various temptations: because your salvation is not yet complete. You are justified (made right with God), but you are still being sanctified (made like God). Total freedom from sin and temptation will come not on the day that your faith finally gets "strong enough" – but on the Day that Christ returns and gives you a new, imperishable body (1 Corinthians 15:53-57).

3) Your identity is not in your fallen desires. You are not defined, even in part, by your fleshly inclinations. Don't identify and view yourself through the lens of your sexuality, but through the lens of your union to Jesus. You're not some different species of Christian. You're not a gay Christian. You are just a Christian (2 Corinthians 5:16-17). You are not the fallen desires you inherited from your first father, Adam. You are the righteousness of God in Christ (2 Corinthians 5:21).

4) You are not alone in your suffering. Sometimes it feels like you're the only Christian that suffers to the degree you do, but this couldn't be more off base. You are not the only one who bears a heavy cross in this life. Your brothers around the world face various, yet equally difficult sufferings. (1 Peter 5:9). Don't give into self-pity; every Christian battles the flesh and has to die to themselves in various ways as they follow Christ (Luke 9:23).

5) God sovereignly rules over your temptations and will not allow them to ultimately defeat you. Your ceaseless wrestling with these desires isn't beyond the grasp of your omnipotent Savior. It may feel at times that the evil inside and around you is going to ultimately overtake you, but Christ who is in you is greater than all the evil, sin, and temptation in and around you (1 John 4:4). Though God allows you to be tempted by these forces, he does not allow you to be tempted beyond your ability to withstand (1 Corinthians 10:13). You *can* resist and you *can* have victory. So fight! And when you don't fight as you should and you stumble (this will happen), don't wallow in the defeat or fear God's judgment. You are justified by the blood of Jesus. All your sins are covered. So get back up and keep fighting. He who called and justified you will not allow your sin to ultimately defeat you. He *will* sustain you to glory (Romans 8:30).

6) God can transform your sexuality. God is not powerless to give you natural sexual desires – even if just for one man or woman whom he's destined to be your spouse. Though heterosexual desire isn't a promise of the gospel, it is not bad to hope for it. And though heterosexual marriage isn't a certainty for anyone, it is not bad to pray God will bless you with it! He has done it for others and he can do it for you. The Lord is a pro at speaking into existence things that don't exist (Romans 4:17). Nothing is impossible for him (Matthew 19:26).

7) Singleness isn't a curse. If God doesn't give you marriage and he calls you be single for the duration of your earthly life, know that he is doing this for your good and joy. God cares for you. If it were better for you to have marriage in this life, he would give it to you. For mysterious reasons that you aren't entitled to know, he may deem singleness the best fit for you. This isn't a curse. It's a freedom and a blessing through which you will serve the Lord more efficiently than you ever could in marriage (1 Corinthians 7:32-38).

8) You can live a full and joyful life without sex. If you're unmarried, your obedience to God in this season of life entails celibacy. Restraining yourself from sexual activity can feel – well, restraining. And it is. You are biologically wired to express yourself sexually, but right now, if you're not married to someone of the opposite gender, it's not an option. Is this hard? Yes. Does this sacrifice rob you of fullness of life? Heck no. Jesus, Paul, and many more like them lived full and joyous lives in the grace of God . . . yet they didn't have sex. It is the pleasures of knowing God – not sex – that truly satisfy the human soul (Psalm 16:11). Eternal life is not found in being romantically or sexually fulfilled, but in knowing and communing with God and his Son Jesus (John 17:3).

9) God will redeem your struggle for his glory. Though the battle with same-sex attraction can be a grueling one, know this: God has a divine purpose for allowing it to continue in your life. Maybe it's to keep you reliant on him. Maybe it's to make your more empathetic toward the struggles and needs of others. Maybe it's to keep you in tune with the brokenness of this world so you keep your eyes on the prize: eternity with Jesus in a new and perfect world. Whatever the case, know for certain that God allows no thorn without a divine purpose (2 Corinthians 12:17). God is using this struggle for your good (Romans 8:28).

10) It won't always be this way. Your struggle will end. The sin inside of you responsible for these attractions will once and for all be obliterated by the redeeming power of God. When Christ comes again, you will no longer just want to be like him but you *will* be like him (1 John 3:2). You will be sinless. You will be perfect. Hold fast to the hope set before you and stand firm in the gospel of your salvation. He who began a good work in you will bring it to completion (Philippians 1:6).

Never Give Up

Many have tried to change their desires, praying, studying the Bible, listening to lectures, putting suggestions into practice, but there has been little success.

There are stories and claims by many thousands who have left the homosexual life and are now living a changed life. Some have made the transition easy enough while others have had a real fight on your hands. We must realize, if we want to please God, we have to conform to his moral standards, setting aside the former lifestyle, even if it is the most difficult thing we ever face. Do not conform yourselves to the standards of this world, but let God transform you inwardly by a complete change of your mind. Then you will be able to know the will of God, what is good and is pleasing to him and is perfect. Know that God is well aware of the struggle, the mental anguish that you are going through, and he has compassion for you. (1 John 3:19-20) If we keep God's laws, there is great reward. (Psalm 19:11) If you prayerfully approach the Bible, the right church leader and an excellent Christian counselor, you will enjoy the best life possible until Christ returns; after that, paradise.

Therefore, continue to rely on God, as you fight those desires. (Gal. 6:9) As Paul said, "Let love be genuine. Abhor what is evil; hold fast to what is good." (Rom. 12:9, ESV) In time, even if it seems like a long time, the desires will begin to fade. Just imagine, after the great tribulation, Armageddon, there will be the thousand-year reign of Christ, where your imperfection becomes perfection. After you are 50,000 years into an eternal life, will this not seem like a momentary thing of little significance?

Review Questions

- Why are our young ones afraid to take a stand against homosexuality?

- How does God view homosexuality?

- How can we avoid any type of homosexual practice?

- How can we avoid the pornography trap?

- How can we can we deal with the self-abuse of masturbation?

- What is destructive self-talk and how can we get control over it?

CHAPTER 4 Homosexuality – Genes or learned?

Some argue that same-sex attraction is brought about through socialization. Somebody acquires a personality or traits through their background (nurture), impacted by family, friends, school, work, and so on. Others would argue that same sex attraction is brought about because one is genetically predisposed (nature).[122] They may say, "I am born this way, it is not my fault, why should I be punished, or miss out on love, because of inheriting a genetic predisposition?" We will take on the science of such an issue herein but not as a scientist. Below is a brief article from WebMD News from Health Day by Randy Dotinga

Genetics of Homosexuality in Men

Researchers able to make accurate predictions 70 percent of time in study of twins

THURSDAY, Oct. 8, 2015 (HealthDay News) -- Scientists are reporting that they've linked the way genes in certain regions of the human genome work to influence sexual orientation in males.

The findings don't explain how such variations in the workings of these genetic regions might affect sexuality in one or both genders. But the authors of the new study say they've been able to use this information to successfully predict the sexual orientation of male identical twins 70 percent of the time, compared to the 50 percent that would be expected by chance.

Twins have the same genes, so something else -- such as the way genes operate -- may explain those who don't have the same sexual orientation, the authors suggested.

---

[122] "A **genetic predisposition** (sometimes also called **genetic** susceptibility) is an increased likelihood of developing a particular disease based on a person's **genetic** makeup. A **genetic predisposition** results from specific **genetic** variations that are often inherited from a parent." – What does it mean to have a genetic predisposition to a ..., http://ghr.nlm.nih.gov/handbook/mutationsanddisorders/predisposition (accessed April 16, 2016).

"Sexual orientation seems to be determined very early in life," said study lead author Tuck Ngun, a postdoctoral researcher at the David Geffen School of Medicine of the University of California, Los Angeles. "Based on these findings, we can say that environmental factors might play a role in sexual orientation."

But he doesn't mean the social environment in which we grow up, such as how we're treated by our parents.

"Instead, we are referring to differences that the twins could have experienced in the womb," Ngun explained.

Several past studies have linked sexual orientation to specific genetic regions, "but what's still a mystery is the specific genes that are involved," Ngun said. "Sexual attraction is a fundamental drive across all species but it is something that is poorly understood on the genetic level, particularly in humans."

In the new study, researchers sought to better understand the links between how genes work -- not just the existence of certain genes or genetic variations -- and sexual orientation.

The investigators looked at identical twins because they share the same DNA. However, genes are also affected by the environment each twin experiences, so they're not clones of each other in terms of how their bodies work, according to the researchers.

The researchers began with information on 140,000 genetic regions and narrowed them down to five regions that appear to have the ability to predict -- 70 percent of the time -- whether an identical male twin is gay or straight based on how genes in those regions work or "express" themselves.

The researchers reached that level of accuracy by seeing if they could predict sexual orientation in 10 pairs of male gay twins and 37 male pairs in which one twin is gay and the other is straight, the study said.

"We weren't expecting 100 percent since we are only looking at a small part of the overall picture," Ngun said.

The genetic regions in question play various roles in the body, Ngun explained, including affecting sexual attraction.

Qazi Rahman, a senior lecturer in cognitive neuropsychology at King's College London in the United Kingdom, who studies sexual orientation, praised the study. While it's small, the study's design is strong, he said.

Rahman added that the study "tells us something about possible environmental differences -- albeit biological differences in the environment -- which might explain the sexual orientation of men who share the same genome."

Some people in the LGBT community have expressed concern about research into the biological roots of sexual orientation because they fear it could be used to target gays and even abort fetuses who seem likely to not be heterosexual. "I am gay, so these questions have a lot of resonance with me on a personal level," study lead author Ngun said.

"I do think we have to tread carefully because the potential for abuse is there. Although I think it's highly unlikely that the findings of this particular research study would lead to a genetic test, future research could ultimately lead to something like that," he added.

Society is going to have to work together, Ngun suggested, "to ensure research on sexual orientation is not misused."

The study is scheduled to be presented Thursday at the annual meeting of the American Society of Human Genetics in Baltimore. Research presented at meetings hasn't yet undergone peer review, and is generally considered preliminary until published in a peer-reviewed journal.[123]

This author would argue that the science is irrelevant to the Christian faith. Let us err on the side of those who say that, for some it is genetic, and they are predisposed toward same-sex attraction. If we concede this, it does nothing to remove the Bible's position on same-sex relationships. Remember, the Bible says that we are all mentally bent toward wickedness. What we should understand is that some lean toward different things in this mental bent and others lean heavily in other directions. By tentatively erring on this side of some being genetically predisposed, we can

---

[123] Scientists Get Closer to Genetics of Homosexuality in Men, http://consumer.healthday.com/health-technology-information-18/genetics-news-334

better help them, and better understand their struggles. Lastly, because we accept genetic predisposition, this does not exclude their gaining control over their body and mind, as well as they being able to take off the old person and put on the new person. Moreover, it does not exclude that many same-sex attraction cases are socialized.

Further, we could respond that the Bible does not address the genetic predisposition of same-sex attraction, but then again it does not deal with the mental issues of bipolar either. It is not a science textbook, nor is it a mental health guide. Thus, we should not look for it to resolve the specifics. However, it does address certain thinking and individual actions. Therefore, the Bible might not explicitly address the genetic, but it does address same-sex acts.

Another response might be that some have argued that addictive personalities are genetically predisposed (gambling, drugs, alcohol, intense opposite sex attraction, and pedophilia), as well as anger and rage are also viewed as genetic. Giving these ones the same benefit of the doubt as to the leanings being genetic, would we approve of a man that beats his wife, or another man that sexually abuses women, because they may be predisposed to those desires. Certainly not, we would send him to Christian counseling, and expect him to get control over his body and mind, by putting on the mind of Christ. Would we excuse a man who is genetically predisposed as a pedophile, who acts on his sexual desire for children? No, we would scream, lock him up and throw away the key. We would acknowledge that the wife beater and the pedophile struggle with these desires, and we would expect that they would not put themselves in an innocent appearing situations. Moreover, we would expect them through redemptive therapy by way of biblical counseling to get and maintain control over themselves. Remember, God feels the same way about homosexuality as the other above sins. We would expect that those with anger issues, those suffering from alcoholism, and those preferring child-sex (pedophile) would get control over themselves and avoid such unsavory activity. God's Word expects the same from those who have same-sex attraction.

Again, the Bible does not directly disclose that same-sex attraction is genetic. However, it could be inferred from God's curse of Canaan, (the forefather of the Canaanites), the grandson of Noah, who, it appears, sexually assaulted Noah when he was unconscious from alcohol. It can be inferred that we inherit leanings and dispositions. Certainly, we inherit sin, i.e., imperfection. (Rom. 5:12) In addition, the Bible does say that some of our imperfect traits are deeply ingrained. (2 Cor. 10:4-5) Therefore, if homosexuality is predisposed to some, this does not equate that "God made me this way." It only means it is imperfection passed on like any other. Thus, the fault lies with Satan and Adam.

Thomas R. Schreiner hits the balance perfectly

Sons and Daughters of Adam

As noted earlier, the biblical prohibition on homosexuality is questioned, because we allegedly have knowledge about homosexuality that was not available to biblical writers. For instance, it is sometimes said that homosexuality is genetic, and biblical writers were not cognizant of this truth. It is not my purpose here to delve into the question of the genetic character of homosexuality. The scientific evidence supporting such a conclusion, however, is not compelling. Most studies yield the rather common sense conclusion that homosexuality is the result of both nature and nurture, and cannot be wholly explained by genetic factors.[124]

However, I do want to look at the perspective of the Scriptures, relative to so-called genetic characteristics. Even if some sins could be traced to our genetics, it would not exempt us from responsibility for such sins. The Scriptures teach that all human beings are born into this world as sons and daughters of Adam, and hence they are by nature children of wrath (Eph. 2:3). They are dead in trespasses in sins (Eph. 2:1, 5), and have no inclination to seek God or to do what is good (Rom. 3:10–11). We come into the world as those who are spiritually dead (Rom. 5:12, 15), so that death reigns over the whole human race (Rom. 5:17). Indeed,

---

[124] See, e.g., Stanton L. Jones & Mark A. Yarhouse, *Homosexuality: The Use of Scientific Research in the Church's Moral Debate* (Downers Grove: InterVarsity, 2000); Jeffrey Satinover, *Homosexuality and the Politics of Truth* (Grand Rapids: Baker, 1996); Schmidt. *Straight and Narrow?*, 131–59; Gagnon, *Homosexual Practice*, 396–432.

human beings are condemned by virtue of Adam's sin (Rom. 5:16, 18). Such a radical view of sin in which we inherit a sinful nature from Adam means that sinful predispositions are part of our personalities from our inception. Hence, even if it were discovered that we are genetically predisposed to certain sinful behaviours like alcoholism or homosexuality, such discoveries would not eliminate our responsibility for our actions, nor would it suggest that such actions are no longer sinful. The Scriptures teach that we are born as sinners in Adam, while at the same time they insist we should not sin and are responsible for the sin we commit. We enter into the world as slaves of sin (Rom. 6:6, 17), but we are still morally blameworthy for capitulating to the sin that serves as our master.[125]

Below is a brief article from Probe Ministries by Sue Bohlin

Is Animal Homosexuality Proof that It's Normal?

First of all, I would encourage her to ask with humility and softness (i.e., no edge in her voice) where she can find the studies that "prove" the prevalence of homosexuality in animals. People toss off assertions all the time (such as, "science has proven homosexuality is genetic") but when we ask where the articles are, they don't have an answer. They're just parroting what they've heard.

Same-sex behavior DOES exist in the animal kingdom, for a number of reasons. Usually, it's either playful antics, or dominance behavior to assert hierarchy. For one male to mount, or attempt to mount, another male is a very powerful way to communicate his higher position in the "pecking order" of the community. But if you bring in a female in heat, suddenly the male-male behavior is abandoned in favor of the female. Sometimes males mount other males in a type of practice before the females come into heat.

Secondly, I have read of same-sex attachments in animals, but the fact that they exist doesn't make it normal any more than the fact that cystic fibrosis or diabetes exists makes those diseases normal. From a Christian perspective, we live in a fallen world, and that falleness extends to the entire creation on the planet. It

[125] Thomas R. Schreiner, "A New Testament Perspective on Homosexuality," *Themelios* 31, no. 3 (2006): 70–75.

would make sense that things would go wrong even among the animals. For instance, I understand that a hormonal imbalance can result in homosexual behavior in some animals. Here are links to a couple of articles concerning that. Note the naturalistic bias underlying them: "What is, is normal and natural and therefore to be embraced."

http://www.noglstp.org/bulletin/1997spring.html

http://www.libchrist.com/other/homosexual/sheepandanimals.html)

Even from a godless evolutionary perspective, there is no benefit to homosexual behavior since those who engage in it do not reproduce, and from an evolutionary perspective, the only purpose in life is to make babies (the bottom line for the more scientific-sounding "survive and reproduce").

I recently discovered an excellent article on the "animal homosexuality myth" at the NARTH (National Association for the Research and Treatment of Homosexuality) website. This article points out that we can find occurrences of "homosexuality," cannibalism and infanticide in the animal kingdom, but the fact that these aberrant behaviors exist should not lead us to deduce that they are acceptable and normal HUMAN behaviors to engage in! www.narth.org/docs/animalmyth.html[126]

The Origin of Our Troubles

As we have evidenced repeatedly throughout this book, humanity's troubles began with Satan, Adam, and Eve. Certainly, there is no direct responsibility of any of Adam's offspring for Adam's sin. Nevertheless, "just as sin came into the world through one man, and death through sin, and so death spread to all men because all sinned." – Romans 5:12, ESV.

Our imperfection puts us at an apparent weakness. However, that does not mean that we are absolved of our responsibility. Jesus stated, "God so loved the world, that He gave His only begotten Son, that whoever believes in Him shall not perish, but

---

[126] Is Animal Homosexuality Proof that It's Normal?, https://www.probe.org/is-animal-homosexuality-proof-that-its-normal/ (accessed April 25, 2016).

have eternal life." (John 3:16, NASB) Paul wrote, "Since by a man came death, by a man also came the resurrection of the dead. For as in Adam all die, so also in Christ all will be made alive." – 1 Corinthians 15:21-22, NASB.

Jesus said of himself, "just as the Son of Man did not come to be served, but to serve, and to give His life a ransom for many." (Matt. 20:28, NASB) Paul was extremely grateful for the ransom sacrifice of Jesus Christ. He wrote, "Wretched man that I am! Who will deliver me from this body of death? Thanks be to God through Jesus Christ our Lord! So then, I myself serve the law of God with my mind, but with my flesh I serve the law of sin." (Rom. 7:24, 25) The apostle John writes, "My little children, I am writing these things to you so that you may not commit a sin.[127] But if anyone does sin, we have an advocate with the Father, Jesus Christ the righteous one" – 1 John 2:1, UASV.

Philippians 4:13 Updated American Standard Version (UASV)

[13] I can do all things through him who strengthens me.

Paul spoke from experience. He had been through the extremes: surplus and poverty. He knew how to weather the dangers of both. This was his secret. Greek and Roman religions had secret initiation rites. Some religions and philosophies prided themselves on secret knowledge. Paul had a different kind of secret. His secret was his reliance on Christ, a reliance gained through his Christian experience. Stoics relied on personal will to gain contentment. Paul did not claim such personal inner strength. His strength came from Jesus living in him. Paul was in Christ and thus content no matter what his circumstances.

J. Vernon McGee writes:

Whatever Christ has for you to do, He will supply the power. Whatever gift He gives you, He will give the power to exercise that gift. A gift is a manifestation of the Spirit of God in the life of the believer. As long as you

---

[127]   Gr., *hamartete,* a   verb   in   the   aorist   subjunctive.   According to *A Grammar of New Testament Greek*, by James H. Moulton, Vol. I, 1908, p. 109, "the Aorist has a 'punctiliar' action, that is, it regards action as a *point:* it represents the point of entrance . . . or that of completion . . . or it looks at a whole action simply as having occurred, without distinguishing any steps in its progress."

function in Christ, you will have power. He certainly does not mean that he is putting into your hand unlimited power to do anything you want to do. Rather, He will give you the enablement to do all things in the context of His will for you (McGee, *Thru the Bible*, V:327–8).

The Christian life is not only difficult; it is also impossible unless we acquire the power to live it through Christ. To be sure, this truth does not come naturally to us but must be learned.[128]

Life is evidence that we must struggle with major hostile powers, as well as our own sinful tendencies and Satan's efforts to move us off the path of salvation by getting us to stop obeying God. (1 Pet. 5:8) It is also very possible that our genes will affect us in one way or another. Nevertheless, we are certainly not helpless. True Christians have the Father, the Son and the Holy Spirit, as well their gift, the Bible, not to mention, the Christian congregation. – 1 Timothy 6:11-12; 1 John 2:1.

Review Questions

- Is not homosexuality genetically predisposed? Explain.

- How is Thomas R. Schreiner's response to a genetic predisposition an absolutely balanced response?

- Is animal homosexuality proof that it's normal?

- What is the origin of our troubles?

- How can we do all things through him who strengthens us?

---

[128] (Anders, Holman New Testament Commentary: vol. 8, Galatians, Ephesians, Philippians, Colossians 1999, 264)

CHAPTER 5 The Pornography Trap

A 50-year-old married physician views Internet pornography for hours at home, masturbating five to seven times a day, then begins surfing porn sites at the office and risks destroying his career.

A woman spends four to six hours a day in Internet chat rooms and having cybersex, and eventually starts arranging to meet online strangers for casual sex in the real world.

A man spends many hours a day downloading porn, filling multiple hard drives, and devotes a separate computer just to pornography.

A married couple views pornographic movies together as part of their loving relationship, but the husband starts spending more time watching and less time with his wife, who feels left behind and rejected.

These scenarios are real-life examples of pornography addiction, a compulsive behavior that falls within the category of sex addiction.[129]

Pornography addiction or problematic pornography use is a behavioral addiction characterized by compulsive, repeated use of pornographic material until it causes serious negative consequences to one's physical, mental, social, and/or financial well-being. Addiction to Internet pornography is a form of cybersex addiction.

Symptoms and Diagnosis

Diagnostic criteria do not exist for pornography addiction or problematic porn viewing. A study on problematic Internet pornography viewing used the criteria of viewing Internet pornography more than three times a week during some weeks, and viewing causing difficulty in general life functioning.

---

[129] http://www.sfgate.com/health/article/Porn-addiction-destroys-relationships-lives-3272230.php

In 1990 Aviel Goodman proposed a general definition of all types of addictions in order to extend the specific disorders included in the DSM-III-R. While not explicitly in the context of pornography, Goodman explains his criteria for addiction as a "process whereby a behavior, that can function both to produce pain and to provide escape from internal discomfort, [and] is employed in a pattern characterized by (1) failure to control the behavior (powerlessness) and (2) continuation of the behavior despite significant negative consequences (unmanageability)."[130]

According to the San Francisco Chronicle, "If people want to escape feelings of low self-esteem, shame, isolation or the pressures of life, work or relationships, pornography is a place to get lost and feel wanted, imagining the perfect partners who always desires them - and whom they can always satisfy."[131] The Chronicle goes on to say that the risk of job loss and spousal loss is very high with those who are truly addicted to pornography.

Dr. Brown further says, "All too often, sexual addicts risk losing important relationships, being plagued with diseases, and place their jobs and careers on the line. For the addict, it is less about the desire and more about fulfilling a compulsive need."

Prevalence

Though no studies have been conducted on prevalence of pornography addiction, research on Internet addiction disorder indicates rates may range from 1.5 to 8.2% in Europeans and Americans.[132] Internet pornography users are included in Internet users, and Internet pornography has been shown to be the Internet activity most likely to lead to compulsive disorders.[133] A study found that 17% of people who viewed pornography on the

---

[130] Goodman, Aviel (1990). "Addiction: Definition and implications". Addiction 85 (11): 1403–8.

[131] http://www.sfgate.com/health/article/Porn-addiction-destroys-relationships-lives-3272230.php#ixzz2N3ZSi4o7

[132] Weinstein, A.; Lejoyeux, M. (2010). "Internet Addiction or Excessive Internet Use". The American Journal of Drug and Alcohol Abuse 36 (5): 277–283.

[133] Meerkerk, G. J.; Eijnden, R. J. J. M. V. D.; Garretsen, H. F. L. (2006). "Predicting Compulsive Internet Use: It's All about Sex!". CyberPsychology & Behavior 9 (1): 95–103.

Internet met criteria for problematic sexual compulsivity.[134] A survey found that 20–60% of a sample of college-age males who use pornography found it to be problematic.[135]

Status as Addiction

In 2011, the American Society of Addiction Medicine published a definition of addiction that for the first time stated that addiction includes pathological pursuit of all kinds of external rewards and not just substance dependence.

The status of pornography addiction as an addictive disorder, rather than simply a compulsivity, is supported by a growing body of evidence but is still contested by some neuroscientists. The current Diagnostic and Statistical Manual of Mental Disorders (DSM-V) includes a new section for behavioral addictions but includes only one disorder: pathological gambling. Other behavioral addictions were included in "Conditions for further study". A 2011 paper by Donald Hilton and Clark Watts argued that studies demonstrating the effect of sexual experiences on neuroplasticity indicate the existence of process addiction, and specifically focused on pornography addiction as an area requiring further study. In a letter to the editor, Rory Reid, Bruce Carpenter, and Timothy Fong responded by arguing that the studies on neuroplasticity used correlational data, and thus could not be used to establish causation. In a commentary included with the letter to the editor, Hilton and Watts pointed to research connecting a marker of addiction, to sexual experience, and claimed that researchers who reject the research they cite are biased against research which connects neuromodulation to behavioral addictions.

Online Pornography

Psychologists who see pornography as addictive may consider online, often Internet pornography more addictive than ordinary

[134] Cooper, A., Delmonico, D. L., & Burg, R. (2000). Cybersex user, abusers, and compulsives. Sexual Addiction and Compulsivity, 7, 5–29.

[135] Twohig, M. P.; Crosby, J. M.; Cox, J. M. (2009). "Viewing Internet Pornography: For Whom is it Problematic, How, and Why?". Sexual Addiction & Compulsivity 16 (4): 253.

pornography because of its wide availability, explicit nature, and the privacy that online viewing offers. Some claim that addicts regularly spend extended periods of time searching the Internet for new or increasingly hardcore pornography.[136]

Some clinicians and support organizations recommend the voluntary use of Internet content-control software, Internet monitoring, or both, to manage online pornography use.

Sex researcher Alvin Cooper and colleagues suggested several reasons for using filters as a therapeutic measure, including curbing accessibility that facilitates problematic behavior and encouraging clients to develop coping and relapse prevention strategies. Cognitive therapist Mary Anne Layden suggested that filters may be useful in maintaining environmental control. Internet behavior researcher David Delmonico noted that, despite their limitations, filters may serve as a "frontline of protection."[137]

Treatment

Cognitive-behavioral therapy has been suggested as a possible effective treatment for pornography addiction based on its success with Internet addicts though no clinical trials have been performed to assess effectiveness among pornography addicts as of 2012. Acceptance and commitment therapy has also been shown to be a potentially effective treatment for problematic Internet pornography viewing.[138]

Damage to Us Spiritually

Colossians 3:5 Updated American Standard Version (UASV)

5 Therefore, Put to death therefore what is earthly in you: sexual immorality, impurity, passion, evil desire, and covetousness, which is idolatry.

---

[136] Downs, Martin F.; Louise Chang, MD (reviewer) (August 30, 2005). "Is Pornography Addictive? Psychologists debate whether people can have an addiction to pornography."

[137] Delmonico, David L. (1997). "Cybersex: High tech sex addiction". Sexual Addiction & Compulsivity 4 (2): 159.

[138] http://en.wikipedia.org/wiki/Pornography_addiction

In telling believers to **put to death** certain behaviors, Paul is calling for complete extermination, not careful regulation. What must go? Paul gives us an "outside in" perspective. He starts with external actions and then moves to the internal drives which cause the conduct. In his "vice lists" Paul mentions three categories of behavior: (1) perverted passions, (2) hot tempers, (3) sharp tongues.

First on the list is **sexual immorality** (*porneia*), a broad, general term for all kinds of illicit sexual behavior. God created sex to be enjoyed by one woman and one man in the confines of marriage. Any sexual activity that does not fit that definition is not to be part of a believer's life. The perverted passion list continues with mention of **impurity**. This reminds us that immorality is "unclean" or dirty and incompatible with the purity of our Savior. Believers are not to be slaves of their **lust** or **evil desires.**[139]

Matthew 5:27-28 Updated American Standard Version (UASV)

27 "You have heard that it was said, 'You shall not commit adultery';[140] **28** but I say to you that everyone who looks at a woman with lust[141] for her has already committed adultery with her in his heart.

Again, this verse is mean for heterosexual relationships; however, what was meant can be useful in controlling same-sex desires, so it will be adapted below.

In verse 28 of Matthew chapter 5, you will notice the phrase **"lustful intent,"** keying in on the word "intent." This is not a woman walking along who catches sight of a beautiful woman and

---

[139] Max Anders, vol. 8, Kendell H. Easley, vol. 12, Galatians, Ephesians, Philippians, Colossians, Holman New Testament Commentary, 329 (Nashville, TN: Broadman & Holman Publishers, 1998).

[140] Ex. 20:14; Deut. 5:17

[141] ἐπιθυμία [Epithumia] to strongly desire to have what belongs to someone else and/or to engage in an activity which is morally wrong–'to covet, to lust, evil desires, lust, desire.'– Johannes P. Louw and Eugene Albert Nida, *Greek-English Lexicon of the New Testament: Based on Semantic Domains* (New York: United Bible Societies, 1996).

has an indecent thought, which she then dismisses. It is not even a woman in the same situation that has an indecent thought, who goes on to entertain and cultivate that thought. No, this is a woman that is staring, gazing at a woman with the intent of lusting, and is looking at the woman, with the intention of peaking her interest and desire, to get her to lust.

Verse 25 of chapter 26 in Proverbs warns the son against just that, do not get "lustful intent" in your heart because of her beauty. The same is true of a man not getting "lustful intent" in his heart because of the beauty of another man. Yes, even when the evil man is seeking to flame such desires. Aside from the fact that it violates God's Law, for mere moments of immediate gratification at a very inexpensive price, you are risking your eternal life.

When we view pornography, let alone take up the time to get addicted, we are out for self-gratification, and we are, in no way, reflecting the Christian quality of love. The apostle Paul wrote,

1 Thessalonians 4:3-7 Updated American Standard Version (UASV)

[3] For this is the will of God, your sanctification; that is, that you abstain from sexual immorality;[142] [4] that each of you know how to possess his own vessel[143] in sanctification and honor, [5] not in lustful passion, just as also the Gentiles who do not know God; [6] that no man transgress and wrong his brother in the matter because the Lord is an avenger in all these things, just as we also told you before and solemnly warned you. [7] For God has not called us for impurity, but in sanctification.

Pornography especially takes selfish or unfair advantage of women and children, and young men, who are likely in abusive situations, for the personal gain of self-gratification. Simply objectifying them for your gratification is demeaning them. If you are using their images, you are also supporting whatever company exploits them, taking advantage of their circumstances. Just taking advantage of images, makes you indifferent, at worst a hater of

---

[142] Gr *porneia, fornication*

[143] I.e. body

women and a sexual deviant, toward the very people group that the Mosaic Law and Jesus Christ tried to protect.

Breaking the Habit

Some early Christians, prior to finding Christ, were 'unrighteous, sexually immoral, adulterers, men who practice homosexuality, and drunkards' However, they "were washed, you were sanctified, you were justified in the name of the Lord Jesus Christ and by the Spirit of our God." – 1 Corinthians 6:9-11.

Psalm 55:22 Updated American Standard Version (UASV)

22 Cast your burden on the Lord,
   and he will sustain you;
he will never permit
   the righteous to be shaken.

This begs the question, how do we throw our burdens on Jehovah (i.e., the Father), and how does he sustain us. How it is that he will not permit the righteous to be moved? In addition, if we are looking at porn, are we not unrighteous? Let us get ever closer to the answer.

1 Corinthians 10:13 Updated American Standard Version (UASV)

13 No temptation has overtaken you but such as is common to man; and God is faithful, who will not allow you to be tempted beyond what you are able, but with the temptation will provide the way of escape also, so that you will be able to endure it.

Many Christians, even very mature ones, as well as those leading congregations, have succumbed to pornography. Therefore, you should not feel alone in your battle to get control over your vessel.

Hebrews 4:12 Updated American Standard Version (UASV)

12 For the word of God is living and active and sharper than any two-edged sword, and piercing as far as the division of soul and spirit, of both joints and marrow, and able to judge the thoughts and intentions of the heart.

This verse contains four statements about God's Word. First, it is **living.** God is a **living** God (Heb. 3:12). His message is dynamic

122

and productive. It causes things to happen. It drives home warnings to the disobedient and promises to the believer. Second, God's Word is **active,** an emphasis virtually identical in meaning with the term **living.** God's Word is not something you passively hear and then ignore. It actively works in our lives, changes us, and sends us into action for God.

Third, God's Word penetrates the **soul and spirit.** To the Hebrew people, the body was a unity. We should not think of dividing the soul from the spirit. God's message is capable of penetrating the impenetrable. It can divide what is indivisible. Fourth, God's message is discerning. **It judges the thoughts and attitudes of the heart.** It passes judgment on our feelings and our thoughts. What we regard as secret and hidden, God brought out for inspection by the discerning power of his Word.[144]

Proverbs 2:1-6 Updated American Standard Version (UASV)

¹ My son, if you receive my words
   and treasure up my commandments with you,
² making your ear attentive to wisdom
   and inclining your heart to discernment;[145]
³ For if you cry for discernment[146]
   and raise your voice for understanding,
⁴ if you seek it like silver
   and search for it as for hidden treasures,
⁵ then you will understand the fear of Jehovah
   and find the knowledge of God.
⁶ For Jehovah gives wisdom;
   from his mouth come knowledge and understanding;

Now, let us return to our questions, and provide answers. How do we throw our burdens on God?

We do so, by going to him fervently in prayer, asking him for help with the problem that we are trying to overcome. Our adding this in our prayers repeatedly shows him our deep concern.

---

[144] Thomas A. Lea, vol. 10, *Hebrews & James*, Holman New Testament Commentary, 72 (Nashville: Broadman & Holman Publishers, 1999).

[145] The Hebrew word rendered here as "discernment" (*tevunah*) is related to the word *binah*, translated "understanding." Both appear at Proverbs 2:3.

[146] See 2.2 ftn.

How does he sustain us?

God sustains us by the Word of God, which contains the very knowledge of God, as explained in Hebrews 4:12 above. Thus, we need to discover the Bible verses that are applicable, and we then need to know what the author meant by the words that he used, as should have been understood by his original readers. In other words, we need to discover the original meaning. Then, we need to find the pattern of meaning that would apply to us. This is called working on behalf of our prayers. However, we are not done yet. We must be obedient to the Word of God. If we obey 50 percent, we will get 50 percent results. If we apply it 100 percent into our lives, we will get 100 percent results.

1 John 5:2 Updated American Standard Version (UASV)

² By this we know that we love the children of God, when we love God and do his commandments.

2 John 1:6 Updated American Standard Version (UASV)

⁶ And this is love, that we walk according to his commandments. This is the commandment, just as you have heard from the beginning, that you should walk in it.

> What is love? It plays itself out in the real world in obedience. The essence of love is that we keep God's commandments. This glorifies God, is best for others, and is best for us. Everything God asks of us is intended to give something good to us or keep us from harm. First John presented the same emphasis on love and the same link between love and obedience. (Walls and Anders 1996, 237)

How it is that he will not permit the righteous to be moved?

God said he would never 'permit the righteous to be moved.' What is meant by 'move'?" It means to stumble or fall down spiritually or get into a practice of sin that you seem to be in. In other words, God will help you to become stable, steadfast, or unmovable, not giving into sin. **If we are looking at porn, are we not unrighteous?**

No, this is not the case. We are all sinners, and God hates sin. However, he hates the **unrepentant** practice of sin. The unrighteous person is the one who lives in sin unrepentantly. If you are reading this, and you have been praying, trying to find a way to get control over yourself; then, you are not unrepentant. God makes allowance for our inherited sin from Adam, which means he understands our human weaknesses.

Thus, the steps are (1) Go to god fervently in prayer, (2) act in harmony with that prayer, by (3) research what the Bible offers toward recovery, (4) apply what you learn, and (5) get your stride again if you stumble, or get up when you fall down.

How often do you come across pornography?

- Never
- Sometimes,
- Rarely
- Daily,
- Weekly

Where do you come across pornography?

- Television,
- Stores,
- Internet,
- Cell phone,
- Email,
- Work,
- School,
- Other

Do you see a pattern of how these encounters come about, and how you deal with them?

Is there a pattern to your encounters?

Do you find yourself depressed or angry, so you look at pornography, because of the feeling that override the depression, even though you know, even worse depression is on the horizon for failing to be faithful? Do you receive email attachments from friends that contain pornography?

The good thing about the internet is that its filters are far better than ten years ago, In order to get a popup, or end up with wrong pages; you need to be very specific in your search. For example, if you Google "race cars," there will be links and images the movement that you get a few letters in. However, if you Google the word "porn," it will do nothing until you hit enter. The same is true with email, like Yahoo and Gmail. The ads in the margins are only reflective of sites that you have been visiting.

How do you react the moment that your eyes see pornography?

- You turn away immediately so that you could barely describe what you saw

- You look at it for a moment before turning away, and could better explain what you saw

- You continue to look until your desires lead you to search for more

The foremost thing that will help you to overcome the habit of viewing pornography is to appreciate the seriousness of it, as well as what your actions mean to you, to God, to your spouse, to your family, and to the victims in the images. You have to get to the point where you "hate evil."—Psalm 97:10.

Remove yourself from whatever results in the viewing of pornography.

Proverbs 22:3 Updated American Standard Version (UASV)

³ The prudent sees danger and hides himself,
but the simple go on and suffer for it.

Be determined that you will not let your eyes fall upon pornography, and if they do unintentionally, you will immediately turn away. When surfing the internet, this is especially important. Each time when encounter someone that stimulates us sexually, it just continues to feed our desires. Each person is tempted when he is lured and enticed by his own desire.

Job 31:1 Updated American Standard Version (UASV)

¹ I have made a solemn promise
never to look with lust at a woman [or man].

Depending on your circumstances, you can apply the following as best you can.

- You only get on the internet when another is in the room

- You will place the computer in a public space

- You will leave your office door open

- You will immediate close out or delete anything inappropriate

- You will find a sponsor that can talk with you when you are feeling weak, stressed, or have stumbled

Review Questions

- Is pornography an addiction and what effect does it have on its victims?

- How can we break the habit?

- How does God sustain us?

- If we are looking at porn, are we not unrighteous? Explain

- Where can we come across pornography?

- How do we react the moment that our eyes see porn?

- What can we do to remove ourselves from pornography?

CHAPTER 6 The Self-Abuse of Masturbation

Masturbation is the sexual stimulation of one's own genitals, usually to the point of orgasm.

Is masturbation serious? Some Bible scholars view masturbation, saying, "The Hebrew and Christian Bibles are silent, neither denouncing nor encouraging the practice. The biblical story of Onan is traditionally linked to referring to masturbation and condemnation thereof, but the act described by this story is coitus interruptus, not masturbation."[147] Protestant "Theologians toward the middle of the 20th century began revising previous teachings, and some today even take pro-masturbation viewpoints. Some view it as an act of self-indulgence and even a sin of the flesh and believe that the practice is principally considered a sin because of its invitation to lust.[148] Those who view it within the range of allowable sexual behavior encourage it as a guard against adultery, pre-marital sex, or other forms of non-allowable sexual behavior, and as a method of balancing differing libidos between spouses."[149]

Before delving into the problems of masturbation, it is best that we consider some things first. It was God, who gave men and women, the natural desires of sexual attraction, as well as the physical pleasures, which are a result of stimulating certain parts of the body. However, Adam and Eve naturally leaned toward good, and would, therefore, have perfect control over their sexual desires. In fact, they did not even have clothes and went around naked. The first couple was together for a very long time in the Garden of Eden, before they sinned, and were expelled. It would seem that they never had relations throughout that time, as they would have likely procreated, and had children in the Garden of

---

[147] Coogan, Michael (October 2010). God and Sex. What the Bible Really Says (1st ed.). New York, Boston: Twelve. Hachette Book Group. p. 110.

Ellens, J. Harold (2006). "6. Making Babies: Purposes of Sex". Sex in the Bible: a new consideration. Westport, Conn.: Praeger Publishers. p. 48.

[148] Miller, Jeff (2008). "Masturbation". Bible.org.

[149] Wright, Anne (2009). Grandma's Sex Handbook. Intimate Press. pp. 123–146.

Eden. [150] Their desire for sexual attraction would not have been dysfunctional as that of imperfect humans after the fall, when sin entered the world. They were busy carrying out the duties that God had given them, like naming the animals, caring for the garden, knowing there was an eternity for the procreation, but knowing that they would sin one day. – Romans 5:12.

Because Adam and Eve rebelled against the sovereignty of God, sin entered into the world, this means sexual desires were just the opposite of their descendants, for we have inherited the disease of sin, missing the mark of perfection. (Gen. 6:5, AT) "When the Lord saw that the wickedness of man on the earth was great and that **the whole bent of his thinking was never anything but evil . . . ."** (Gen. 8:21, AT) ". . . **the bent of man's mind may be evil from his very youth. . . .**" (Jer. 17:9, ESV) The **heart is deceitful** above all things, and it is exceedingly corrupt: who can know it?

The main reason for sexual intercourse between a man and a woman is to procreate and fill the earth. Being that God is the Creator of all, including humans, he has the right to set the moral standards of what is good and what is bad. Of Course, Adam and Eve disregarded this, when their rebellion demonstrated that they felt that they did not need his standards, but could determine for themselves what is good and what is bad. The Bible is quite clear that sexual relations are to be between one man and one woman, who are married. Anything outside of that would be adultery if married, or fornication if unmarried.

The imperfect human lacks the self-control that perfect Adam and Eve displayed. Those who are single have sexual desires that are not able to be satisfied. In fact, the male human body has a way of dealing with such stress to the body, which is by nocturnal emission of semen. Is masturbation another way for single men and women, to deal with the stress and frustration of pent up sexual desires? No. While it is true, that masturbation does no physical harm if practiced in moderation. However, as Christians, we are

---

[150] For a discussion on the length of the creation days, please see, http://bible-translation.net/page/part-2-genesis-1-1-is-the-earth-only-6-000-to-10-000-years-old-are-the-creative-days-literally-only-24-hours-long

not concerned with the physical aspect, but rather the spiritual aspect.

The Bible on Masturbation

The Bible condemns quite clearly such sexual sins as fornication, adultery, homosexuality, and bestiality; masturbation is not mentioned. (Genesis 39:7-9; Leviticus 18:20, 22-23; 1 Corinthians 6:9-10) Another factor to consider is that the language of the New Testament, Koine Greek, contained several words to describe the practice masturbation in the Greek-speaking world, but they are not used in the New Testament.

While the opinion of most physicians is that masturbation is harmless physically, it seems that the human conscience rejects it, as most are not as comfortable talking about masturbation as they are about another bodily function, like washing your hands. If you doubt me, the next time you are at a restaurant, and the women excuse themselves to freshen up, when they return, ask them if they masturbated. If it is as natural, you will not have any reservations about asking, and they will not have any embarrassed or angry looks on their face. This may sound extreme, but it makes the point.

Adam and Eve were created in the image of God and were a reflection of his qualities and attributes. Even after the fall, in our state of imperfection, all humans still maintain a good measure of that image. We all have a moral nature, which produces the faculty of conscience. This moral nature and associated conscience are seen in that most countries have laws that are based on the Bible's moral values, do not kill, do not steal, and do not commit adultery, and so on. Why is it that most people feel guilty, ashamed, dirty, embarrassed, or abnormal when discussing masturbation? It is the conscience that God gave us.

Put to Death Evil Desire

Colossians 3:5 Updated American Standard Version (UASV)

⁵ Therefore, Put to death therefore what is earthly in you: sexual immorality, impurity, passion, *evil desire*, and covetousness, which is idolatry.

The ... two words belong together. "Lust" (*epithymia*) and "passions" (*pathos*) or "evil desires," as translated in the NIV, generally refer to strong desires gone bad. Although the word can, on occasion, be used of an honorable desire (1 Tim 3:1), the normal use is negative. It refers most often to the misdirected fulfillment of bodily appetites, usually sexual appetites. A passion is uncontrolled and habitual lust. When lust goes unchecked, a passion for what is forbidden arises. Habits are formed which feed each other. Lust encourages passion, and passion produces more perverted lust.[151]

"Deaden, therefore, your body members," urges the Bible, "as respects . . . **sexual appetite**." (Col. 3:5) This "sexual appetite" is not the new sexual sensations that most youths feel during puberty, of which there is no need to be ashamed. "Sexual appetite" exists when these feelings are intensified so that one loses control. Such sexual appetite has led to gross sexual immorality, as described by Paul at Romans 1:26-27.

However, does not masturbation "put to death" these "evil desires"? Hardly, in order to masturbate, one must feed his mind on evil desires, as well as pornographic images. Like any addiction, it takes stronger content to achieve the same gratification. If you drink one beer a day, soon you will have to move on to two, to get the same feeling. If you look at pornographic images, soon they will have to be viler, to achieve the same results. Eventually, you will need the real thing because the imagination is not achieving the same outcome. The world is full of opportunity, where you will find yourself aroused in a wrong moment or an inconvenient time, and you will commit fornication if single, or adultery if married.

Your Thoughts Will Lead You Astray

Moreover, your using women or men objectively in your imagination will carry over into the real world. Masturbation means that you need to view and think of women as a tool, as a

---

[151] Richard R. Melick, Jr, vol. 32, Philippians, Colossians, Philemon, The New American Commentary, 291 (Nashville: Broadman & Holman Publishers, 1993).

means to an end, as opposed to sensitive human beings. In addition, you will start to see your own body as an object as well, a means to self-gratification. Self-abuse is self-centered. The person loses sight of love and moves toward sexual pleasures. Our Creator intended man and woman to find their sexual satisfactions within the marriage bed, between one man and one woman, and within expressions of love.

How Does God View our Human Weaknesses?

Psalm 86:5 Updated American Standard Version (UASV)

⁵ For you, O Jehovah, are good, and ready to forgive,
and abundant in lovingkindness to all who call upon you.

When we slip up and fall short, succumbing to masturbation, we certainly feel guilty, which is appropriate. However, we do not want to beat ourselves down to where anxiety and stress cause future failures.

1 John 3:20 Updated American Standard Version (UASV)

²⁰ in whatever our heart condemns us; for God is greater than our heart and knows all things.

We may find ourselves falling short on masturbation many times, as it has a stronger hold on us than we may have realized. This results in our feeling guilty, ashamed, dirty, embarrassed, or abnormal. We do not feel worthy of God's Love. We need not think that God is no longer forgiving us, as this is exactly what Satan would like. The fact that you feel as distraught as you do means that God still loves you, and you have not committed the unforgivable sin. Simply be steadfast in the process of overcoming this habit, and continue fervently to go to God in prayer, begging him for forgiveness and cleansing and help. However, we as imperfect humans can be accredited a righteous standing before God, being accepted back into the family of God. **He makes allowances** for our imperfection.

Below is how he views a repentant sinner,

Psalm 103:8-14 Updated American Standard Version (UASV)

8 Jehovah is compassionate and gracious,
  slow to anger and abounding in lovingkindness.
9 He will not always find fault,
  nor will he keep his anger forever.
10 He does not deal with us according to our sins,
  nor repaid us according to our iniquities.
11 For as high as the heavens are above the earth,
  So great is his lovingkindness toward those who fear him.
12 As far as the east is from the west,
  so far does he remove our transgressions from us.
13 As a father has compassion on his children,
  so Jehovah has compassion on those who fear him.
14 For he himself knows our formation;
  he remembers that we are dust.

Isaiah 38:17 Updated American Standard Version (UASV)

17 Look, it was for my welfare
  that I had great bitterness;
but in love you have delivered my soul
  from the pit of destruction,
for you have cast all my sins
  behind your back.

Micah 7:18-19 Updated American Standard Version (UASV)

18 Who is a God like you, pardoning iniquity
  and passing over transgression
  for the remnant of his inheritance?
He does not retain his anger forever,
  because he delights in lovingkindness.
19 He will again have compassion on us;
  he will tread our iniquities underfoot.
You will cast all our sins
  into the depths of the sea.

You will notice in Psalm 103:12, that God removes the sins of the repentant one as far as the east is from the west. The picture being painted is, to the human mind that is the farthest you can remove something as there is no greater distance. In Isaiah 38, we are given another visual, God throwing our sins behind his back, meaning he can no longer see them, as they are out of sight, thus out of mind. In Micah, our last example, we see that God hurls all of the sins of a repentant person into the depths of the sea. In the setting of the ancient person, this meant that retrieving them was literally impossible. In other words, God has removed them, never to be retrieved or brought to mind ever again. This was the viewpoint that he had before Jesus ever even offered himself as a ransom sacrifice.

However, just because God is so forgiving, this will never justify sinning unrepentantly, as his patience will wear out, or the evil age of Satan will end when we least expect it. He hopes that you will continue to work toward setting aside the habit of masturbation, as it is an unclean habit.

Review Questions

- Is masturbation serious?

- Who gave men and women, the natural desires of sexual attraction, as well as the physical pleasures, which are a result of stimulating certain parts of the body, and how has imperfect man abused these gifts?

- What do the Scriptures say about the mental bent of imperfect man and his heart (inner person)?

- What is the main reason for sexual intercourse between a man and a woman?

- Even though the Bible does not mention masturbation as a sexual sin with fornication, adultery, homosexuality, and bestiality, how do we know that it is biblical wrong?

- How do we put to death evil desires?

- How do our thoughts lead us astray?

- How does God view our human weaknesses?

- How does God view a repentant sinner?

CHAPTER 7 Can the Bible Help Us Cope With Loneliness?

Intense feelings of loneliness can be so overwhelming it could lead to alcoholism, drug abuse, even suicide. If it drags on for weeks, it would be best to seek the help of a Christian counselor. The world seems so crowded in the 21st century, especially because of the internet, one might ask, how could anyone feel alone? First, it should be noted upfront that some feelings of loneliness are appropriate at certain times. For example, the husband is away on a business trip, or a child heads off to college, or the elderly husband or wife is left at home while the other has to go to a nursing home.

Some believe that "if I just surround myself with friends and family members, I will get over this bout of loneliness.' While this may provide a measure of distraction, it does not always solve the problem, because there is a void, something is missing. We cannot spend time with friends every minute of every day. Some have even made the error of believing that marriage would be the answer, so they rush into a marriage, which ends up as a life of loneliness, as a married person. One has to conquer the missing component of his or her loneliness before that can enjoy the relationship of another.

The Correct Mindset

The Bible does offer its readers, who correctly apply its counsel, practical advice on how to cope with loneliness. While we have all felt the pain of loneliness, some more so than others, being alone is not necessarily equal to loneliness. Even Jesus wanted some alone time, Matthew 14:13 tells us that Jesus 'withdrew to a secluded place to be by himself.' He wanted the alone time to rest from the crowds, to meditate and pray.

Mark 6:31 English Standard Version (ESV)

³¹ And he said to them, "Come away by yourselves to a desolate place and rest a while." For many were coming and going, and they had no leisure even to eat.¹⁵²

If our circumstances have us living alone, we not view it from a lonely perspective. What we tell ourselves in our self-talk about our being alone, will develop into how we feel. What we need to do is view our alone time, as a blessing from God, and take a few moments, reflecting on how we use our alone time. Are we simply looking for ways to fill the time, before our next encounter with people? Alternatively, we could contemplate on how we might better use this alone time, to make the most out of it.

We can use our alone time, to take care of our responsibilities around the house. If we work hard all day, we can use some of our alone time to recharged physically, emotionally, and spiritually, by taking a long hot bath, planning a movie and a snack that is mentally encouraging and healthy. We can use some of our alone time, for personal Bible study, to prepare for Christian meetings. The apostle Paul tells us "the word of God is living and active, sharper than any two-edged sword, piercing to the division of soul and of spirit, of joints and of marrow, and discerning the thoughts and intentions of the heart." – Hebrews 4:12.

True Friends

Proverbs 18:24 English Standard Version (ESV)

²⁴ A man of many companions may come to ruin,
but there is a friend who sticks closer than a brother.

---

¹⁵² With this verse, Mark resumes his narrative about the disciples whom Jesus had sent out. The disciples returned and they had an exciting tale to tell. But the crowds were increasing by such large numbers (partly due to the disciples' actions) that they had not even had a chance to eat. The large crowds suggest that Jesus and his disciples were probably in Capernaum.

Jesus knew how tiring ministry can be. He knew what it felt like to heal people, to have the press of the crowds upon him, to preach from town to town until his voice was hoarse, to get so caught up in God's business that daily needs were forgotten. His compassion reached out to the disciples, and he encouraged them to come away from the crowds to get some rest. – (Cooper 2000, 105)

While alone time is great for getting things done, digging into the Word of God, and rebooting for the next day, we were designed for companionship. In other words, humans were designed to be people persons. While being with a group, having a good time, can be refreshing, it need not always be a group to set aside feelings of loneliness. It can simply be a few close friends, who help you see that you are truly not alone.

There are some, who struggle to make friends. We may want to do a little self-examination, as to why we struggle to acquire friends and maintains that friend after that. Some want an enormous amount out of friendship while they do not reciprocate hardly anything in return. These ones suck the very life out of a friendship because they are excessively needy. They tend to isolate themselves until they cannot stand it any longer, and then call on a friend, to which they go on and on in a rapid-fire conversation about one problem after another.

Proverbs 18:1 English Standard Version (ESV)

¹ Who ever isolates himself seeks his own desire;
he breaks out against all sound judgment.

If we are suffering from loneliness, we may want to start with self-examination. What am I doing with my downtime? How can I use it more wisely? How can I look at it in a different light? Who are my real friends, and am I giving them as much as I am getting? Do I demonstrate that I am as interested in them, as they are in me? Alternatively, Do I tend to focus all of the attention on myself? If we are to disrupt the phase of loneliness, we will have to become more of a giver, and less of a receiver.

Philippians 2:4 English Standard Version (ESV)

⁴ Let each of you look not only to his own interests but also to the interests of others.

Looking out for our own interests comes naturally. We need, and receive, no instruction for that. We are instructed to look out for **the interests of others**. We are to keep an eye out to discover ways we can help others even when they do not see they need such help. The apostle stated in Galatians 6:2: "Carry each other's burdens, and in this way you will fulfill the law of Christ."[153]

If we were to "look out for" the interests of others, this would include an emotional and spiritual reflection of or plotting for the best time to demonstrate our interest in them. Thus, we can consider our family, our friends, and congregation members, reflecting on their needs, plotting how we might fill those needs. If all of us look out for the needs of others, be it mental, emotional, physical or spiritual needs; then, others will meet our needs.

If we are to have a close, intimate friend, we must first be a close, intimate friend. Jesus said, "Give, and it will be given to you ... For with the measure you use it will be measured back to you." (Luke 6:38) In addition, the apostle Paul says Jesus said, "'it is more blessed to give than to receive.'"--Acts 20:35

We are Never Ever Truly Alone

Matthew 5:3 English Standard Version (ESV)

[3] "Blessed are the poor in spirit, for theirs is the kingdom of heaven.

> In any century, a poor person has little reason to be happy, based on outward circumstances. Jesus, however, clarified in the first words of his sermon that he was not speaking of physical poverty, but spiritual poverty—**poor in spirit**. The beginning of repentance is the recognition of one's spiritual bankruptcy—one's inability to become righteous on one's own. The blessing or happiness that belongs to the poor in spirit is because such a person is, by his admission, already moving toward participating in God's kingdom plan, acknowledging his need for a source of salvation outside himself. Old Testament uses of this concept would have been familiar to Jesus' listeners and Matthew's readers. (Familiar Scriptures would have included Pss. 40:17; 69:29–30, 33–34; Isa. 57:15; 61:1; 66:2, 5.)[154]

---

[153] http://biblia.com/books/hntc69ga/Php2.4

[154] http://biblia.com/books/hntc61mt/Mt5.3

Yes, we need to be aware of our spiritual needs. We were created with the need of developing a friendship with our Creator. One thing is for certain, humans may fail us, but God never will. Therefore, we can feel secure in that friendship, like no other. Jesus said,

John 16:32 English Standard Version (ESV)

32 Behold, the hour is coming, indeed it has come, when you will be scattered, each to his own home, and will leave me alone. Yet **I am not alone, for the Father is with me**.

Our friendship with God can quench our loneliness. However, this will not be the case, if we treat God like was stated above, expecting him to be the only giver in the friendship. We must develop the friendship with God, by getting to know him, to draw closer to him.

Psalm 34:8 American Standard Version (ASV) 8 Oh taste and see that Jehovah is good: Blessed is the man that takes refuge in him.	**John 17:3** English Standard Version (ESV) 3 And this is eternal life, that they know you the only true God, and Jesus Christ whom you have sent.

While the above counsel can get one out of the pits of loneliness, it is paramount that we seek help, if we are falling deeper and deeper into depression, especially if we have had thoughts of hurting ourselves.[155]

Review Questions

- How serious is intense loneliness?

- What mistaken belief about loneliness do some have?

- What is the correct mindset that we should have when it comes to loneliness?

- How does the Bible describe a true friend?

---

[155] www.aacc.net/

- If we struggle to make friend, why is a little self-examination important?

- What does the Bible say about isolating oneself? What questions should we ask ourselves?

- How does looking out for the interests of others help us?

- Why are we truly never alone?

- Why is all of this only temporary in the grand scheme of things?

CHAPTER 8 Why has God Permitted Wickedness and Suffering?

The big issue that drove me to Agnostcism [Dr. Bart D. Ehrman is now an atheist] has to do not with the Bible, but with the pain and suffering in the world. I eventually found it impossible to explain the evil so rampant among us--whether in terms of genocides (which continue), unspeakable human cruelty, war disease, hurricanes, tsunamis, mudslides, the starvation of millions of innocent children, you name it--if there was a good and loving God who was actively involved in this world. **Misquoting Jesus (p. 248)**

As you will see with this chapter, Ehrman starts with the wrong premise. **Point One,** he begins with, "If God is a God of love, who has the power to fix anything, how can there have been such horrific pain and suffering in imperfection over the last 6,000 years?" **Point Two,** he also starts with the premise "God is responsible for everything that happens." If one starts with the wrong premise, there is no doubt he will reach the wrong conclusion(s). **Point One** is dealt with below, but Ehrman is looking through the binoculars from the wrong end, the big side through the small. When you do that, you get a narrow, focused outlook. God looks through the binoculars the right way, and can see the big picture. Ehrman can only see a fraction and a moment of time, 70 years – 80 years, while God sees everything that has happened the for more than 6,000 years in great detail, and he can see what the outcome would be if he had handled things in different ways.

Point Two, people often misunderstand suffering and evil. God is responsible for everything, but not always directly. If he started the human race, and we end up with what we now have, he is essentially responsible. Likewise, people who have a child are responsible for their child committing murder 21 years into his life because they procreated and gave birth to the child. The mother and father are **in**directly responsible. King David commits adultery with Bathsheba and has her husband Uriah killed to cover it up, and impregnates Bathsheba, but the adulterine child, who remains nameless, died. Is God responsible for the death of that child? We

141

can answer yes and no to that question. He is responsible in two ways: **(1)** He created humankind, so there would have been no affair, murder, adulterine child if he had not. **(2)** He did not step in and save the child, when he had the power to do so. However, he is not directly responsible, because he did not make King David and Bathsheba commit the acts that led to the child being born, nor did he bring an illness on the adulterine child. He just did not step in to save the child at a time that had a high rate of infant deaths.

The reason why people think God does not care about us is the words of religious leaders. When a tragedy strikes, what do pastors and Bible scholars often say? When the terrorist attacks occurred on September 11, 2001, with thousands dying in the Twin Towers of the World Trade Center in New York City, many ministers said: "It was God's will. God must have had some good reason for doing this." When religious leaders make these comments, or similar ones, they are blaming God for bad things that happen. Yet, the disciple James wrote, "Let no one say when he is tempted, 'I am being tempted by God,' for God cannot be tempted with evil, and he himself tempts no one." (James 1:13) God never directly causes what is bad. Indeed, "Far be it from God that he should do wickedness, and from the Almighty that he should do wrong." (Job 34:10)

Human history has been inundated with pain and suffering on an unprecedented scale, much of which they have brought on themselves. The question that has plagues people is, "Why would a loving God allow it to start, and worse, why allow it to go on for over 6,000 years?" Many apologist scholars have struggled to answer this question because they overanalyze it opposed to looking for the answer in God's Word. Therefore, to answer this question we must go back to Adam and Eve at the time of the first sin. Many have read this account, but I will list the texts as a refresher.

Genesis 2:17 English Standard Version (ESV)

¹⁷ but of the tree of the knowledge of good and evil you shall not eat, for in the day that you eat of it <u>you shall surely die</u>."

As you can see, humankind's continued existence in a paradise with perfection was dependent upon obedience, his continued acceptance of God as his sovereign.

Genesis 3:1-5 English Standard Version (ESV)

¹ Now the serpent was more crafty than any other beast of the field that the LORD God had made. He said to the woman, "Did God actually say, 'You shall not eat of any tree in the garden'?" ² And the woman said to the serpent, "We may eat of the fruit of the trees in the garden, ³ but God said, 'You shall not eat of the fruit of the tree that is in the midst of the garden, neither shall you touch it, lest you die.'" ⁴ But the serpent said to the woman, "<u>You will not surely die</u>. ⁵ For God knows that when you eat of it your eyes will be opened, and you will be like God, knowing good and evil."

Later Bible texts establish Satan using a serpent as his mouthpiece, like a ventriloquist would a dummy. Note that Satan contradicts the clear statement made to Adam in Genesis 2:17, "You will not surely die." Backing up a little, we see Satan ask an inferential question, "Did God actually say, 'You shall not eat of any tree in the garden'?" First, he overstates what he knows to be true, not "any tree," just one tree. Second, Satan infers, "I can't believe that God would say . . . how dare he say such.' Notice too that Eve has been told so thoroughly about the tree that she even goes beyond what Adam told her, not just that you "do not eat from it,' no, 'you do not even touch it!' Then, Satan lied and slandered God as a liar by saying "they would not die." To make matters worse, he infers God is withholding good from them, and they would be better off to rebel, being like God, "knowing good and bad." This latter point is not knowledge of good and bad. It is the self-sovereignty of choosing good and bad for oneself and created creatures acting in a rebellious manner. What was symbolized by the tree is well expressed in a footnote on Genesis 2:17, in *The Jerusalem Bible* (1966):

This knowledge is a privilege which God reserves to himself and which man, by sinning, is to lay hands on, 3:5, 22. Hence it does not mean omniscience, which fallen man does not possess; nor is it moral discrimination, for unfallen man already had it and God could not refuse it to a rational being. It is the power of deciding for himself what is good and what is evil and of acting

143

accordingly, a claim to complete moral independence by which man refuses to recognise his status as a created being. The first sin was an attack on God's sovereignty, a sin of pride.

The Issues at Hand

(1) Satan called God a liar and said he was not to be trusted, as to the issue of life or death.

(2) Satan's challenge questioned the right and legitimacy of God's rightful place as the Universal Sovereign.

(3) Satan suggested people would remain obedient to God only as long as their submission to God benefitted them.

(4) Satan said humans could walk on their own, with no need for dependence on God.

(5) Satan argued man could be like God, choosing for himself what is right and wrong.

(6) Satan claimed God's way of ruling was not in the best interests of humans, and they could do better without God.

Job 1:6-11 English Standard Version (ESV)

⁶ Now there was a day when the sons of God came to present themselves before the LORD, and Satan also came among them. ⁷ The LORD said to Satan, "From where have you come?" Satan answered the LORD and said, "From going to and fro on the earth, and from walking up and down on it." ⁸ And the LORD said to Satan, "Have you considered my servant Job, that there is none like him on the earth, a blameless and upright man, who fears God and turns away from evil?" ⁹ Then Satan answered the LORD and said, "Does Job fear God for no reason? ¹⁰ Have you not put a hedge around him and his house and all that he has, on every side? You have blessed the work of his hands, and his possessions have increased in the land. ¹¹ But stretch out your hand and touch all that he has, and he will curse you to your face."

Job 2:4-5 English Standard Version (ESV)

⁴ Then Satan answered the LORD and said, "Skin for skin! All that a man has he will give for his life. ⁵ But stretch out your hand

and touch his bone and his flesh, and he will curse you to your face."

This general reference to "a man," as opposed to specifically naming Job, suggests all men and women will only obey God when things are good, but when the slightest difficulty arises, he will not obey. If you faced intense trials, would you prove your love for your heavenly Father and show you preferred his rule to that of any other?

God Settles the Issues

Satan did not challenge one thing: the power of God. Satan did not suggest God was unable to destroy him as an accuser of God's creatures. He challenged God's way of ruling, not his right to rule. Therefore, this moral issue must be resolved.

An illustration of how God chose to deal with the problem can be demonstrated in human terms. A neighbor down the street slandered a man who had a son and a daughter. The slanderer said this other man was not a good father, that he withheld good from his children, and was overbearing to the point of being abusive. The slanderer stated the children would be better off without the father. He further argued the children had no real love for their father, and only obeyed him because he provided food and shelter. How should the father deal with these false and slanderous accusations? If he went down the street and pummeled the slanderer, it would only validate the lies, making neighbors believe he is telling the truth.

The answer lies within his family, they can serve only as his witnesses. (Prov. 27:11; Isa. 43:10) If the children stay obedient and grow to be successful adults, turning out to be loving, caring, honest people with spotless character, it proves the accusations were false. If the children accept the lies, rebel, and grow up to be despicable people, it just validates they would have been better off by staying with the father. So, God chose to deal with the issues. The issues that were raised must be settled beyond all reasonable doubt.

If God had destroyed the rebellious three: Satan, Adam, and Eve, he would not have resolved the issues of whether man could walk on his own, if he would be better off without his Creator, God's rulership were not best, and God were hiding good from man. In addition, there was an audience of untold billions of angelic creatures watching this. If God destroyed without settling things, these spirit creatures would be following God out of dreadful fear, not love, fear of displeasing God. Moreover, say he did destroy them, and started over and ten thousand years later, now with billions of humans now on earth, the issues were raised again. God would be forced to destroy billions of people again, and again, and again throughout time until he settled these issues.

God has allowed time to pass and the issues to be resolved. Man thought he was better off without God and could walk on his own. In addition, man has attempted every rulership imaginable, and one must ask, "Have they proven themselves better than rulership under the sovereignty of their Creator?" (Prov. 1:30-33; Isa. 59:4, 8) Sadly, the issues must be taken to the brink of destroying man (Rev. 11:18), otherwise, the argument would be that if given enough time, they could have changed things. If a man goes up to the point of destroying himself and Armageddon comes at the last minute, it would set case law, solve the issue, and the Bible would serve as the example forever. If the issues of God's sovereignty or the loyalty of his creatures, angelic or human, is ever questioned again, the Holy Bible will serve as a law established based on previous verdicts of not guilty.

What Have Been the Results?

(1) God does not cause evil and suffering. He does not cause injustices. (Rom. 9:14)

(2) The fact God has allowed evil, pain, and suffering has proved that independence from God has not brought about a better world. (Jere. 8:5, 6, 9)

(3) God's permission of evil, pain, and suffering has also proved that Satan has not been able to turn all humans away from God. (Ex. 9:16; 1 Sam. 12:22; Heb. 12:1)

(4) The fact God has permitted evil, pain, and suffering to continue has provided proof that only God, the Creator, has the capability and the right to rule over

humans for their eternal blessing and happiness. (Eccles. 8:9)

(5) Satan has been the god of this world since the sin in Eden, over 6,000 years, and how has that worked out for man, and what has been the result of man's desire for independence from God and his rule? (Matt. 4:8-9; John 16:11; 2 Cor. 4:3-4; 1 John 5:19; Psalm 127:1)

Satan's impact on the earth's activities has carried with it conflict, evil, and death, and his rulership has been by means of deception, power, and his own self-interest. He has demonstrated himself an unfit ruler of everything. Therefore, God is now vindicated in putting an end to this corrupted rebel, along with all who have shared in his evil deeds. – Romans 16:20.

God has tolerated evil, sickness, pain, suffering, and death until our day in order to settle all the issues raised by Satan. We are self-centered in thinking this has only pained us. Imagine you are holding a rope on a sinking ship that 20 other men, women, and children are clinging to, when your child loses her grip and falls into the ocean. You can either hold the rope, saving 20 people, or you can let go and attempt to rescue your daughter. God has been watching the suffering of billions from the day of Adam and Eve's sin. Moreover, it has been his great love for us, which causes him to cling to the rope of issues, saving us from a future of repeated problems. He will not allow evil to remain forever. He has set a fixed time (Acts 17.31) when he will end this wicked system of Satan's rule.

Daniel 11:27 Holman Christian Standard Bible (HCSB)

²⁷ The two kings, whose hearts are bent on evil, will speak lies at the same table but to no avail, for still the end will come <u>at the appointed time</u>.

Unlike what many people may think (the world that lies in the hands of Satan), being obedient to God is not difficult. We simply must set aside our pride and accept the wisdom of God is so far greater than our own, and accept that he has worked for the good of obedient humans because he loves each one of us.

Matthew 7:21 Holman Christian Standard Bible (HCSB)

21 "Not everyone who says to Me, 'Lord, Lord!' will enter the kingdom of heaven, but [only] the one who does the will of My Father in heaven.

1 John 2:15-17 Holman Christian Standard Bible (HCSB)

15 Do not love the world or the things that belong to the world. If anyone loves the world, love for the Father is not in him. Because everything that belongs to the world, 16 the lust of the flesh, the lust of the eyes, and the pride in one's lifestyle, is not from the Father, but is from the world. 17 And the world with its lust is passing away, but the one who does God's will remains forever.

As Christians, there is a love we must not have. We must "not love the world or anything in it." Instead, we must keep ourselves from becoming infected by the corruption of unrighteous human society that is alienated from God. We must not breathe in its mental disposition or be moved by its sinful dominant attitude. (Eph. 2:1, 2; James 1:27) If we demonstrate the views of the world that oppose God, "the love of the Father" would not be in us. – James 4:4.

Review Question

- How is it that Bart D. Ehrman starts with the wrong premise?

- What issues did Satan raise in the Garden of Eden and in heaven with God?

- How did God settle the issues Satan had raised?

- What has been the results?

CHAPTER 9 Why is Life So Unfair?

On December 14, 2012, 20-year-old Adam Lanza fatally shot twenty children and six adult staff members in a mass murder at Sandy Hook Elementary School, in the village of Sandy Hook in Newtown, Connecticut. Before driving to the school, Lanza shot and killed his mother Nancy at their Newtown home. As first responders arrived, he committed suicide by shooting himself in the head.[156]

Parents, who sent their children to school that morning, never expected that by the end of the day, Adam Lanza would have murdered them. Worse still, there were signs that, if paid attention to, things may have not turned out the way they did. These parents are certainly, what comes to mind when we think of life being unfair.

Unfairness the World Over

The world is full of these type of accounts the world over. We have social depravities everywhere we look. In the United States, there are hundreds of thousands living in homeless shelters, under bridges, eating at soup kitchens, and many have young children with them as well. On the other hand, the United States throws away more food than any other country. Sadly, the hungry in the United States, while truly unfair, rates very low when one considers the inhumane conditions of other countries. In some countries, like Mexico, you have a millionaire living in a mansion, with a poor person living in a shack next door, and a person living in a car, living next door to him. Almost two billion people live in such hopeless poverty and inhuman conditions that those in the Western part of the world could never relate.

Poverty is defined as a state of want; lacking means; inadequacy. Poverty "brings hunger, disease, high infant mortality, homelessness, and even war." Poverty "falls on the more vulnerable groups in society, such as women, the elderly, minority groups,

---

[156]http://en.wikipedia.org/wiki/Sandy_Hook_Elementary_School_shooting

and children." About 1 billion people around the world live on less than $1 a day.[157]

God's View of Fairness

Leviticus 19:15 English Standard Version (ESV)

[15] "You shall do no injustice in court. You shall not be partial to the poor or defer to the great, but in righteousness shall you judge your neighbor.

The New American Commentary (Leviticus) says, "Even though those who are disadvantaged are to be treated properly, no special favors are to be given to the poor in judicial settings (19:15; see Exod 23:3). All proceedings are to be characterized by justice, just as God is just (Job 36:3; Pss 85:10; 89:14; 97:2; 119:42; Isa 42:6; 45:18, 19; Jer 11:20; Hos 2:19)."[158] The irony is, one of the charges Satan made against God was that he is unfair. In addition, he said God was not rightly exercising his sovereignty. Then, he was believing that God was going to fairly hear his case and deal with his rebellion in a fair and just way. In other words, he believed God would allow him to live if Satan could prove the charges he had raised. Thus, Satan's charge of God being unfair was self-defeating in that he depended on him to be fair in hearing the issues. God is just and impartial.

Deuteronomy 32:4 English Standard Version (ESV)

[4] "The Rock, his work is perfect,
    for all his ways are justice.
A God of faithfulness and without iniquity,
    just and upright is he.

"This word [**rock**], representing the stability and permanence of God, was placed at the beginning of the verse for emphasis and was followed by a series of phrases which elaborated the attributes of God as the rock of Israel. It is one of the principal themes in this song (see vv. 15, 18, 30, 31), emphasizing the unchanging nature of

---

[157] ttp://prezi.com/8duqy_es2rmu/inadequate-living-conditions-around-the-world/

[158] (Rooker, Leviticus: The New American Commentary 2001, p. 258)

God in contrast to the fickle nature of the people."[159] All of God's actions are perfect in that he expresses his attributes of justice, wisdom, love, and power in perfect balance.

Acts 10:34-35 English Standard Version (ESV)

[34] So Peter opened his mouth and said: "Truly I understand that God shows no partiality, [35] but in every nation anyone who fears him and does what is right is acceptable to him.

Kenneth O. Gangel writes, "Cornelius and his family already were worshipers of God and thus had some prior preparation for the gospel. Peter could have assumed such knowledge on their part and not have to start by first introducing the basic monotheistic message of faith in God as he did when preaching to pagan Gentiles. Peter's sermon at Cornelius's basically followed the pattern of his prior sermons to the Jews but with several significant differences. One is found at the very outset, where he stressed that God shows no favoritism, accepts people from every nation, and that Jesus is "Lord of all." This emphasis on the universal gospel is particularly suited to a message to Gentiles. Peter's vision had led him to this basic insight that God does not discriminate between persons, that there are no divisions between "clean" and "unclean" people from the divine perspective. The Greek word used for favoritism (v. 34) is constructed on a Hebrew idiom meaning *to lift a face.*[160] Peter saw that God does not discriminate on the basis of race or ethnic background, looking up to some and down on others. But God does discriminate between those whose behavior is acceptable and those whose attitude is not acceptable. Those who reverence God and practice what is right are acceptable to him (v. 35; cf. Luke 8:21)." (Polhill 2001, p. 261)

---

[159] MacArthur, John (2005-05-09). *The MacArthur Bible Commentary* (Kindle Locations 9334-9337). Thomas Nelson. Kindle Edition.

[160] For God's judgment on the basis of one's conduct, see also Gen 4:7; Rom 2:6; Rev 20:12f. For God's impartiality cf. Eph 6:9; Col 3:25, Jas 2:1, 9; 1 Pet 1:17; Rev 22:12. The idiom "lifting a face" pictures God as an oriental monarch lifting the face of a petitioner. To lift the petitioner's face is to receive him or her with favor (cf. Esth 4:11; 5:2, where the custom is different but the import is the same).

From Where Does Unfairness Stem?

Genesis 2:17 Updated American Standard Version (UASV)

[17] "but from the tree of the knowledge of good and evil you shall not eat, for in the day that you eat from it you shall surely die."

"The tree of the knowledge of good and evil," resulted in man's failure to respect God's decree and his sovereignty, which brought man's fall.

Genesis 3:4-5 Updated American Standard Version (UASV)

[4] And the serpent **[Satan the Devil]** said to the woman, "You shall not surely die. [5] For God knows that when you eat of it your eyes will be opened, and you will be like God, knowing good and evil." knowing good and evil.

[6] So when the woman saw that the tree was good for food, and that it was a delight to the eyes, and that the tree was to be desirable to make one wise, and she took of its fruit and ate, then she also gave some to her husband when with her, and he ate.

Satan the Devil, a very powerful angelic spirit person rebelled against God, seeking glory and power for himself. He use the serpent hanging from the tree, like a ventriloquist uses a dummy to project his voice to deceive Eve and inevitably cause Adam to rebel.

Genesis 3:24 Updated American Standard Version (UASV)

[24] So he drove the man out, and at the east of the garden of Eden he placed the cherubim and a flaming sword that turned every way to guard the way to the tree of life.

The New American Commentary (Genesis) says, "Such imagery effectively depicts the excommunication of the man and woman from the presence of God. Later Israel was all too aware that an audience with God was the exclusive privilege of Aaron's lineage and only at the invitation of God once a year. Our parents squandered what men and women have longed to regain ever since. However, not all is lost since God initiates for Israel a new way into his presence but at the costly price of innocent blood. In spite of man's inability to obtain life through the garden's tree, the tabernacle revealed at Sinai enabled Israel to live with God, though imperfectly. The means and extent of access to God's presence was altered because of sin, but divine mercy overtook the wayward man and woman. For their future generations provision was afforded through Israel. This all, however, only foreshadowed the perfect and final passage into the presence of God by the very body of Jesus Christ, whose blood cleanses us so that we might know life through his death (Heb. 9:6–14)." (Mathews 2001, p. 258)

John 8:44 English Standard Version (ESV)

[44] You are of your father the devil, and your will is to do your father's desires. He was a murderer from the beginning, and does not stand in the truth, because there is no truth in him. When he lies, he speaks out of his own character, for he is a liar and the father of lies.

John MacArthur writes, "Jesus' words refer to the fall when Satan tempted Adam and Eve and successfully killed their spiritual life (Gen. 2:17; 3:17–24; Rom. 5:12; Heb. 2:14)."[161]

Revelation 12:9 English Standard Version (ESV)

[9] And the great dragon was thrown down, that ancient serpent, who is called the devil and Satan, the deceiver of the whole world, he was thrown down to the earth, and his angels were thrown down with him.

The MacArthur Bible Commentary says, "Satan and his demons were cast out of heaven at the time of their original rebellion, but still have access to it (cf. Job 1:6; 2:1). That access will then be denied, and they will be forever barred from heaven. Devil and Satan. Cf. 20:2. Devil comes from a Greek verb meaning "to slander" or "to falsely accuse." He is a malignant liar (John 8:44; 1 John 3:8). His accusations against believers (v. 10) are unsuccessful because of Christ our Advocate (1 John 2:1). Satan, meaning "adversary," or "enemy," appears especially in Job and the Gospels. deceives the whole world. As he has throughout human

---

[161] MacArthur, John (2005-05-09). *The MacArthur Bible Commentary* (Kindle Locations 47425-47426). Thomas Nelson. Kindle Edition.

history, Satan will deceive people during the Tribulation (cf. 13:14; 20:3; John 8:44). After his temporary release from the bottomless pit at the end of the Millennium, he will briefly resume his deceitful ways (20:8, 10)."[162]

Unfairness in the Last Days

Revelation 12:12 English Standard Version (ESV)

[12] Therefore, rejoice, O heavens and you who dwell in them! But woe to you, O earth and sea, for the devil has come down to you in great wrath, because he knows that his time is short!"

The Holman New Testament Commentary (Revelation) says, "Satan's overthrow means that his accusations can never again ascend to the throne of God. This is great news for all the holy angels. It is cause for **you who dwell in** the heavens to **rejoice**. What brings heavenly joy causes **woe to the earth and the sea**. More terrors await them from the sea beast and from the land beast that the dragon will call up. The dragon is **filled with fury**, for he has never before been so utterly defeated. He recognizes this as a sign: **his time is short** to damage God and his people, so he must act quickly with renewed energy. (Easley 1998, p. 213)

Daniel 12:4 English Standard Version (ESV)

[4] But you, Daniel, shut up the words and seal the book, until the time of the end. Many shall run to and fro, and knowledge shall increase."

The angel "Gabriel therefore was instructing Daniel to preserve "the words of the scroll," not merely this final vision146 but the whole book147 for those who will live at "the time of the end" when the message will be needed. This future generation will undergo the horrors of the tribulation ("time of distress") and will need the precious promises contained in the Book of Daniel–that God will be victorious over the kingdoms of this world and that the suffering will last for only a brief time–to sustain them." (Miller 1994, p. 321)

---

[162] MacArthur, John (2005-05-09). The MacArthur Bible Commentary (Kindle Locations 67207-67213). Thomas Nelson. Kindle Edition.

2 Timothy 3:1-5 English Standard Version (ESV)

¹ But understand this, that in the last days there will come times of difficulty. ² For people will be lovers of self, lovers of money, proud, arrogant, abusive, disobedient to their parents, ungrateful, unholy, ³ heartless, unappeasable, slanderous, without self-control, brutal, not loving good, ⁴ treacherous, reckless, swollen with conceit, lovers of pleasure rather than lovers of God, ⁵ having the appearance of godliness, but denying its power. Avoid such people.

The MacArthur Bible Commentary says, "**3:1 the last days.** This phrase refers to this age, the time since the first coming of the Lord Jesus. See note on 1 Timothy 4:1. perilous times. Perilous is used to describe the savage nature of two demon-possessed men (Matt. 8:28). The word for times had to do with epochs, rather than clock or calendar time. Such savage, dangerous eras or epochs will increase in frequency and severity as the return of Christ approaches (v. 13). The church age is fraught with these dangerous movements accumulating strength as the end nears. Cf. Matthew 7:15; 24:11, 12, 24; 2 Peter 2:1, 2. **3:2–4** This list of attributes characterizing the leaders of the dangerous seasons is a description of unbelievers similar to the Lord's in Mark 7:21, 22. **3:5 having a form of godliness but denying its power.** Form refers to the outward shape or appearance. Like the unbelieving scribes and Pharisees, false teachers and their followers are concerned with mere external appearances (cf. Matt. 23:25; Titus 1:16). Their outward form of Christianity and virtue makes these indivduals all the more dangerous."[163]

Unfairness Removed

Romans 16:20 English Standard Version (ESV)

²⁰ The God of peace will soon crush Satan under your feet. The grace of our Lord Jesus Christ be with you.

---

[163] MacArthur, John (2005-05-09). The MacArthur Bible Commentary (Kindle Locations 60742-60751). Thomas Nelson. Kindle Edition.

Do Not Love the World

1 John 2:15-17 English Standard Version (ESV)

¹⁵ Do not love the world or the things in the world. If anyone loves the world, the love of the Father is not in him. ¹⁶ For all that is in the world, the desires of the flesh and the desires of the eyes and pride of life, is not from the Father but is from the world. ¹⁷ And the world is passing away along with its desires, but whoever does the will of God abides forever.

The End of the Age

Matthew 24:1-3 English Standard Version (ESV)

¹ Jesus left the temple and was going away, when his disciples came to point out to him the buildings of the temple. ² But he answered them, "You see all these, do you not? Truly, I say to you, there will not be left here one stone upon another that will not be thrown down." ³ As he sat on the Mount of Olives, the disciples came to him privately, saying, "Tell us, when will these things be, and what will be the sign of your coming and of the end of the age?"

Here in verse three, we have Jesus and the disciples taking a seat on the Mount of Olives, looking down on the temple below. The temple compound was the ninth wonder of the ancient world. Jesus had just told the disciples that this marvel was going to be so devastated in a coming destruction, "there will not be left here one stone upon another that will not be thrown down." Looking down, the disciples asked Jesus what they thought to be but one question, not knowing the answer that Jesus would give, showed it to be three separate questions. Of course, the initial question **(1)** was their wondering when the destruction that Jesus spoke of was coming. There second portion of that question was **(2)** what will be the sign of your coming. The third portion of the question was **(3)** the end of the age.¹⁶⁴ Herein, we will focus on questions **(2)**

---

¹⁶⁴ Whether one sees this as two questions or three questions is not that big of a difference. If it is two questions; then, the coming/presence of Christ and the end of the age are being treated as one event. However, if there are three; then, the coming/presence of Christ and the end of the age are being treated as two events. Either way, you have Christ's coming/presence and the end of the age. If the Greek word *parousia* carries the sense of both the arrival of Christ and his presence for a time before the end of the age, as explained

and **(3)**. In short, **(1)** the destruction of Jerusalem took place in 70 C.E., just 37-years after the death, resurrection, and ascension of Christ.

They ask these questions about the destruction of Jerusalem and the temple, his own second coming (... [*parousia*], presence, common in the papyri for the visit of the emperor), and the end of the world. Did they think that they were all to take place simultaneously? There is no way to answer. At any rate Jesus treats all three in this great eschatological discourse, the most difficult problem in the Synoptic Gospels. ... It is sufficient for our purpose to think of Jesus as using the destruction of the temple and of Jerusalem which did happen in that generation in a.d. 70, as also a symbol of his own second coming and of the end of the world (... [*sunteleias tou aiōnos*]) or consummation of the age. In a painting the artist by skilful perspective may give on the same surface the inside of a room, the fields outside the window, and the sky far beyond. Certainly in this discourse Jesus blends in apocalyptic language the background of his death on the cross, the coming destruction of Jerusalem, his own second coming and the end of the world. He now touches one, now the other. It is not easy for us to separate clearly the various items.[165]

In "what will be the sign of your **coming**," the Greek word behind "coming" (*parousia*) needs a little more in-depth explaining.

Parousia ... lit., "a presence," *para*, "with," and *ousia*, "being" (from *eimi*, "to be"), denotes both an "arrival" and a consequent "presence with." For instance, in a papyrus letter a lady speaks of the necessity of her parousia in a place in order to attend to matters relating to her property there. Paul speaks of his *parousia* in Philippi, Phil. 2:12 (in contrast to his *apousia*, "his absence"; see absence). Other words denote "the arrival" (see *eisodos* and *eleusis*, above). *Parousia* is used to describe the presence of Christ with His disciples on the Mount of Transfiguration, 2 Pet. 1:16.

---

by *Vine's Expository Dictionary*, this seems to better support it being a three part question. How long that interval is between the arrival, the presence and the conclusion, no one can truly know.

[165] A.T. Robertson, *Word Pictures in the New Testament* (Nashville, TN: Broadman Press, 1933), Mt 24:3.

When used of the return of Christ, at the rapture of the church, it signifies, not merely His momentary "coming" for His saints, but His presence with them from that moment until His revelation and manifestation to the world. In some passages the word gives prominence to the beginning of that period, the course of the period being implied, 1 Cor. 15:23; 1 Thess. 4:15; 5:23; 2 Thess. 2:1; Jas. 5:7-8; 2 Pet. 3:4. In some, the course is prominent, Matt. 24:3, 37; 1 Thess. 3:13; 1 John 2:28; in others the conclusion of the period, Matt. 24:27; 2 Thess. 2:8.[166]

"What will be the sign of your coming" As we can see from the context of Matthew 24 and Vine's *Expository Dictionary*, parousia, describes not only the arrival of Christ, but his presence as well. This does not give us the sense of a coming and some swift departure. Rather, the presence aspect is a period of time that we cannot know the exact length of, so it does no good even to speculate by adding adjectives, like a "lengthy" or "short" presence.

"the end of the age" What is meant by the Greek word *aion*, which is translated "age." It refers to a certain period of time, an epoch, or age.

aion (αἰών, 165), "an age, era" (to be connected with *aei*, "ever," rather than with *ao*, "to breathe"), signifies a period of indefinite duration, or time viewed in relation to what takes place in the period.[167]

What period of time is being referred to here? If we look at God's use of Moses to help in the Exodus of his people from Egypt, and Moses penning of the Mosaic Law, we would say that from the Exodus to the sacrifice ransom death of Christ was an "age" (period of time or epoch) where the Israelite nation was the only way to God. Then, Jesus entered humanity into another age by his

---

[166] The reader should be aware that the Greek word parousia does mean presence, the word is derived from para (with) and ousia (being). However, it does not denote the idea of invisible as the Jehovah Witnesses attest to. See W. E. Vine, Merrill F. Unger, and William White Jr., *Vine's Complete Expository Dictionary of Old and New Testament Words* (Nashville, TN: T. Nelson, 1996), 111.

[167] W. E. Vine, Merrill F. Unger, and William White Jr., *Vine's Complete Expository Dictionary of Old and New Testament Words* (Nashville, TN: T. Nelson, 1996), 19.

ransom sacrifice, which runs up unto his second coming/presence and the end of this age of Christianity.

Jesus answers this two or three-part question throughout the rest of Matthew 24 and chapter 25. Matthew gives us Jesus' presentation of the events that lead to Jesus coming and presence, to set up his kingdom to rule **over** the earth for a thousand years. Most will be shocked by my saying "over" the earth, as almost all translations render Revelation 5:10 as "and you have made them a kingdom and priests to our God, and they shall reign **on** the earth."

epí [2093] is in the genitive and can range from: "on, upon; over; at, by; before, in the presence of; when, under, at the time of;"[168] Below you are going to find a list of the genitive epi within Revelation that has a similar construction.

If we are to establish that some translations are choosing a rendering because it suits their doctrine, we must compare how they render the same thing elsewhere. I do believe that the English is a problem in trying to say, "They shall reign **on** the earth." First, because this is not a location issue: i.e., "where." The genitive *epi* is dealing not with where, but with authority over, which is expressed by having it over ... not on ...

Please also take special note that the context of all of these epi genitives that follow the active indicative verb and then are followed by the genitive definite article and noun are dealing with authority.

The verb "to reign" is properly used of kings and queens, and here implies complete power over the world and its inhabitants. So another way of expressing this is "and they shall rule over the world and its inhabitants" or "they shall have power over ...."[169]

Revelation 5:9-10 has a high level of theological content. It either says that Jesus and his co-rulers are going to over the earth, or on the earth. It is theological bias to have several cases of similar

[168] William D. Mounce, Mounce's Complete Expository Dictionary of Old & New Testament Words (Grand Rapids, MI: Zondervan, 2006), 1150.

[169] Bratcher, Robert G.; Hatton, Howard: A Handbook on the Revelation to John. New York: United Bible Societies, 1993 (UBS Handbook Series; Helps for Translators), S. 105

context and the same grammatical construction, rendering the verses the same every time, yet to then render one verse contrary to the others, simply because it aligns with one's theology. Please see Revelation 2:26; 6:8; 9:11; 11:6; 13:7; 14:18; 16:9; 17:18, and then look at Revelation **5:10**. Nowhere in Scripture does it say that Jesus is going to rule over the earth.

Signs of the End of the Age

Matthew 24:4 New American Standard Bible (NASB)

⁴ And Jesus answered and said to them, "See to it that no one misleads you.

Jesus' disciples, like any other Jew of the day, would have seen the destruction of Jerusalem in 70 C.E., the first century Jewish historian, Josephus, tells us 1,100,000 Jews were killed in the destruction of Jerusalem, with another 97,000 taken captive. (War VI. 9.3)[170] Therefore, here in advance (33 C.E.), Jesus wanted his disciples to be on the watch, to not be misled, as though the destruction of Jerusalem (66-70 C.E.) also meant "the end of the age."

Matthew 24:5 English Standard Version (ESV)

⁵ For many will come in my name, saying, 'I am the Christ,' and they will lead many astray.

Yes, this would be one of the ways that many coming in Jesus' name would have led the disciples astray, claiming to be the Christ (Hebrew *Messiah*), namely the "anointed one." Therefore, it would not be Christians alone, who would be filling this role as false christs/messiahs/anointed ones.

"From Josephus it appears that in the first century before the destruction of the Temple [in 70 C.E.] a number of Messiahs arose promising relief from the Roman yoke, and finding ready followers ... Thus about 44, Josephus reports, a certain impostor, Theudas, who claimed to be a prophet, appeared and urged the people to

---

[170] Flavius Josephus and William Whiston, *The Works of Josephus: Complete and Unabridged* (Peabody: Hendrickson, 1987).

follow him with their belongings to the Jordan, which he would divide for them. According to Acts v. 36 (which seems to refer to a different date), he secured about 400 followers. Cuspius Fadus sent a troop of horsemen after him and his band, slew many of them, and took captive others, together with their leader, beheading the latter ... Another, an Egyptian, is said to have gathered together 30,000 adherents, whom he summoned to the Mount of Olives, opposite Jerusalem, promising that at his command the walls of Jerusalem would fall down, and that he and his followers would enter and possess themselves of the city. But Felix, the procurator (c. 55-60), met the throng with his soldiery. The prophet escaped, but those with him were killed or taken, and the multitude dispersed. Another, whom Josephus styles an impostor, promised the people "deliverance and freedom from their miseries" if they would follow him to the wilderness. Both leader and followers were killed by the troops of Festus, the procurator (60-62; "Ant." xx. 8, § 10). Even when Jerusalem was already in process of destruction by the Romans, a prophet, according to Josephus suborned by the defenders to keep the people from deserting announced that God commanded them to come to the Temple, there to receive miraculous signs of their deliverance. Those who came met death in the flames.

Unlike these Messiahs, who expected their people's deliverance to be achieved through divine intervention, Menahem, the son of Judas the Galilean and grandson of Hezekiah, the leader of the Zealots, who had troubled Herod, was a warrior. When the war broke out he attacked Masada with his band, armed his followers with the weapons stored there, and proceeded to Jerusalem, where he captured the fortress Antonia, overpowering the troops of Agrippa II. Emboldened by his success, he behaved as a king, and claimed the leadership of all the troops. Thereby he aroused the enmity of Eleazar, another Zealot leader, and met death as a result of a conspiracy against him (ib. ii. 17, § 9). He is probably identical with the Menahem b. Hezekiah mentioned in Sanh. 98b, and called, with reference to Lam. i. 17, "the comforter ["menaḥem"] that should relieve" (comp. Hamburger, "R. B. T." Supplement, iii. 80). With the destruction of the Temple the appearance of Messiahs ceased for a time. Sixty years later a politico-Messianic movement of large proportions took place with

Bar Kokba at its head. This leader of the revolt against Rome was hailed as Messiah-king by Akiba, who referred to him. *The Jewish Encyclopedia* lists 28 false Messiahs between the years 132 C.E. and 1744 C.E.[171]

Matthew 24:6 English Standard Version (ESV)

⁶ And you will hear of wars and rumors of wars. See that you are not alarmed, for this must take place, but the end is not yet.

There have been religious leaders that have been misled by the two Great Wars of the 20th century, World War I and II, associating each of them with the "end of the age." The First Jewish–Roman War (66–73 C.E.),[172] at times called The Great Revolt, could have misled the disciples into thinking that the end was imminent. Therefore, Jesus tells them that they should not be alarmed, and that the end is not yet. This counsel of Jesus has had to be applied from First Jewish–Roman War to the two Great Wars of the 20th century, every time a war came along, which seems to be an end all for humanity. Nevertheless, this one sign alone is not enough to signal the end, because imperfect humans are prone to war.

Matthew 24:7 English Standard Version (ESV)

⁷ For nation will rise against nation, and kingdom against kingdom, and there will be famines and earthquakes in various places.

Here Jesus expounds on his previous comments about war, because the conflicts of humankind have been so pervasive that there was a need for a reference book, *Dictionary of Wars* by George C. Kohn. Therefore, while we should take note of current events, wars, rumors of wars and even kingdom against kingdom is not enough alone to suppose that the end is here. Therefore, Jesus

---

[171] Vol. X, pp. 252-255.

[172] The Second Jewish–Roman War (132–135 C.E.) Simon Bar Kokba, who claimed to be the long awaited Messiah, led a revolt against Roman Emperor Hadrian (76-139), for setting up a shrine to Jupiter (supreme Roman god), on the temple site in Jerusalem, as well as outlawing circumcision and instruction of the Law in public.

adds yet another two signs, famines and earthquakes. These two have been a part of humankind's history. Of course, the impact is going to be far greater with seven billion living people on earth, as opposed to a hundred million in 100 C.E. Nevertheless, these are just the beginning. It seems that a war between the Islamic state and Christian nations is inevitable.

Matthew 24:8 English Standard Version (ESV)

⁸ All these are but the beginning of the birth pains.

Wars, rumors of wars, kingdoms again kingdom, famines and earthquakes are just the beginning of the things to come. However, they are not the goal post that the end is imminent. Such tragedies being merely a "beginning of the birth pains," the end was "not yet." Men likely cannot appreciate this verse, because the woman only knows the pain of giving birth to a child. It is the most natural thing in her life and yet the most painful. Therefore, consider that what comes after this metaphorical concept is going to be far more painful for humankind. These pains will grow in severity until the birth of the end of the age, and the return of Jesus. Nevertheless, like any other birth that has finally reached the end, the joy of a newborn child makes one forget the prior pains. This is true after the tribulation, the joys from the Kingdom will outweigh the previous pains.

Matthew 24:9 English Standard Version (ESV)

⁹ "Then they will deliver you up to tribulation and put you to death, and you will be hated by all nations for my name's sake.

Verse 9 of the new section, 9-12, begins with "then" (Greek *tote*), which brings the reader into another section of signs, offering us more of the lines in the fingerprint, the full picture that we are in the time of to the end. "Then" can have the meaning coming *after, or at the same time*, or it could mean simply *therefore*. It would seem that "then" is best understood as meaning 'at the same time,' because these signs, as well as those that we covered in 4-7, and those coming in verse 10 are of a composite sign. Meaning, you are looking for a time when they are all happening, and on a worldwide scale.

163

Who are "they" that deliver Christians up to tribulation? It would those Christians of verse 5, who were led astray, abandoning the Christian faith. The last 30 years, this has truly seen the abandonment of Christianity, as well as much tribulation for those that have remained faithful. What I am primarily referring to is liberal Christianity (80 percent of Christianity), who has abandoned the biblical truth, for the lie, so they can maintain a good relationship with the world, and progressivism. Christianity has never been more hated than it is today. Sadly, conservative Christians have been deeply opposed and persecuted by liberal Christianity, atheists, not to mention Islam and other religions.

Verse 9 says they will deliver you over (ESV), or hand you over (HCSB), to tribulation. If one is handed over, he must first be seized and then delivered to those, who are seeking to do him harm, even death. Why are the Christians hated so? Former Christians and liberal Christians hate the stand that conservative Christians take by truly living by God's Word, in a world that is anything but. Radical Islam is simply trying to impose themselves on everyone who stands in their way of dominating the world. Thus, being handed over is a result for one's true faith in Jesus Christ.

Matthew 24:10 English Standard Version (ESV)

¹⁰ And then many will fall away and betray one another and hate one another.

While early Christianity suffered horrible deaths through being martyred for simply being a Christian, the hatred today is just as vile by those that slaughter Christians around the world. Nevertheless, persecution through social media, news media, and by way of lawsuits, and protests in the streets, has become the new form of persecution in the Western world. Many have fallen away from Jesus, becoming apostates toward their former brothers and sisters, loathing their very existence.

Matthew 24:11 English Standard Version (ESV)

¹¹ And many false prophets will arise and lead many astray.

What is a prophet? The primary meaning is one who proclaims the word of God, a spokesperson for God. Therefore, a false prophet would be a spokesperson giving the impression that he is a spokesman for God, but really he is far from it. These ones are very subtle and deceptive in their ability to present themselves as a person representing God. Some modern day examples would be, Jim Bakker, Kenneth Copeland, Benny Hinn, T.D. Jakes, Joyce Meyer, Juanita Bynum, Creflo Dollar, Eddie Long, Pat Robertson, and Joel Olsteen. Of course, these are just some of the televangelists, who are false prophets, with tens of millions of followers. Other false prophet religious leaders have tens of millions of followers as well. Then, there are charismatic Christian denominations that numbered over 500 million followers. These ones claim gifts of God (faith healing, speaking in tongues, etc.), which clearly are anything but. The true Christians are falling away in great numbers, being led astray by these false prophets, and those who have not, need to remain awake!

Matthew 24:12 English Standard Version (ESV)

¹² And because lawlessness will be increased, the love of many will grow cold.

The world we live in is overflowing with murders, rapes, armed robberies and assaults, not to mention war. It has grown so pervasive that many have grown callused to seeing the newspapers, websites and television news filled with one heinous crime, one after another. In looking at just one city in the United States, in 2012, 532 people were murdered in the city of Chicago, with a population of 2.7 million. However, in San Pedro Sula of the country Honduras, 1,143 people were murdered with only a population of 719,447. Statistics from the United Nations report 250,000 cases of rape or attempted rape annually. However, it must be kept in mind that because of the savagery of the times, in "many parts of the world, rape is very rarely reported, due to the extreme social stigma cast on women who have been raped, or the fear of being disowned by their families, or subjected to violence, including honor killings."¹⁷³

Verse 12 says that the love of "the love of many will **grow cold**," and indeed it has. There are atrocious crimes against individuals, groups, nations, which would cripple the mind of anyone living decades ago. However, because of seeing it every

---

¹⁷³ http://en.wikipedia.org/wiki/Rape_statistics

day, all day long, the world has grown hardened to the lawlessness that exists around them. Christians carry the hope of salvation in their heart, which Jesus addresses next.

Matthew 24:13 English Standard Version (ESV)

13 But the one who endures to the end will be saved.

What are we to endure? We are to endure while we maintain our walk with God through false Christs who will lead many astray, the wars, and the natural disasters. We are to endure while we maintain our walk with God through the loss of many of our spiritual brothers and sisters who fall away, the betrayal of former Christians, and the hatred of humankind who is alienated from God. We are to endure while we maintain our walk with God through false prophets that have arisen and lead many astray, the increase of the lawlessness in this world, and the love of humanity growing colder. Yes, each of us, who survives to the end of the Christian era, to the return of Christ, will be saved from Jesus' destruction of the wicked. However, we are not to simply sit around, we have a work to accomplish that is the last sign of the end of the age.

Matthew 24:14 English Standard Version (ESV)

14 And this gospel of the kingdom will be proclaimed throughout the whole world as a testimony to all nations, and then the end will come.

This is the last of the signs that Jesus gave that should concern us, as it is directly related to the end of the age, and the return of Christ, namely '**the gospel of the kingdom being proclaimed throughout the whole world**.' Jesus makes it very clear what he meant by "the whole world," by then saying "all nations" (Gk., *ethnos*). What Jesus meant here was more directed toward all races, not so much the "nations" that we know the world to be divided into today. Therefore, Jesus speaking of the whole world was a reference to "**a body of persons united by kinship, culture, and common traditions, *nation, people*.**"[174] Today,

---

[174] William Arndt, Frederick W. Danker, and Walter Bauer, *A Greek-English Lexicon of the New Testament and Other Early Christian Literature* (Chicago: University of Chicago Press, 2000), 276.

while for the most part, nations are made up of different races, the world is also becoming a melting pot.

In the phrase "**testimony** to all nations," we find the Greek word *martyrion*, which was a legal term of "**that which serves as testimony or proof,** *testimony, proof*."[175] The testimony here that is to be shared by Christ's disciples has to with Jesus and the kingdom. Evidence, proof, testimony has the ability to overcome the false reasoning of those in the world, to win them over, as well as convict those who refuse to see the evidence for what it is. Elsewhere Jesus said very clearly,

Matthew 11:15	Matthew 13:9	Matthew 13:43
English Standard Version (ESV)	English Standard Version (ESV)	English Standard Version (ESV)
[15] He who has ears to hear, let him hear.	[9] He who has ears, let him hear."	[43] Then the righteous will shine like the sun in the kingdom of their Father. He who has ears, let him hear.

No One Knows That Day and Hour

Matthew 24:36 English Standard Version (ESV)

[36] "But concerning that day and hour no one knows, not even the angels of heaven, nor the Son, but the Father only.

While none of us can know the precise time of Jesus' return, we do know that we are to be busy in the work that he has given us. Regardless of the time left, how will you use it? Here is how we should use our time before Christ's return. We should **live as though it is tomorrow**, but **plan as though it is 50-years away**. What do we mean by this? We live as though Christ is returning tomorrow, by walking with God, having a righteous standing before him. We plan as though it is 50-years away by living a life that makes strategies for a long-term evangelism that

---

[175] IBID, 619.

fulfills our end of the great commission. (Matt 24:14; 28:19-20; Ac 1:8)

Our sinful nature would not do well if we knew the exact day and hour. We do badly enough when we simply think Christ's return is close. You have had religions that have set dates for Christ's return, or are constantly saying, 'the end is near!' The ones who set actual dates for Christ's return: quit their jobs, sell their homes, take all their money out of the bank, and take their kids out of school, either (1) to have a good time before the end, or (2) to spend the last couple years yelling from the rooftops that "the end is coming!"

Those who are constantly saying, 'the end is near,' are similar, in that they do not take job promotions, because it would cut into their evangelism, they do not allow their children to have university educations or plan careers, because to them the end is near. Nevertheless, these groups are at least concerned about their evangelism, but fail to realize, we do not know when the end is coming.

We need to find a way in the time that remains, be it 5 years, 50 years, or 500 years, to encourage and foster "sincere brotherly love," and to display "obedience to the truth." What do we need to be obedient to? **(1)** We need to clean up the household of Christianity. **(2)** We need to then, carry out the great commission that Jesus assigned, to preach, to teach, and to make disciples! (Matt 24:14; 28:19-20; Ac 1:8) It is our assignment, in the time remaining, to assist God in helping those with a receptive heart, to accept the good news of the kingdom. Yes, we are offering those of the world, the hope of getting on the path of salvation, an opportunity at everlasting life. Just because we do not know the day or the hour, does not mean that we should be less urgent about this assignment. Remember Jesus' illustration,

Matthew 24:43 English Standard Version (ESV)

⁴³ But know this, that if the master of the house had known in what part of the night the thief was coming, he would have stayed awake and would not have let his house be broken into.

Moreover, remember Jesus' question,

Luke 18:8 English Standard Version (ESV)

⁸ I tell you, he will give justice to them speedily. Nevertheless, when the Son of Man comes, will he find faith on earth?"

If we were to consider the chaos within Christianity today, the 41,000 different denominations of Christianity, all believing differently, could we honestly say that Jesus would truly find the faith?

Fairness Restored

Isaiah 2:1-4 Updated American Standard Version (UASV)

¹ The word that Isaiah the son of Amoz saw concerning Judah and Jerusalem.

² It will come to pass in the latter days
    that the mountain of the house of Jehovah
will be established on the top of the mountains,
    and will be lifted up above the hills;
and all the nations will stream to it,
³   and many peoples will come, and say:
"Come, let us go up to the mountain of Jehovah,
    to the house of the God of Jacob,
that he may teach us concerning his ways
    and that we may walk in his paths."
For the law[176] will go forth from Zion,
    and the word of Jehovah from Jerusalem.
⁴ He will judge between the nations,
    and will correct matters for many peoples;
and they shall beat their swords into plowshares,
    and their spears into pruning hooks;
nation shall not lift up sword against nation,
    neither shall they learn war anymore.

On these verses, Trent C. Butler writes, "**2:1.** This section begins with another introduction much like Isaiah 1:1, but this one only introduces the following sermons, not the entire book. What

---

[176] Or *instruction* or *teaching*

follows is a vision, what Isaiah … saw. Interestingly, the first part of this vision also appears in Micah 4:1–5. The form of this sermon sounds like a call to worship introduced by a prophetic announcement of salvation. Apparently Isaiah and his younger contemporary Micah both used the same call to worship from the Jerusalem temple to speak to God's people. This would mean that God used the temple hymnody as a source for his inspired word."

"**2:2.** While the destruction of Jerusalem dominated chapter 1, the city's function as the center of salvation for all nations introduces this section. The last days are still within world history with separate nations acting. Israel used the same language as her Near Eastern neighbors in talking about the national temple as the highest mountain on earth where the deity fights battles for his people (cp. Pss. 46; 48). The prophet Isaiah applied this language to the temple in Jerusalem even though Jerusalem was obviously not the highest of the mountains Israel could see. Jerusalem would be high and lifted up because God was at work there, causing his purpose for the world to be realized in historical events. The emphasis is not on the height of Jerusalem. The emphasis is on the unheard-of foreign nations coming to Jerusalem to worship. God's hope always encompasses the world, not just one small nation (see Gen. 12:1–4)."

"**2:3–4.** The prophet, as he often did, took up the popular theology of the people's hymnody and subtly shifted it from present to future tense. Only in the last days would Zion occupy such an exalted position. God would no longer battle the nations. Jerusalem could no longer glory in the hope that nations would march to her with large gifts and tribute for her victorious king. The prophetic hope is that God's word will become the world's weapon. Military academies and weapons will vanish. People will learn to live according to God's ways. They will obey his teachings. Nations will come to Jerusalem, not because a victorious king forces them to, but because they are attracted to Jerusalem by the God who lives there and the wisdom he gives there. No longer will they have to fight to settle their differences. In Jerusalem God will be the great Mediator who settles all human disputes without battle. Military weapons will become obsolete. The world's only war will be on poverty and hunger."[177]

Isaiah 11:3-5 Updated American Standard Version (UASV)

³ And he will delight in the fear of Jehovah,
And he will not judge by what his eyes see,
  Nor make a decision by what his ears hear;
⁴ But with righteousness he shall judge the poor,
  And decide with fairness for the meek of the earth;[178]
And he shall strike the earth with the rod of his mouth,
  And with the breath of his lips he shall kill the wicked.
⁵ Righteousness shall be the belt of his waist,
  And faithfulness the belt of his loins.

On these verses, Trent C. Butler writes, "The wise king would enter the royal courtroom to judge his nation correctly. As judge, the king would be empowered with the breath of his lips, the same word translated "Spirit" in verse 2. By this he would protect the poor from the wicked, establishing the economic justice so central to prophetic preaching. The new age established by the new king would bring righteousness, a dominant theme for Isaiah. Coupled with faithfulness, this clothed the king for his royal reign."[179]

Isaiah 42:1 English Standard Version (ESV)

¹ Behold my servant, whom I uphold,
  my chosen, in whom my soul delights;
I have put my Spirit upon him;
  he will bring forth justice to the nations.

On this verse, Trent C. Butler writes, "This is the first of four "Servant Songs" in Isaiah 40-55 (49:1–6; 50:4–9; 52:13–53:12). Here God formally presented the servant to an audience, although both the name of the servant and the nature of the audience remain mysteriously unclear. We do not have to find answers to all

---

[177] Anders, Max; Butler, Trent (2002-04-01). Holman Old Testament Commentary - Isaiah (p. 29-30). B&H Publishing.

[178] "The Messiah will reverse Israel's earlier dealings with the underprivileged (3:14, 15; 10:2)." – MacArthur, John (2005-05-09). The MacArthur Bible Commentary (Kindle Locations 27444-27445). Thomas Nelson. Kindle Edition.

[179] Anders, Max; Butler, Trent (2002-04-01). Holman Old Testament Commentary - Isaiah (p. 83). B&H Publishing.

our questions about the servant. We need to understand that he is God's chosen one, God takes great delight in him, and God upholds or supports him."

"The servant's mission surprised Israel and it surprises us. His mission was not to deliver Israel from captivity and exile. The mission was for the nations. The servant gained power for his mission from the divine Spirit just as earlier rulers and prophets had. (For Spirit of God, see "Deeper Discoveries," chs. 62-64.) The servant's task was to bring justice to the nations. (For justice, see "Deeper Discoveries," ch. 1.) Justice involves a much broader meaning than the English term. In verse 4 it stands parallel to Torah, law or teaching. It is the verdict handed down by a judge (2 Kgs. 25:6); the whole court process (Isa. 3:14); the gracious and merciful judgment of God (Isa. 30:18); or the natural right and order claimed by a person or group of persons (Exod. 23:6)."

"In our text, the term for the servant's mission apparently encompasses a broad meaning. It refers to the natural world order and the rights expected by the nations of the earth within that order. God restores that order with its natural rights through his gracious and merciful judgment on the basis of his law or teaching."[180]

Isaiah 35:3-7 English Standard Version (ESV)

³ Strengthen the weak hands,
and make firm the feeble knees.
⁴ Say to those who have an anxious heart,
"Be strong; fear not!
Behold, your God
will come with vengeance,
with the recompense of God.
He will come and save you."

⁵ Then the eyes of the blind shall be opened,
and the ears of the deaf unstopped;
⁶ then shall the lame man leap like a deer,
and the tongue of the mute sing for joy.
For waters break forth in the wilderness,

---

[180] Anders, Max; Butler, Trent (2002-04-01). Holman Old Testament Commentary - Isaiah (p. 232). B&H Publishing.

and streams in the desert;
⁷ the burning sand shall become a pool,
    and the thirsty ground springs of water;
in the haunt of jackals, where they lie down,
    the grass shall become reeds and rushes.

On these verses, Trent C. Butler writes, "The revelation of God's glory provided the background for a new prophetic commission (vv. 3-4; cp. ch. 6). If God could change the dry wasteland so radically, how much more he could do so for humanity! The prophet was called to encourage the weak and feeble. Their reason for fear would vanish. God would come in vengeance. The divine appearance would destroy the enemy (34:8) but bring salvation to the people of God. Such salvation is not limited to a spiritual realm. The sick and disabled would find all their reasons for having an inferiority complex destroyed."[181]

Isaiah 65:20-23 English Standard Version (ESV)

²⁰ No more shall there be in it
an infant who lives but a few days,
    or an old man who does not fill out his days,
for the young man shall die a hundred years old,
    and the sinner a hundred years old shall be accursed.
²¹ They shall build houses and inhabit them;
    they shall plant vineyards and eat their fruit.
²² They shall not build and another inhabit;
    they shall not plant and another eat;
for like the days of a tree shall the days of my people be,
    and my chosen shall long enjoy the work of their hands.
²³ They shall not labor in vain
    or bear children for calamity,
for they shall be the offspring of the blessed of the Lord,
    and their descendants with them.

On these verses, Trent C. Butler writes, "The injustices of life would disappear. Long life would be the rule for God's people, death at a hundred being like an infant's death that could only be explained as the death of a sinner. All of God's people would live

---

[181] Anders, Max; Butler, Trent (2002-04-01). Holman Old Testament Commentary - Isaiah (p. 191). B&H Publishing.

to a ripe old age and enjoy the fruits of their life. The age of Messiah would clearly have dawned (cp. 11:6–9). No longer would people lose their property and crops to foreign invaders. Each of God's faithful people would enjoy the works of their hands. Labor would be rewarded in the field and in the birth place. Every newborn would escape the "horror of sudden disaster" (author's translation; NIV, misfortune). Curses would disappear. Every generation would be blessed by God."[182]

Psalm 37:7-11 English Standard Version (ESV)

⁷ Be still before the Lord and wait patiently for him; fret not yourself over the one who prospers in his way, over the man who carries out evil devices!

⁸ Refrain from anger, and forsake wrath!
Fret not yourself; it tends only to evil.
⁹ For the evildoers shall be cut off,
but those who wait for the Lord shall inherit the land.

¹⁰ In just a little while, the wicked will be no more;
though you look carefully at his place, he will not be there.
¹¹ But the meek shall inherit the land
and delight themselves in abundant peace.

On these verses, Stephen J. Lawson wrote, "David repeated his original advice: Do not fret when men succeed. He returned to the earlier thought of verse 2—sinners who seem to flourish for a season will eventually be destroyed (Eccl. 3:16–17). To point this out, he used a series of contrasts between the godly and the ungodly. **Refrain from anger**, he declared, because these **evil men** in the final day would be cut off and die before entering eternity damned. **But those who hope in the LORD**—the meek—**will inherit the land** (cp. Matt. 5:5). This indicated the fullness of God's blessing."[183]

---

[182] Anders, Max; Butler, Trent (2002-04-01). Holman Old Testament Commentary - Isaiah (p. 374). B&H Publishing.

[183] Anders, Max; Lawson, Steven (2004-01-01). Holman Old Testament Commentary - Psalms: 11 (p. 199). B&H Publishing.

Revelation 21:3-4 English Standard Version (ESV)

³ And I heard a loud voice from the throne saying, "Behold, the dwelling place of God is with man. He will dwell with them, and they will be his people, and God himself will be with them as their God. ⁴ He will wipe away every tear from their eyes, and death shall be no more, neither shall there be mourning, nor crying, nor pain anymore, for the former things have passed away."

On these verses, Kendell Easley wrote, "For the third and final time John hears **a loud voice from the throne** (16:17; 19:5). The word for **dwelling** is traditionally translated "tabernacle" or "tent." When the Israelites had lived in the wilderness after the exodus, God's presence was evident through the tent (Exod. 40:34). Part of the reward for Israel's obedience to God was, "I will put my dwelling place [tabernacle] among you, and I will not abhor you. I will walk among you and be your God, and you will be my people" (Lev. 26:11–12). Israel's disobedience, of course, led finally to the destruction of the temple."

"The permanent remedy began when God became enfleshed in Jesus: "The Word became flesh and made his dwelling among us" (John 1:14). A form of the same verb translated "made his dwelling" in John 1:14 is now used by the heavenly voice: **he will live with them**. Here, then, is the final eternal fulfillment of Leviticus 26."

"**They will be his people, and God himself will be with them and be their God** is a divine promise often made, particularly in context of the new covenant (Jer. 31:33; 32:38; Ezek. 37:27; 2 Cor. 6:16). In eternity, it will find full completion in its most glorious sense. One striking note here is that the word translated "people," while often singular in Revelation (for example, 18:4), here is plural, literally "peoples." This points to the great ethnic diversity of those in heaven."

"The great multitude who came out of the Great Tribulation received the pledge of many blessings including the final removal of any cause for **tears** (7:15–17). Now this promise extends to every citizen-saint of the New Jerusalem. The picture of God himself gently taking a handkerchief and wiping away all tears is overwhelming. It pictures the removal of four more enemies:

- **death**—destroyed and sent to the fiery lake (20:14; 1 Cor. 15:26)

- **mourning**—caused by death and sin, but also ironically the eternal experience of those who loved the prostitute (18:8)

- **crying**—one result of the prostitute's cruelty to the saints (18:24)

- **pain**—the first penalty inflicted on mankind at the Fall is finally lifted at last (<u>Gen. 3:16</u>)"

"All these belonged to **the old order of things** where sin and death were present. The last thought could also be translated, "The former things are gone." No greater statement of the end of one kind of existence and the beginning of a new one can be found in Scripture." (Easley 1998, p. 395)

Resurrection of Life and Judgment

John 5:28-29 English Standard Version (ESV)

²⁸ Do not marvel at this, for an hour is coming when all who are in the tombs will hear his voice ²⁹ and come out, those who have done good to the resurrection of life, and those who have done evil to the resurrection of judgment.

When Jesus returns, he will bring many angels, and wipe out the wicked. However, the righteous will not be destroyed, and the righteous prior to Jesus first coming back in the first century, will receive a resurrection. The unrighteous, which had never had the opportunity to know God, will also be resurrected for a chance to hear the Good News, and then, they will be judged on what they do during the millennial reign of Christ. (Acts 24:15) Therefore, the punishment for sin is death, the punishment for those, who "keep on sinning deliberately after receiving the knowledge of the truth, there no longer remains a sacrifice for sins," i.e., eternal death. However, "there will be a resurrection of both the just and the unjust [i.e., those who never heard the Good News]." – Acts 24:15

In death, Scripture show us as being unable to praise God. The Psalmist tells us, "For in death there is no remembrance of you; in Sheol [gravedom] who will give you praise?" (Psa. 6:5) Isaiah the prophet writes, "For Sheol [gravedom] cannot thank you [God], death cannot praise you; those who go down to the pit cannot hope for your faithfulness. 'It is the living who give thanks to you, as I do today; a father tells his sons about your faithfulness.'" – Isaiah 38:18-19.

Passing Over from Death to Life

John 5:24 English Standard Version (ESV)

²⁴ Truly, truly, I say to you, whoever hears my word and believes him who sent me has eternal life. He does not come into judgment, but has passed from death to life.

Regeneration is God restoring and renewing somebody morally or spiritually, where the Christian receives a new quality of life. This one goes from the road of death over to the path of life. (John 5:24) Here he becomes a new person, with a new personality, having removed the old person. (Eph. 4:20-24) **This does not mean** that the imperfection is gone, and the sinful desires are removed, but that he now has the mind of Christ, the Spirit and the Word of God to gain control over his thinking and his fleshly desires. Therefore, if one has truly experienced a conversion it will be evident by the changes in one's new personality from the old personality, his life, and his actions. If this is the case, he will be fulfilling the words of Jesus, "let your light shine before others, so that they may see your good works and give glory to your Father who is in heaven." (Matt. 5:16)

Can we see one as truly a man of faith, a committed Christian, who attends the meetings, but never carries out any personal study, never shares the gospel with another, never helps his spiritual brothers or sisters (physically, materially, mentally, or spiritually), nor helps his neighbor, or any of the other things one would find within a man of faith? James had something to say about this back in chapter 1:26-27, "If anyone thinks he is religious and does not bridle his tongue but deceives his heart, this person's religion is worthless. Religion that is pure and undefiled before

177

God, the Father, is this: to visit orphans and widows in their affliction, and to keep oneself unstained from the world." One who does not possess real faith, will not help the poor, he will not separate himself from worldly pursuits, he will favor those that he can benefit from (the powerful and wealthy), and ignore those than he cannot make gains from (orphans and widows), he will not know the love of God, nor his mercy. (Jas. 2:8, 9, 13)

Titus 3:5 Lexham English Bible (LEB)

⁵ he saved us, not by deeds of righteousness that we have done, but because of his mercy, **through the washing of regeneration** and renewal by the Holy Spirit,

The Greek word *polingenesia* means to a renewal or rebirth of a new life in Christ, by the Holy Spirit. Jesus told Nicodemus, "unless someone is born of ... Spirit, he is not able to enter into the kingdom of God." (John 3:5). At the moment a person is converted, he is regenerated or renewed, passing over from death to life eternal. Jesus explains this at John 5:24, "the one who hears my word and who believes the one who sent me has eternal life, and does not come into judgment, but has passed from death into life." The principal feature of rebirth of a new life in Christ, by the Holy Spirit, regeneration, is the passing over from death to life eternal.

At that point, the Spirit dwells within this newly regenerated one. From the time of Adam and Eve, God has desired to dwell with man. God fellowshipped with Adam in the Garden of Eden. After Adam's rebellion, he chose faithful men, to walk with him in their life course, to communicate with them. Enoch, Noah, and Abraham walked with God. In the Hebrew language the tabernacle is called *mishkan* meaning "dwelling place." In both the tabernacle and the temple, God was represented as dwelling with the people in the Most Holy. He also dwelt with the people through the Son, "And the Word became flesh and dwelt among us, and we have seen his glory, glory as of the only Son from the Father, full of grace and truth." (John 1:14) After Jesus' ascension, God dwelt among the Christians, by way of the Holy Spirit, in the body of each individual Christian, which begins at conversion.

Review Questions

- What are the living conditions for most of the earth?

- What is God's view of fairness?

- From where does this unfairness stem?

- How is this unfairness to unfold in the last days?

- Who will remove this unfairness?

- What did Jesus say about the end of the age?

- What are some of the signs of the end of the age?

- How should we deal with the fact that we do not know the day and hour?

- What is the resurrection of life and judgment?

- What does it mean to pass over from death to life?

CHAPTER 10 Does God Step in and Solve Our Every Problem Because We are Faithful?

Praising God as the Grand Savior

Psalm 42 depicts for us the circumstances of a Levite, one of the offspring's of Korah, who found himself in exile. His inspired words can be very beneficial to us in preserving thankfulness for friendship with fellow Christians and continuing steadfastly while going through hostile conditions.

Thirsting for God as a Deer Thirsts for Water

The psalmist stated,

Psalm 42:1-2 English Standard Version (ESV)

¹ As a deer pants for flowing streams,
so pants my soul for you, O God.
² My soul thirsts for God,
for the living God.
When shall I come and appear before God?

A female deer cannot survive long without water. If water is low, the deer will risk its life going out of cover to get at the lifesaving water, even though she knows that the prey could attack at any moment. Like the deer that longs for water because it is a matter of life or death, the psalmist longed for God. The word "pants" in the Hebrew means "to have a keen, consuming desire for." His driving passion was not for people, possessions, or prosperity but for God."[184]

The Bible lands are a dry country, where the vegetation wastes away rapidly throughout the dry season, and water is a very valuable commodity, as it is limited in the extreme. That is why the Psalmist says that he was a 'soul thirsting for God.' He had been going without his essential spiritual needs being satisfied, that is the freedom of going to the sanctuary; therefore, he asks when he might again "appear before God."

He had been confined because of persecution, which prevented him from having contact with his fellow believers, which resulted in intense sadness, unhappiness and hopelessness, as verse three indicates.

Psalm 42:3 English Standard Version (ESV)

³ My tears have been my food
day and night,
while they say to me all the day long,
"Where is your God?"

---

[184] Anders, Max; Lawson, Steven (2004-01-01). *Holman Old Testament Commentary - Psalms: 11* (p. 224). B&H Publishing.

Because of this hostile situation, the Psalmist was depressed to the point of being unable to eat. Therefore, his 'tears were his food.' Yes, "day and night" tears would roll down his cheeks into his mouth. His isolation and distress were not enough, as his enemies aggravated his wounds by provoking, ridiculing, in a hurtful or mocking way, as they would say all day long, "Where is your God?" He needed to find a way to reassure himself during this time of difficulty, to not be overrun by sorrow and heartache.

Why am I in Despair?

Psalm 42:4-6 English Standard Version (ESV)

4 These things I remember,
as I pour out my soul:
how I would go with the throng
and lead them in procession to the house of God
with glad shouts and songs of praise,
a multitude keeping festival.

5 Why are you cast down, O my soul,
and why are you in turmoil within me?
Hope in God; for I shall again praise him,
my salvation 6 and my God.

My soul is cast down within me;
therefore I remember you
from the land of Jordan and of Hermon,
from Mount Mizar.

Here we find the Psalmist not living in the moment of suffering, but rather remembering a time before he was in exile. He 'pours out his soul,' reaching the depths of his inner self with such passion, as he reminisces within about the former days. The Levite recalls in his mind what life was like when he was in his land, as he lived and worshiped with his brother and sister Israelites, as they walked "to the house of God," to celebrate the festival. Initially, these memories did not bring joy, but the pain of knowing they were a thing of the past, deeply missed.

Then, he asked himself, "Why are you cast down, O my soul and why are you in turmoil within me"? At that moment, he realized that his hope of salvation was not in himself, but in God.

Therefore, the sweet memories truly brought him relief! He knew that if he patiently waited, God would act in his behalf. He then knew that his unfavorable conditions were not going to define his faith that, in time God would aid him in his time of need. When that moment would happen, he would "praise him" for 'his salvation' and being 'his God.' He might have been far removed from the sanctuary, but the Psalmist kept his God at the forefront of his mind.

If we ever find ourselves in difficult times, unrelenting times, we need to follow the pattern set by the Psalmist. We need to remember that God is well aware of our circumstances, and he will not forsake us. We must realize that the issues that were raised by Satan in the Garden of Eden, the sovereignty of God, the rightfulness of his rulership, and the issues raised by Satan to God in the book of Job, the loyalty of God's creatures, are greater than we are.

Proverbs 3:25-26 Lexham English Bible (LEB)

25 Do not be afraid of sudden panic,
or the storm of wickedness that will come.
26 [Jehovah] will be your confidence
and guard your foot from capture.

Before delving into the rest of Psalm 42, let us take a moment to establish what these verses do not mean. Should we understand that these verses or any others in Scripture teach that because we are wisely walking with God that he will miraculously step in to protect each servant personally from difficult times, diseases, mental disorders, injury or death? No. These sorts of miracles are the extreme exception to the rule. Of the 4,000 plus years of Bible history, from Adam to Jesus, with tens of millions of people living and dying, we have but a few dozen miracles that we know of in Scripture. Even in Bible times, miracles were not typical, far from it. Hundreds of years may pass with no historical record of a miracle happening at all.

If we are wisely walking with God, we can be confident that bodily disease, mental disorders, injury or early death is far less likely than if we were not. Moreover, we can draw on the resurrection hope. Does God miraculously move events to save us out of difficult times or miraculously heal us? Yes, he certainly can, but it is an extreme exception to the rule. He miraculously heals those who are going to play a significant role in his settling of the issues that were raised in the Garden of Eden.

What God's Word teaches us is this, that if we walk by using discernment and exercising sound judgment from Scripture, unless unexpected events befall us, we can be sure that we will not stumble into the difficulties that the world of humankind alienated from God faces every day. Conversely, the wicked do not have this protection as they reject the Word of God as foolish. In other words, Christians live by the moral values of Scripture, which gives them an advantage over those who do not. Therefore, God answers our prayers by our faithfully acting in behalf of those prayers, by applying Scripture in a balanced manner. If we have not taken in a deep understanding of God's Word, how can we have the Spirit inspired wisdom, the very knowledge of God to guide and direct us in our ways? Just because we are not being rescued when we feel that we should, this does not mean that we have lost faith, or that God is displeased. Even though the Psalmist had no doubt that Jehovah God was coming to his aid, he still experienced grief.

Psalm 42:7 English Standard Version (ESV)

⁷ Deep calls to deep
  at the roar of your waterfalls;
all your breakers and your waves
  have gone over me.

Yes, the Psalmist's surroundings of his exile were very beautiful; however, they brought him back to the reality of his difficulty! Verse 7 may very well be describing the snow on Mount Hermon when it melts. Marvelous waterfalls are fashioned, which pour into the Jordan, causing it to increase in size. It is as though one wave is speaking to another wave. This extraordinary spectacle of power brought to the Psalmist's mind that he had been consumed by distress as if being overcome by a flood. Nevertheless, his faith in God does not waiver.

Psalm 42:8 English Standard Version (ESV)

8 By day [Jehovah]¹⁸⁵ commands his steadfast love,
and at night his song is with me,
a prayer to the God of my life.

There is no doubt in the Psalmist's mind that Jehovah God will engulf him with his steadfast love, freeing him of anxiety. This will empower him to praise God in song and to offer a prayer of thanks 'to the God of his life.'

The Korahite Levite thinks,

Psalm 42:9-10 English Standard Version (ESV)

9 I say to God, my rock:
"Why have you forgotten me?
Why do I go mourning
because of the oppression of the enemy?"
10 As with a deadly wound in my bones,
my adversaries taunt me,
while they say to me all the day long,
"Where is your God?"

Then, it seems that the Psalmist slips, even though he views God as 'his rock,' a place of protection from one's enemies. Yes, he now asks, "Why have you forgotten me?" Yes, the Psalmist was allowed to remain in his circumstances of sadness, feeling depressed, as his enemies took pleasure in what appeared to be a victory. The psalmist speaks of himself as being criticized in an unbearable way. So malicious was the mockery and disdain that it could be likened 'as with a deadly wound in his bones.' However, the Levite again comes to himself with self-talk, challenging his irrational thinking with rational thinking.

---

¹⁸⁵ Translations take liberties with God's personal name, by removing it and replacing it with the title LORD in all caps. There is no rational reason, or Scriptural grounds for doing so. In fact, Scripture shows just the opposite.—See the American Standard Version Isaiah 42:8; Malachi 3:16; Micah 4:5; Proverbs 18:10; Joel 2:32; Ezekiel 36:23; Exodus 9:16; Malachi 1:11; Psalm 8:1;148:3.

Wait for God

Psalm 42:11 English Standard Version (ESV)

¹¹ Why are you cast down, O my soul,
and why are you in turmoil within me?
Hope in God; for I shall again praise him,
my salvation and my God.

It is not the troubles of the Psalmist, which actually caused him to feel bad. It is what he told himself that contributed to how he felt. Self-talk is what we tell ourselves in our thoughts. In fact, self-talk is the words we tell ourselves about people, self, experiences, life in general, God, the future, the past, the present; it is specifically all the words we say to ourselves all the time. Destructive self-talk, even subconsciously, can be very harmful to our mood: causing mood slumps, our self-worth plummeting, our body feeling sluggish, our will to accomplish even the smallest of things is not to be realized and our actions defeat us.

Intense negative thinking of the Psalmist led to his feeling forsaken, resulting in painful emotions, and depressive state. However, his thoughts based on a good mood were entirely different from those based on his being upset. Negative thoughts that flooded his mind were the actual contributors of his self-defeating emotions. These very thoughts were what kept the Psalmist sluggish and contributed to his feeling abandoned. Therefore, his thinking was also the key to his relief.

Every time the Psalmist felt down because of his irrational self-talk, he attempted to locate the corresponding negative thought he had to this feeling. It was those thoughts that created his feelings of low self-worth. By offsetting them and replacing them with rational thoughts, he actually changed his mood. The negative thoughts that move through his mind did so with no effort, and were the easiest course to follow, because imperfect human tendencies gave him that way of thinking, a pattern of thinking. However, the Psalmist challenged those irrational thoughts of being forsaken with rational ones, saying that he would hope in God and that he would continue to praise him as in the end God is his salvation, even if that salvation comes in the form of a resurrection.

The centerpiece to it all is our Christlike mine. Our moods, behaviors and body responses result from the way we view things (fleshly or spiritual). It is a proven fact that we cannot experience any event in any way, shape, or form unless we have processed it with our mind first. No event can depress us; it is our perception of that event that will contribute to intense sadness, even depression. If we are only sad over an event, our thoughts will be rational, but if we are depressed or anxious over an event, our thinking will be bent and irrational, distorted and utterly wrong.

If we are to remain rational in our thinking, we need to grasp the fact that God does not always step in when we believe he should, nor is he obligated to do so. As was stated earlier, he has greater issues that need resolving, which have eternal effects for the whole of humankind. There is far more times that when God does not step in, meaning that our relief may come in the hope of the resurrection. However, for his servants that apply his Word in a balanced manner, fully, God is acting in their best interest by way of his inspired, inerrant Word.

Review Questions

- Christian leaders and charismatic Christians overly attributed actions to God, what impact has it had?

- Does God always step in and solve faithful Christian's problems? Explain.

CHAPTER 11 Those Who May Dwell with God

Is that even possible? What does it mean to dwell with Jehovah God anyway? It means that you can be God's friend. Jesus half-brother James tells us in his letter, "Abraham believed God, and it was counted to him as righteousness, and he was called a friend of God." (James 2:23, ESV) The above chapter title is figurative language that means all have the opportunity of developing such a relationship with God that he or she has access to God in prayer and worship. Let us start by meditatively reading the Psalm 15:1-5 in its entirety, and then we will do a verse-by-verse discussion of the Psalm. Read it first meticulously, emphatically hitting the ten dos and the don'ts, or conditions that give ones access to God as a friend, enabling them to approach him freely in their prayer and worship.

Psalm 15 Updated American Standard Version (UASV)

A Psalm of David.

15

O Jehovah, who may be a guest[186] in your tent? Who shall dwell on your holy mountain?

² He **who walks blamelessly** and **does what is right**
and **speaks truth** in his heart;
³ who **does not slander** with[187] his tongue
and **does no evil** to his neighbor,
nor takes up a reproach against his friend;
⁴ in whose eyes **a vile person is despised**,
but who[188] **honors those** who fear Jehovah;
who **swears to his own hurt** and does not change;
⁵ who does **not put out his money at interest**,[189]

---

[186] Lit *sojourn*

[187] Lit *according to*

[188] Lit *he*

[189] I.e. **not** to the destitute

and does **not take a bribe** against the innocent.
He who does these things shall never be shaken.

We Walk Blamelessly and Do What is Right

The Hebrew word rendered "blameless" is *tamim*, is not a reference to a perfect condition, one without sin; it is simply living an exemplary moral life, a life that is whole or sound. When the *tamim* is used in reference to humans that live during this time of imperfection, it is meant in a relative sense, not as an absolute. If we look at all of the good characteristics and qualities of the Bible, which all Christians are subject to possessing, it must be in a balanced manner. He is not expected to be perfect in all of them. He is expected to meet a certain level of competence of each, not being out of balance. He would not be kind in the extreme to others, but lack self-control in private. What does "walking" signify here? It is used in a figurative sense of following a certain course of action, life course, which is outlined in God's Word, to the extent that he finds favor in God's eyes. – Psalm 1:1; 3 John 1:3-4.

We Speak the Truth in Our Heart

How does a Christian 'speak the truth in his heart?' It means that he is consistent in what he says, he is not double hearted (Psalm 12:2), (literally, with a heart and a heart), attempting to live one way in an outward sense, while concealing another life, or deceptively saying one thing, while in his mind, he is thinking something else entirely. – 1 Chronicles 12:33

Some Christians might not out and out lie, but they speak half-truths, to avoid and discomfort that may come from telling the complete truth. Christian students cheat on their tests while their Christian parents alter the figures on their taxes to make the bottom line look better. These fall short in that they are not whole or sound when it comes to the truth. The apostle Paul said, "Do not lie to each other, since you have taken off your old self with its practices and have put on the new self, which is being renewed in knowledge in the image of its Creator." (Colossians 3:9, 10) We must ask ourselves, are we completely honest in our dealings with others? Moreover, are we completely honest with ourselves? If we are, this will affect the next condition that must be met in order to be able freely to approach God in our prayers and worship.

We Do Not Slander With Our Tongue

To slander someone is to say something false or malicious (intentionally harmful) that damages somebody's reputation. The Hebrew verb *ragal* is a reference to the lowest part of the leg, the body part upon which a person or animal stands, the foot (regel). It is used both literally and figuratively. It has the meaning "to foot it," in other words, "to go about." The Israelites were commanded, "You shall not go about with slander among your people." (Lev. 19:16) We are robbing a person of his good name if we slander him, deliberately trying to do harm to his or her reputation. We can help to bring slander to a halt, by refusing to listen to it, and especially not spreading it on to another. If it is of such paramount importance that we control our speech, is it not, much more important that we control what we do?

We Do No Evil to Our Neighbor

We will fare far better in life if we apply the words of Jesus, which are in harmony with Psalm 15:3: "In all things, whatever you want that people should do to you, thus also you do to them." (Matt 7:12, LEB) It is simple, we must avoid doing anything bad to other people, but it must also be a heart condition of how we feel. The Psalmist said, "O you who love Jehovah, **hate evil**: He preserves the souls of his saints; He delivers them out of the hand of the wicked."(Ps 97:10, ASV) Therefore, if we are to be a friend of God like Abraham and many other holy ones of the past, we must live by the moral standards that he created within us.

This removing of bad from our lives would fall to not doing anyone wrong when we have dealings with them. This would include what we say, as well as what we do, in our dealings with others, doing nothing to bring them any kind of harm. That is avoiding the bad, but we also need to embrace doing the good for the people that enter our lives as well. This can be as small as driving in a courteous way when we are on the road. Are we in such a hurry that we do not pause to let another driver in our lane, or out of a parking lot into traffic. We can also do good by helping the elderly, help raise the spirits of the downhearted, comfort the grieving. What does the Psalmist address next?

We Do Not Reproach Our Friends

Bringing reproach on another is criticizing him or her to another for something they may have done wrong. Each of us makes mistakes, and we would hope that our friends would overlook these small imperfect moments in our lives. It is ironic, if we make a mistake, we hope the friend ignores it and does not share it with others. However, when others are the ones that make a mistake, we can be quick to share that moment of imperfection with others. There are some in the Christian congregation, who will share minor embarrassing weaknesses of others, to sidestep their own issues, or to build themselves up, while tearing down others. However, this type of spirit does not belong to a friend of God, who throws our transgressions into the sea (so that they are so far down that they will never be seen again). One who casts our transgressions as far off as the sunrise is from the sunset (the greatest distance possible), who throws our transgressions behind his back (so he is unable to see them).--Micah 7:19; Psalm 103:12; Isaiah 38:17

Proverbs 17:9 Updated American Standard Version (UASV)

⁹ Whoever covers   a   transgression   seeks   love, but he who repeats a matter separates close friends.

We are to Despise Vile Persons

A vile person is one who would have no value in the life of the true worshipers, who is unclean, lacking honesty or moral integrity, or morally corrupts. A true worshiper has to have dealings with those who practice sin in this world, but does not bond with such a person in any kind of social setting or friendship. He realizes that such an association would defile him. When a man with a white glove shakes hands with a man wearing a glove that is covered in dirt, the clean white glove does not rub off on the dirty glove; it is always the dirt coming off onto the clean glove.--1 Corinthians 5:6; 15:33

191

There is a tendency to overlook the defiled man if he is wealthy, famous, in a position of power. (Jude 16) We must come to the realization that friendship with God is impossible for those who become friends with those who are vile (wicked in their ways). We are to hate the wicked ones ways, anything that is contrary to the moral standard of God. (Rom. 12:9) So bad was Israel's king Jehoram that the prophet Elisha told him:

2 Kings 3:14 Updated American Standard Version (UASV)

14 And Elisha said, "As the Lord of hosts lives, before whom I stand, were it not that I have regard for Jehoshaphat the king of Judah, I would neither look at you nor see you.

If we want to be considered a friend of God, then, we will adopt his values and morals to the extent that we are uncomfortable around wrongdoers. We will have dealings only to the extent that we have to because we live in this world. As Paul said 'we must live in this world, but we need not be a part of it.' On the other hand, those we invite into our lives, as friends should be chosen based on their walk with God, not because they are wealthy, popular, or influential. We will choose our friends based on the love we have for our heavenly Father because we fear the idea of ever hurting him.

We Honor Those Who Fear God

This fear of God is not the dread that we would have of say being dangled over the edge of a cliff, or cowering in a closet as our house is being robbed by several criminals, or having a cruel employer that makes our life a living torture chamber. No, the fear of Jehovah is a reverential fear of displeasing him, because our love for him is like that of a loving father, but only greater. It is like a son, who imitates his father, so too we want to be like our heavenly Father, as we are made in his image.

Proverbs 1:7 Updated American Standard Version (UASV)

7 The fear of the Lord is the beginning of knowledge; fools despise wisdom and instruction.

This love for him, moves us to apply his Word more fully in our lives, it serves as a daily guide in all that we do. We realize that the values and morals that he has placed in our conscience are refined by his Word, and will help us be able to determine between what is good and what is bad. For example, one who lives by these values would apply all the Bible principles that would make him an excellent worker, meaning he would be productive, honest, and looking to be of help to all on the job site. Fellow workers may view this as attempts at seeking favor with management, looking to get ahead, so they ridicule this one. Others may feel that he is making them work harder, or look bad in the boss's eyes, so they despise him. What they do not realize is that these are his qualities as a person of God, and he has none of the evil intentions that fellow workers may suspect. Are we honoring persons like this, persons who fear God?

We Keep Our Promises Regardless of the Cost

We keep our promises that we make to Jehovah God himself, as well as to our neighbor, friends, family, employer, and so on, not allowing one word to fail, as this is what God would have done. (1 Kings 8:56; 2 Corinthians 1:20) We do this even if after having made a promise, it turns out that it is going to be more complicated, or more involved than we had originally thought. If we swear to help a neighbor one weekend and then a friend offers us a chance to go to once in a lifetime event, we keep our word. If we promise our wife that we will get something done, we get it done. Even when Joshua was tricked into giving his word to the Gibeonites, he still kept that word once he found out.

Joshua 9:16-19 Updated American Standard Version (UASV)

[16] At the end of three days after they had made a covenant with them, they heard that they were their neighbors and that they lived among them.[190] [17] Then the sons of Israel set out and came to their cities on the third day. Now their cities were Gibeon and Chephirah and Beeroth and Kiriath-jearim. [18] The sons of Israel did not strike them because the leaders of the congregation had sworn to them by Jehovah the God of Israel. And the whole congregation grumbled against the leaders. [19] But all the leaders said to all the

---

[190] *Or within their land*

congregation, "We have sworn to them by Jehovah, the God of Israel, and now we cannot touch them.

Thus, if we make a commitment to another, we are obligated to that promise, and it is our integrity on the line, as well as God's good name, because when we fail to keep a promised, we bring reproach on ourselves, as well as the God that we represent. Jesus said, "Let what you say be simply 'Yes' or 'No'; anything more than this comes from evil." (Matthew 5:37) Especially should all who have dedicated their lives to Christ be ever determined to live up to their promise to be his disciple?

We Lend Our Money without Charging Interest

Of course, money lent for business purposes is an exception to this principle. David in this Psalm was referring to when we give money to those living or falling into poverty. Exodus 22:25 specifically says, "If you lend money to any of my people with you who is poor, you shall not be like a moneylender to him, and you shall not exact interest from him." We also find an account in Nehemiah where he discovered the poor being taken advantage of by others who were using them for ill-gotten gains, and he brought this to a stop.--Nehemiah 5:1-13.

As an aside, of interest is David's choice of words, for the Hebrew word he used is a derivative of another one that signifies "to bite." In other words, those greedy usurers were chewing up and devouring the destitute to line their pockets. We should rather live by the principles that Jesus outlined for us at Luke 14:12-14, "When you give a dinner or a banquet, do not invite your friends or your brothers or your relatives or rich neighbors, lest they also invite you in return, and you be repaid. But when you give a feast, invite the poor, the crippled, the lame, the blind, and you will be blessed, because they cannot repay you. For you will be repaid at the resurrection of the just." If it is our desire to be a friend of God and to dwell with him, we should never take advantage of those who are struggling financially.

We Do Not Take Bribes that Hurt the Innocent

A bribe is to give somebody money or some other incentive to do something, especially something illegal or dishonest, and this has a demeaning and shameful effect. We are told at Deuteronomy 16:19, "You shall not pervert justice. You shall not show partiality, and you shall not accept a bribe, for a bribe blinds the eyes of the wise and subverts the cause of the righteous." We are to be about just and justice alone, not perverting justice. We would never want to accept any incentive to do an innocent person wrong, which deserves justice. The greatest injustice since the fall of man had been when Judas Iscariot accepted a Bribe to betray Jesus Christ! Matthew 26:14-16.

We may believe that we are innocent under this provision, but if we have ever tried to influence another to avoid justice, in any way, we are guilty. The prophet Samuel sets the example for us to follow, "Here I am; testify against me before [Jehovah] and before his anointed. Whose ox have I taken? Or whose donkey have I taken? Or whom have I defrauded? Whom have I oppressed? Or from whose hand have I taken a bribe to blind my eyes with it? Testify against me, and I will restore it to you." They said, 'You have not defrauded us or oppressed us or taken anything from any man's hand.'" (1 Samuel 12:3, 4)

If We Do These Things We Will Stand Firm

King David closes this list of standards or criterion that we are to live by, with "he who does these things shall never be moved." The New Living Translation reads, "Such people will stand firm forever." This is not an absolute; it is relative to the imperfect condition we are in and the imperfect world in which we live. All of these kinds of statements in the Bible, if you do "A" you will get "B" are best understood if you these phrases before the statement: generally speaking, "on the whole," "by and large," or "as a rule" in the front of the verse. "Generally speaking, such people will stand firm forever." Unlike those in the world, who have their flesh as their god, we will fair far better if we do these things to the best of our Christian ability.

Of course, there is far more to being God's friend than what we have covered here in Psalm 15. Jesus brought the servant of God new spiritual light, such as what he said at John 4:23-24 "But the hour is coming and is now here, when the true worshipers will worship the Father in spirit and truth, for the Father, is seeking such people to worship him. God is spirit, and those who worship him must worship in spirit and truth." By following the Bible study program that we have outlined here in this publication, you will discover the deeper things of God, which will enable to draw closer, and become God's friend.

Review Questions

- Who are morally qualified so that may dwell with God?

- If you are to be God's friend, what must you be free of?

- Are you completely honest with yourself and others, speaking the truth in your heart?

- Who should we refuse to listen to?

- What does avoiding evil include?

- How does a Christian look upon upright persons?

CHAPTER 12 Walk Humbly With Your God

Micah 6:8 Updated American Standard Version (UASV)

⁸ He has told you, O mortal man, what *is* good,
and what does Jehovah require of you
but to do justice, and to love kindness,
and to walk humbly with your God?

It is certainly a difficult thing, trying to picture a puny human walk with the Creator of heaven and earth. It would be like setting a piece of sand next to the biggest bolder on earth, and this would not even be close. Of course, we are talking about a metaphorical walk, a life course that a Christian follows, one that is in harmony with Jehovah's values, will and purposes.

Others have done just that, as we learn from Scripture that "Enoch walked with God" and "Noah walked with God." If we truly are a friend of God, like Abraham, we will be living a life that is reflective of that friendship. Jehovah expects nothing less of his servants, than that they 'walk humbly with him.' – Genesis 5:22; 6:9; Malachi 2:4, 6; Micah. 6:8

If we are to walk with God in a system of things that is run by Satan, possessing a mind and body that leans naturally toward sin, it will be necessary for us to have a very close relationship, closer than any human relationship that we may have ever had. We read of Moses that it was, "by faith he left Egypt, not fearing the anger of the king, for he persevered as if he saw the invisible one." (Heb. 11:27) Even though King David had many bumps in his relationship with God, it is said that his "eyes are continually toward Jehovah." Yes, David said, "I have set Yahweh before me always. Because he is at my right hand I will not be shaken." – Psalm 25:15; 16:8, LEB.

Why should we walk with God? First, we do so because he is the giver of life, and the sovereign of the universe. Second, as our Creator, he designed us not to walk alone. How has that been working out for humanity over the past 6,000 plus years? "I know, O [Jehovah], that to the human is not his own way, nor to a person is the walking and the directing of his own step." (Jer. 10:23, LEB) Yes, we were designed to be under the umbrella of his sovereignty, possessing free will, but best served by following his lead. Therefore, our eternal happiness is dependent upon our walking with him.

We can draw comfort from the fact that God created us out of his endless love, making us in such a way, to enjoy life to the fullest extent. It was Adam who rebelled, placing us in this difficult situation. Now Jehovah is moving heaven and earth to get us back to his intended purpose. Jehovah is omniscient (all knowing), which means he knows what is best for us. Having him walk us through this difficult period in human history is the safest way to the end of this wicked system of things. – Proverbs 2:6-9; Psalm 91:1

Further, walking with God should come out of our love for him, not what we can gain from him. We should find true happiness in our friendship with him; otherwise, our motives are not pure. The Scriptures are quite clear about how he feels about our love for him, as he tells us to "Be wise, my child, and make my heart glad, and I will answer him who reproaches me with a word." – Proverbs 77:11, LEB.

Threefold Resistance

When we enter the pathway of walking with our God, we will certainly come across resistance from three different areas. **Our greatest obstacle** is **ourselves**, because we have inherited imperfection from our first parents Adam and Eve. The Scriptures make it quite clear that we are mentally bent toward bad, not good. (Gen 6:5; 8:21, AT) In other words, our natural desire is toward wrong. Prior to sinning, Adam and Eve were perfect, and they had the natural desire of doing good, and to go against that was to go against the grain of their inner person. Scripture also tells us of our inner person, our heart.

Jeremiah 17:9 Updated American Standard Version (UASV)

⁹ The heart is more deceitful than all else,
and desperately sick;
who can understand it?

Romans 7:21-25 Updated American Standard Version (UASV)

²¹ I find then the law in me that when I want to do right, that evil is present in me. ²² For I delight in the law of God according to the inner man, ²³ but I see a different law in my members, warring against the law of my mind and taking me captive in the law of sin which is in my members. ²⁴ Wretched man that I am! Who will deliver me from this body of death? ²⁵ Thanks be to God through Jesus Christ our Lord! So then, I myself serve the law of God with my mind, but with my flesh, I serve the law of sin.

1 Corinthians 9:27 Updated American Standard Version (UASV)

²⁷ but I discipline my body and make it my slave, so that, after I have preached to others, I myself will not be disqualified.

The **second greatest obstacle** is the **world of humankind that is alienated from God**. Its ruler, Satan, designs this world to cater to our fallen flesh. The spirit of this world comes from Satan himself, and if breathed in for too long, we will begin to adopt the same mindset, the same thinking, attitude, conduct, and speech that is opposite of Jehovah God. This poisonous air will paralyze us quite quickly if we entertain it either by thinking on it, or worse still, engaging in it. 1 Corinthians 2:11-16, LEB

1 Peter 4:3-4 Updated American Standard Version (UASV)

³ For the time that has passed *was* sufficient *to do what the Gentiles desire to do*, having lived in licentiousness, *evil* desires, drunkenness, carousing, drinking parties, and wanton idolatries, ⁴ with respect to which they are surprised *when* you do not run with *them* into the same flood of dissipation, *and so they* revile *you*.[191]

---

[191] "**4:3 lewdness . . . abominable idolatries**. Lewdness describes unbridled, unrestrained sin, an excessive indulgence in sensual pleasure. Revelries has the idea of an orgy. The Greek word was used in extrabiblical literature to refer to a band of drunken, wildly acting people, swaggering and staggering through public streets, wreaking havoc. Thus, the pleasures of the ungodly are described here from the perspective of God as despicable acts of wickedness. Though Peter's readers had indulged in such sins before salvation, they must never do so again. Sin in the believer is a burden which afflicts him rather than a pleasure which delights him.

4:4 they think it strange. One's former friends are surprised, offended, and resentful because of the Christian's lack of interest in ungodly pleasures. the same flood of dissipation.

The **third greatest obstacle** is **Satan the Devil and his demon army**. Yes, they are so powerful that one demon could kill hundreds of thousands of humans in very short order. That is why true Christians receive a hedge placed around them by God, protecting them from Satan and the demons. Yes, God's servants receive special protection from this powerful force. (Job 1-2) The only way to weaken that protection is to violate your conscience repeatedly, toy with demonic activities, like horror movies, rap and heavy metal music, games like the wigi-board or dungeons and dragons.

Our human imperfections and the world that caters to them is with us 24/7. True, we can get control over our vessel by putting on the new personality, gaining the mind of Christ, and the help of Holy Spirit. However, it does not take much to drift away, fall away, refuse, draw away, become sluggish, become hardened through deceptive powers, or shrink back from Christian responsibilities. We just need to entertain the wrong thoughts too long, without dismissing them, and then we are on our way. (James 1:14-15) Now, as far as Satan goes, Peter warns us in the extreme to, "Be sober; be on the alert. Your adversary the devil walks around like a roaring lion, looking for someone to devour." (1 Pet. 5:8) Paul also said that were to,

Ephesians 6:11-12 Updated American Standard Version (UASV)

[11] Put on the full armor of God, so that you will be able to stand firm against the schemes of the devil.[192] [12] For our struggle[193] is

---

Dissipation refers to the state of evil in which a person thinks about nothing else. The picture here is of a large crowd running together in a mad, wild race—a melee pursuing sin." – MacArthur, John (2005-05-09). The MacArthur Bible Commentary (Kindle Locations 64155-64162). Thomas Nelson. Kindle Edition.

[192] "**6:11 Put on the whole armor of God**. Put on conveys the idea of permanence, indicating that armor should be the Christian's sustained, life-long attire. Paul uses the common armor worn by Roman soldiers as the analogy for the believer's spiritual defense and affirms its necessity if one is to hold his position while under attack. **wiles**. This is the Greek word for schemes, carrying the idea of cleverness, crafty methods, cunning, and deception. Satan's schemes are propagated through the evil world system over which he rules, and are carried out by his demon hosts. Wiles is all-inclusive, encompassing every sin, immoral practice, false theology, false religion, and worldly enticement. See note on 2 Corinthians 2:11. **the devil**. Scripture refers to him as "the anointed cherub" (Ezek. 28:14), "the ruler of the demons" (Luke 11:15), "the god of this world" (2 Cor. 4:4), and "the prince of the power of the air" (2:2). Scripture depicts him opposing God's work (Zech. 3:1),

not against flesh and blood, but against the rulers, against the powers, against the world-rulers of this darkness, against the wicked spirit forces in the heavenly places.[194]

Threefold Assistance

There is a threefold defense against this threefold opposition to our walking with God. **First**, we have **the Word of God**, which should come in the way of literal translations, like the English Standard Version and New American Standard Bible. Jehovah God gave us this special revelation to guide us through this wicked time. It has the power to make us stronger spiritually, as well as fortify us to accomplish his will and purposes. The Bible should be read daily, in conjunction with our recommended Bible reading program.[195] We also need to use our Bible in all of our religious meetings. If a Scripture is being read, we need to look it up. We also need to use our Bible in our ministry, meaning that we need to formulate texts that can help us to teach others the good news of the Kingdom.

Deuteronomy 17:19 Updated American Standard Version (UASV)

[19] And it shall be with him, and he shall read in it all the days of his life, that he may learn to fear Jehovah his God by keeping all the words of this law and these statutes, and doing them,

---

perverting God's Word (Matt. 4:6), hindering God's servant (1 Thess. 2:18), obscuring the gospel (2 Cor. 4:4), snaring the righteous (1 Tim. 3:7), and holding the world in his power (1 John 5:19)." –MacArthur, John (2005-05-09). *The MacArthur Bible Commentary* (Kindle Locations 57495-57498). Thomas Nelson. Kindle Edition.

[193] Lit., "wrestling."

[194] "**6:12 wrestle.** A term used of hand-to-hand combat. Wrestling features trickery and deception, like Satan and his hosts when they attack. Coping with deceptive temptation requires truth and righteousness. The four designations describe the different strata and rankings of those demons and the evil supernatural empire in which they operate. Satan's forces of darkness are highly structured for the most destructive purposes. Cf. Colossians 2:15; 1 Peter 3:22. not . . . against flesh and blood. See 2 Corinthians 10:3–5. spiritual hosts of wickedness. This possibly refers to the most depraved abominations, including such things as extreme sexual perversions, occultism, and Satan worship. See note on Colossians 1:16. in the heavenly places. As in 1:3; 3:10, this refers to the entire realm of spiritual beings. – MacArthur, John (2005-05-09). *The MacArthur Bible Commentary* (Kindle Locations 57499-57505). Thomas Nelson. Kindle Edition.

[195] http://christianway.us/page/bible-reading-program

As we work our way through the Bible in our Bible reading program, let us not rush, but make sure we understand the author's intended meaning, and how we can apply that in our lives, as well as share it with others. We should be able to see our walking with God, come to life through the historical accounts found all throughout Scripture.

Joshua 1:7-8 Updated American Standard Version (UASV)

⁷ Only be strong and very courageous, being careful to do according to all the law that Moses my servant commanded you; do not turn from it to the right or to the left, so that you may have success wherever you go. ⁸ This Book of the Law shall not depart from your mouth, but you shall meditate on it day and night, so that you may be careful to do according to all that is written in it; for then you will make your way prosperous, and then you will have good success.

Below in Psalm 1:1-3, you will notice in verse 1 that there is a progression of intimacy through walking in the counsel of the wicked, to standing with sinners, to sitting with scoffers. Each level is a sign of spending more time with, being more deeply involved. We should not be involved with any of these three, because this would never be in harmony with a Christian, who is walking with God. Yes, verse 2 helps us to appreciate where our delight is found, the law of Jehovah, to which we read and study in a meditative way, day and night, which simply means on a regular basis. Truly, verse 3 helps us to appreciate the result of avoiding certain ones, and cultivating a love for God's Word, endurance and a strong spiritual health. If we follow the counsel of verses 1-2, we will be able to weather any storm that may come upon us.

The Way of the Righteous and the Wicked

Psalm 1:1-3 Updated American Standard Version (UASV)

1 Blessed is the man
who walks not in the counsel of the wicked,
nor stands in the way of sinners,
    nor sits in the seat of scoffers;
² but his delight is in the law of Jehovah,
    and on his law he meditates day and night.

³ He is like a tree
   planted by streams of water[196]
that yields its fruit in its season,
   and its leaf does not wither.
In all that he does, he prospers.

Second, along with God's Word, are some of the best **Bible study tools** as well as the **Christian congregation**. Paul tells the Ephesians, "Look carefully then how you walk, not as unwise but as wise, making the best use of the time, because the days are evil." (Eph. 5:15-16) Moreover, the Apostle Paul exhorted "let us consider how to stir up one another to love and good works, not neglecting to meet together, as is the habit of some, but encouraging one another, and all the more as you see the Day drawing near." (Heb. 10:24-25)

Third, we have **Holy Spirit**, which sustains us in these difficult days. We need to "Live by the Spirit and reject the deeds of the flesh." If we are to be victorious over our fallen flesh, or fallen imperfection, it will be by way of the Spirit. From our first step of entering the path of salvation, to the continuation of walking on that path of developing our new personality, and taking on the mind of Christ, that is sanctification, we are in need of the Holy Spirit.

Galatians 5:16-26 Updated American Standard Version (UASV)

¹⁶ ¹⁶ But I say, walk by the Spirit, and you will not carry out the desire of the flesh. ¹⁷ For the desires of the flesh are against the Spirit, and the desires of the Spirit are against the flesh, for these are opposed to each other, so that you may not do the things you want to do. ¹⁸ But if you are led by the Spirit, you are not under the law. ¹⁹ Now the works of the flesh are evident, which are: sexual immorality, impurity, sensuality, ²⁰ idolatry, sorcery, enmity, strife, jealousy, fits of anger, rivalries, dissensions, divisions, ²¹ envy, drunkenness, orgies, and things like these. I warn you, as I warned you before, that those who do such things will not inherit the

---

[196] "Here, David is referring to a tree that has been deliberately planted in a choice location; not something, that by chance, has sprung up just anywhere. Consideration and thought has gone into its planting. Such is the planning by God for the life of a Christian."—Bruce Prince.

kingdom of God. ²² But the fruit of the Spirit is love, joy, peace, patience, kindness, goodness, faithfulness, ²³ gentleness, self-control; against such things there is no law. ²⁴ And those who belong to Christ Jesus have crucified the flesh with its passions and desires.

²⁵ If we live by the Spirit, let us also walk by the Spirit. ²⁶ Let us not become conceited, provoking one another, envying one another.

Those who follow the flesh will reap the results of such a course by having unattractive fruits. On the other hand, those who follow the lead of the Spirit will have fruitage that is attractive and beneficial for themselves, family, congregation, friends, and neighbors. One thing that we have to realize by looking at other related texts is, these fruits are not the results of our efforts, are the consequence of having an active faith in Christ, which makes us receptive to them.

Godly Devotion

If we are to walk with God, we need to possess the most important ingredient, FAITH. "Now faith is the reality of what is hoped for, the proof of what is not seen." (Heb. 11:1, HCSB) "Now without faith it is impossible to please God, for the one who draws near to Him must believe that He exists and rewards those who seek Him." (Heb. 11:6, HCSB) However, before we can have the faith that we need to walk with God, we must ask, "Do two walk together unless they have met?" (Amos 3:3, LEB) Yes, if we are to truly going to get to walk with God, we must, "this is eternal life: that they may know You, the only true God, and the One You have sent, Jesus Christ." – John 17:3, HCSB.

The Value of Wisdom

Proverbs 2:1-6 Updated American Standard Version (UASV)

2 My son, if you receive my words
and treasure up my commandments with you,
² making your ear attentive to wisdom

and inclining your heart to discernment;[197]

³ For if you cry for discernment[198]

and raise your voice for understanding,

⁴ if you seek it like silver

and search for it as for hidden treasures,

⁵ then you will understand the fear of Jehovah

and find the knowledge of God.

⁶ For Jehovah gives wisdom;

from his mouth come knowledge and understanding;

> **2:1 my words**. Solomon has embraced God's law and made it his own by faith and obedience, as well as teaching. The wisdom of these words is available to those who, first of all, understand the rich value ("treasure") that wisdom possesses. Appropriating wisdom begins when a person values it above all else.[199]

Once we have studied to the point of coming to know God through knowledge, discernment, and understanding, we will begin to appreciate who he is, what he did for us, and after we had rebelled, what he did to save us. Moreover, after we have begun to live by the principles within his revelation to us, we will begin to love and appreciate him even more, as we see a life of chaos; become a life of order, blessing, and joy, even in this imperfect world. If we are truly to walk with God, we must be in harmony with his will and purposes. "Not everyone who says to me, 'Lord, Lord,' will enter the kingdom of heaven, but the one who does the will of my Father who is in heaven." (Matt 7:21, ESV) Exactly, what is the will and purpose of God? You might be thinking that it is to remove sin and death from his human creation, because of sending his Son, Jesus Christ to ransom those that are receptive to the Gospel. However, this is not the primary purpose of God; it is the vindication of the slanderous accusations made by Satan the Devil, made in the Garden of Eden, and in the book of Job. (Gen 3:1-6; Job 1-2) It is by means of his Son in the

---

[197] The Hebrew word rendered here as "discernment" (*tevunah*) is related to the word *binah*, translated "understanding." Both appear at Proverbs 2:3.

[198] See 2.2 ftn.

[199] MacArthur, John (2005-05-09). The MacArthur Bible Commentary (Kindle Locations 24768-24770). Thomas Nelson. Kindle Edition.

Kingdom of God that is to bring this about. The secondary purpose, which runs alongside is the vindication of his human creation.

Exodus 34:14 Updated American Standard Version (UASV)

[14] for you shall worship no other god, for Jehovah, whose name is Jealous, is a jealous God,[200]

Exodus 34:10-15. In order for God to work on Israel's behalf, she must scrupulously keep the terms of the covenant—observe the law of God. God would rout the enemies who occupied the land of Canaan—enemies whom Israel was not to make treaties with. Israel was to prove her faithfulness to Yahweh by obliterating any trace of foreign gods in her midst. The Lord, whose name is Jealous, demanded complete faithfulness of the Israelites.[201]

Mark 12:30 Updated American Standard Version (UASV)

[30] and you shall love the Lord your God with all your heart, and with all your soul, and with all your mind, and with all your strength.'[202]

Matthew 22:37 heart . . . soul . . . mind. Mark 12:30 adds "strength." The quote is from Deuteronomy 6:5, part of the shema (Heb. for "hear," Deut. 6:4). That verse says "heart . . . soul . . . strength." Some LXX manuscripts add "mind." The use of the various terms does not distinguish among human faculties but

---

[200] God is jealous for His people Israel in sense (1), that is, God is intolerant of rival gods (Exod. 20:5; 34:14; Deut. 4:24; 5:9) One expression of God's jealousy for Israel is God's protection of His people from enemies. Thus God's jealousy includes avenging Israel (Ezek. 36:6; 39:25; Nah. 1:2; Zech. 1:14; 8:2). Phinehas is described as jealous with God's jealousy (Num. 25:11, 13, sometimes translated zealous for God). Elijah is similarly characterized as jealous (or zealous) for God (1 Kings 19:10, 14). *Holman Illustrated Bible Dictionary*, ed. Chad Brand, Charles Draper, Archie England et al. (Nashville, TN: Holman Bible Publishers, 2003), 873.

[201] Anders, Max; Martin, Glen (2002-07-01). *Holman Old Testament Commentary - Exodus, Leviticus, Numbers* (p. 141). B&H Publishing. Kindle Edition.

[202] Quotation from Deuteronomy 6:4–5, which reads, "Hear, O Israel! Jehovah our God is one Jehovah! You shall love Jehovah your God with all your heart and with all your soul and with all your might."

underscores the completeness of the kind of love commanded.[203]

Matthew 6:33 Updated American Standard Version (UASV)

33 But be you seeking[204] the kingdom of God and his righteousness, and all these things will be added to you.

Have we grown so close to God that we understand the issues behind why we were allowed to enter into this period of sin and death, as opposed to just removing those that caused the rebellion, why he has allowed pain and suffering to continue for so long?[205] Are we willing to work toward the same purpose, the vindication of God's great name and reputation, to resolve the issues that were raised? If so, we will seek out what our role in the great commission is (Matt. 28:19-20), and we will carry it out with our whole heart, soul, mind and strength.

> **6:33 kingdom of God**. This phrase means the same as "the kingdom of heaven." See note on 3:2. It refers to the sphere of salvation. Jesus urges listeners to seek salvation—and with it would come the full care and provision of God. Cf. Romans 8:32; Philippians 4:19; 1 Peter 5:7.[206]

God's Case for Justice

If we are to walk with God, we have to be guided by his divine justice. He is holy, so we to must be holy, which means that like him, we separate ourselves from anything that would be at odds with his moral standards. In addition, while he is perfect in an absolute sense, we can do this by loving our enemies and praying for those who persecute us. Even though we are truly insignificant as we walk alongside the Creator of all things, we must be a

---

[203] MacArthur, John (2005-05-09). *The MacArthur Bible Commentary* (Kindle Locations 40258-40261). Thomas Nelson. Kindle Edition.

[204] Gr., *zeteite*; the verb form indicates continuous action.

[205] Why Has God Permitted Wickedness and Suffering:

http://www.christianpublishers.org/suffering-evil-why-god

[206] MacArthur, John (2005-05-09). *The MacArthur Bible Commentary* (Kindle Locations 39077-39079). Thomas Nelson. Kindle Edition.

dispenser of his brand of justice. – Micah 6:8; 1 Peter 1:16; Matthew 5:48.

We must love to do right,[207] but deplore the idea of ever doing what is bad, if we are to continue our walk with God. Satan's world has catered to the fleshly desires that lie within each of us for so long; it is not great thing for us to be tempted in a weak moment, and surrender. Therefore, our best recourse is to cultivate abhorrence for what is bad. Not one of us should ever believe that we are too strong, or that we might never stumble, because the Apostle Paul was not so bold to believe this about himself. – Isaiah 61:8; Psalm 45:7; 97:10; Romans 12:9; 1 Corinthians 9:27; 10:12.

Each of us is well aware of what our particular weakness is. The best defense against any such weakness is to identify it to ourselves outwardly in prayer, regularly. We need to understand how we fall short in this weakness, what is usually going on with us at the time we give in. We need to see if there are innocent-appearing situations that will put us in the line of fire. Once these are understood, we need to avoid them at all costs. If one is an alcoholic, it is all too clear that he would not take a job as a bartender, or rent an apartment above a bar. However, what about the convenient store where you pick up the newspaper, if it has a very large alcohol section. If our weakness has something to do with sex, we would not want to find ourselves in a compromising situation with the opposite sex, or the same sex if this is the tendency. If immoral thoughts enter our mind, they are to be immediately dismissed ("flee fornication"), followed by a prayer. We must self-talk to ourselves about the consequences, quashing all irrational thoughts. – Matthew 10:26; 2 Cor. 10:5; Isa. 52:11.

Love Kindness

If we are to walk with God, we must love kindness. The Hebrew word *checed*, is rendered "loving-kindness, steadfast love,

---

[207] "The Greek word "agape", which is generally translated into the all-rounder English word "love", means simply to seek the other's highest good. We can do this even for those who persecute us."—Bruce Prince.

grace, mercy, faithfulness, goodness, devotion." "This word is used 240 times in the Old Testament, and is especially frequent in the Psalter. The term is one of the most important in the vocabulary of Old Testament theology and ethics."[208] If it were not for God's loving kindness toward his creation, at the rebellion, we would not even be here having this conversation. The Psalmist says, "How precious is your steadfast love, O God! The children of mankind take refuge in the shadow of your wings." (Ps. 26:7) Jeremiah helps us to appreciate that 'in Jehovah God is salvation." (Lam. 3:22-23) And James, the half-brother of Jesus wrote, "the Lord is compassionate and merciful." – James 5:11.

The Apostle Paul gives us the fruitage of the Spirit, "**love**, joy, peace, patience, **kindness**, goodness, faithfulness, gentleness, [and] self-control." If we can take on the quality of Loving-kindness, we will be more sympathetic, empathetic, tolerant, thoughtful, tender and supportive of others, even enemies. When we enter into a difficulty with another, we will have the ability to identify with and understand their feelings or difficulties. Even though it may appear that Jehovah God is far removed from us and our circumstances, he is very much able to identify with our circumstances, especially since he sent his Son to walk in our shoes, so to speak.

Psalm 103:6-14 Updated American Standard Version (UASV)

⁶ Jehovah performs righteous deeds
and judgments for all who are oppressed.
⁷ He made known his ways to Moses,
his acts to the sons of Israel.
⁸ Jehovah is compassionate and gracious,
slow to anger and abounding in lovingkindness.
⁹ He will not always find fault,
nor will he keep his anger forever.
¹⁰ He does not deal with us according to our sins,
nor repaid us according to our iniquities.
¹¹ For as high as the heavens are above the earth,
So great is his lovingkindness toward those who fear him.

---

[208] W. E. Vine, Merrill F. Unger and William White, Jr., vol. 1, *Vine's Complete Expository Dictionary of Old and New Testament Words* (Nashville, TN: T. Nelson, 1996), 142.

¹² As far as the east is from the west,
  so far does he remove our transgressions from us.
¹³ As a father has compassion on his children,
  so Jehovah has compassion on those who fear him.
¹⁴ For he himself knows our formation;
  he remembers that we are dust.

Jesus Christ was the perfect example of an empathetic person. He chose to give up his position in heaven, to come down here and suffer with us, to walk with us, suffer a severe persecution, and a horrendous execution. Remember that Saul (Paul), prior to his conversion was persecuting the Christians and even played a part in the stoning of Stephen. The risen Christ came to Paul on the road to Damascus, as he was heading to arrest more Christians. Paul said to Jesus, "Who are you, Lord?" And he said, "I am Jesus, whom you are persecuting! (Acts 9:5) Jesus' statement means that he was putting himself in the place of those who were being persecuted. In other words, to be persecuting them, was the same as persecuting him.

Once Saul became a Christian, and started using his name Paul, we find him imitating Jesus empathic example. Paul too put himself in the circumstances of those to whom he witnessed.

1 Corinthians 9:19-23 Updated American Standard Version (UASV)

¹⁹ For though I am free from all men, I have made myself a slave to all, so that I may gain more. ²⁰ And so to the Jews I became as a Jew, that I might gain Jews; to those under the law I became as under the law, though I myself am not under the law, that I might gain those under the law. ²¹ To those without law I became as without law, although I am not without law toward God but under the law toward Christ, that I might gain those without law. ²² To the weak I became weak, that I might gain the weak. I have become all things to all men, that I might by all means save some. ²³ But I do all things for the sake of the gospel, that I may become a fellow partaker of it.

Walk Humbly With Your God

Imagine that the Creator of everything is willing to humble himself to walk with us. One would think that is a given (common sense) that, we would humble ourselves to walk with him. What exactly is involved in our humbling ourselves? It means that we are obedient to him as the sovereign of the universe. This should be the first thing we learn before we ever commit ourselves to him. If we are humble in our dealing, we will not be self-important. This means that a wife would recognize the headship of her husband, and that the congregation would recognize the authority of those taking the lead among them. Let us suppose that the wife of a household has better judgment than her husband has. It does not mean that she usurps his position, but then again, it does not mean that the husband is dismissive of her counsel. She can inform him, and he makes the decision based on that added knowledge.

Humility helps us to be submissive to those that have been given responsibility over us. The one with the responsibility could be a husband, a pastor in the congregation, or the superior authorities of the nation where we live. Everyone has someone who is over him or her but God. We need to keep in mind that our greatest goal is to make peace where there may be none, or to preserve peace. Another concern is our unity as a family or as a Christian congregation. Therefore, we must be wise in our dealings with others, considering much beside ourselves. If we have insight that can improve a family decision, or the congregation, it should be given at the appropriate time, and in the right way.

Certainly, if you have ever investigated the Bible a even a little, you know that the wisest course is to walk with God. However, if you have been at it for some time, you may have discovered that it is not always easy to do, when based on your human weaknesses, the wicked world that we live in, in addition to the influence of Satan and his demons. However, we know that it is not too difficult for God, who has given us his **(1)** Word, **(2)** study tools and the Christian congregation, as well as **(3)** the Holy Spirit. Then, he has opened himself up to hearing our every prayer that is in harmony with his will and purposes, giving us a chance to talk with him, especially in time of need.

Review Questions

- What does it mean to walk humbly with your God?

- What threefold resistance to we come across in our walk with our God?

- What threefold assistance do we have in our walk with our God

- What is Godly devotion?

- What do we mean by God's case for justice?

- What does it mean to love kindness?

- What does it mean to walk humbly with your God?

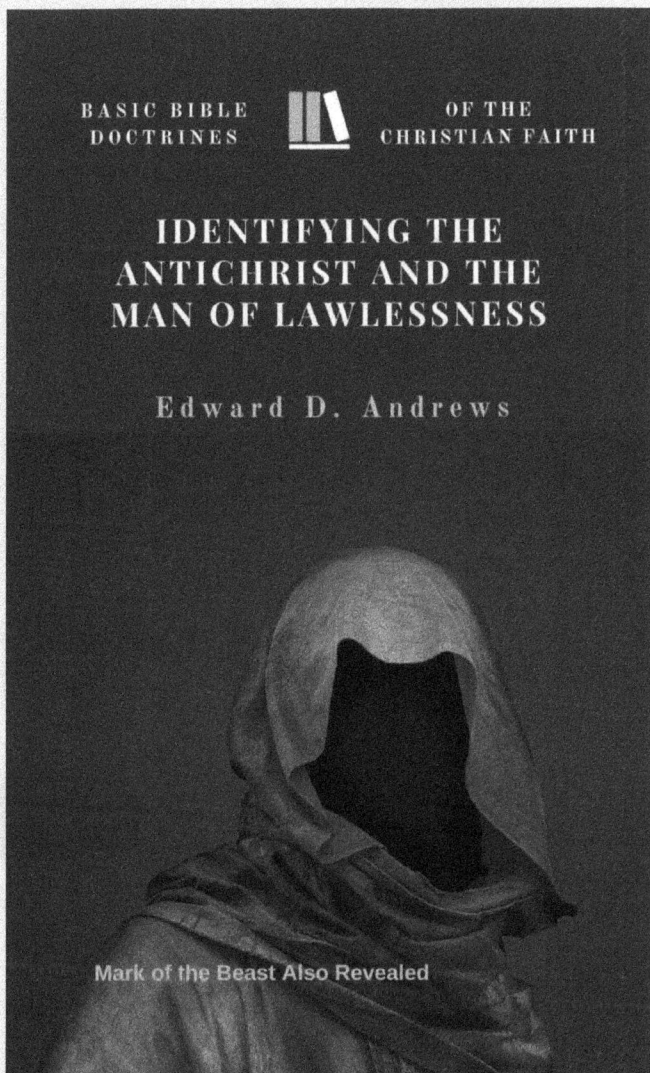

BASIC BIBLE DOCTRINES — OF THE CHRISTIAN FAITH

IDENTIFYING THE ANTICHRIST AND THE MAN OF LAWLESSNESS

Edward D. Andrews

Mark of the Beast Also Revealed

Christian Publishing House
ISBN-10: 0692614702
ISBN-13: 978-0692614709

http://www.christianpublishers.org/apps/webstore/products/show/5355019

BASIC BIBLE
DOCTRINES

OF THE
CHRISTIAN FAITH

WHERE ARE THE DEAD?

Edward D. Andrews

Christian Publishing House
ISBN-10: 0692611126
ISBN-13: 978-0692611128
http://www.christianpublishers.org/apps/webstore/products/show/5341545

BASIC BIBLE DOCTRINES — OF THE CHRISTIAN FAITH

EXPLAINING THE DOCTRINE OF MAN

Edward D. Andrews

Christian Publishing House
ISBN-13: 978-0692695098
ISBN-10: 0692695095
COMING by August 2016

BASIC BIBLE
DOCTRINES

OF THE
CHRISTIAN FAITH

WHAT IS HELL?

Edward D. Andrews

Christian Publishing House
ISBN-10: 0692610170
ISBN-13: 978-0692610176
http://www.christianpublishers.org/apps/webstore/products/show/5346167

BASIC BIBLE
DOCTRINES

OF THE
CHRISTIAN FAITH

EXPLAINING THE
HOLY SPIRIT

Edward D. Andrews

Christian Publishing House
ISBN-13: 978-0692616338
ISBN-10: 0692616330
http://www.christianpublishers.org/apps/webstore/products/sh
ow/6565103

BASIC BIBLE
DOCTRINES

OF THE
CHRISTIAN FAITH

EXPLAINING THE
DOCTRINE OF LAST THINGS

Edward D. Andrews

Christian Publishing House
ISBN-13: 978-0692669891
ISBN-10: 0692669892
http://www.christianpublishers.org/apps/webstore/products/show/6741906

BASIC BIBLE DOCTRINES

OF THE CHRISTIAN FAITH

EXPLAINING THE DOCTRINE OF SALVATION

Edward D. Andrews

Christian Publishing House
ISBN-13: 978-0692616338
ISBN-10: 0692616330
http://www.christianpublishers.org/apps/webstore/products/show/6601413

BASIC BIBLE
DOCTRINES

OF THE
CHRISTIAN FAITH

The SECOND
COMING of CHRIST

Edward D. Andrews

Christian Publishing House
ISBN-10: 0692611134
ISBN-13: 978-0692611135
http://www.christianpublishers.org/apps/webstore/products/show/5383701

BASIC BIBLE DOCTRINES — OF THE CHRISTIAN FAITH

UNDERSTANDING THE CREATION ACCOUNT

Edward D. Andrews

GENESIS 1-4

Christian Publishing House
ISBN-13: 978-0692657072
ISBN-10: 069265707X
http://www.christianpublishers.org/apps/webstore/products/show/6712205

Bibliography

Akin, Daniel L. *The New American Commentary: 1, 2, 3 John.* Nashville, TN: Broadman & Holman , 2001.

Akin, Daniel L., David P. Nelson, and Jr. Peter R. Schemm. *A Theology for the Church.* Nashville: B & H Publishing, 2007.

Aland, Kurt and Barbara. *The Text of the New Testament.* Grand Rapids: Eerdmans, 1987.

Alden, Robert L. *Job, The New American Commentary, vol. 11 .* Nashville: Broadman & Holman Publishers, 2001.

Anders, Max. *Holman New Testament Commentary: vol. 8, Galatians, Ephesians, Philippians, Colossians.* Nashville, TN: Broadman & Holman Publishers, 1999.

—. *Holman Old Testament Commentary - Proverbs .* Nashville: B&H Publishing, 2005.

Anders, Max, and Doug McIntosh. *Holman Old Testament Commentary - Deuteronomy.* Nashville: B&H Publishing, 2009.

Anders, Max, and Steven Lawson. *Holman Old Testament Commentary - Psalms: 11.* Grand Rapids: B&H Publishing, 2004.

Anders, Max, and Trent Butler. *Holman Old Testament Commentary: Isaiah.* Nashiville, TN: B&H Publishing, 2002.

Anderson, Neil T. *Discipleship Counseling: The Complete Guide to Helping Others: Walk in Freedon and Gow in Christ.* Ventura: Regal Books, 2003.

Andrews, Edward D. *BOOKS OF 2 JOHN 3 JOHN and JUDE CPH New Testament Commentary.* Cambridge: Christian Publishing House, 2013.

—. *FOR AS I THINK IN MY HEART—SO I AM: Combining Biblical Counseling with Cognitive Behavioral Therapy.* Cambridge: Christian Publishing House, 2013.

—. *PUT OFF THE OLD PERSON WITH ITS PRACTICES And Put On the New Person.* Cambridge: Christian Publishing House, 2014.

—. *The Text of the New Testament: A Beginner's Guide to New Testament Textual Criticism.* Cambridge, OH: Bible-Translation.Net Books, 2012.

Andrews, Stephen J, and Robert D Bergen. *Holman Old Testament Commentary: 1-2 Samuel.* Nashville: Broadman & Holman, 2009.

Archibald, Hunter, H. *Interpreting the Parables. London:SCM.* Philadephia: Westminster, 1980.

Arndt, William, Frederick W. Danker, and Walter Bauer. *A Greek-English Lexicon of the New Testament and Other Early Christian Literature. 3rd ed.* . Chicago: University of Chicago Press, 2000.

Arnold, Clinton E. *Zondervan Illustrated Bible Backgrounds Commentary Volume 2: John, Acts.* . Grand Rapids, MI: Zondervan, 2002.

—. *Zondervan Illustrated Bible Backgrounds Commentary Volume 3: Romans to Philemon.* Grand Rapids: Zondervan, 2002.

—. *Zondervan Illustrated Bible Backgrounds Commentary Volume 4: Hebrews to Revelation.* Grand Rapids, MI: Zondervan, 2002.

—. *Zondervan Illustrated Bible Backgrounds Commentary: Matthew, Mark, Luke, vol. 1.* Grand Rapids, MI: Zondervan, 2002.

Baer, Daniel. *The Unquenchable Fire.* Maitland, FL: Xulon Press, 2007.

Barclay, William. *The Letter to the Hebrews (New Daily Study Bible).* Louisville, KY: Westminster John Knox Press, 2002.

Barker, Kenneth L., and Waylon Bailey. *The New American Commentary: vol. 20, Micah, Nahum, Habakkuk, Zephaniah.* Nashville, TN: Broadman & Holman Publishers, 2001.

Barnett, Paul. *The Birth of Christianity: The First Twenty Years (After Jesus, Vol. 1)* . Grand Rapids, MI: Wm. B. Eerdmans , 2005.

Barry, John D., and Lazarus Wentz. *The Lexham Bible Dictionary.* Bellingham, WA: Logos Bible Software, 2012.

Benner, David G. *Strategic Pastoral Counseling: A Short-Term Structural Model.* Grand Rapids: Baker Academic, 1992, 2003.

Benner, David G., and Peter C Hill. *Baker Encyclopedia of Psychology and Counseling (Second Edition).* Grand Rapids: Baker Books, 1985, 1999.

Bercot, David W. *A Dictionary of Early Christian Beliefs.* Peabody: Hendrickson, 1998.

Bergen, Robert D. *The New American Commentary: 1-2 Samuel.* Nashville: Broadman & Holman, 1996.

Black, David Alan. *IT"S STILL GREEK TO ME: An Easy-to-Understand Guide t Intermediate Greek.* Grand Rapids: Baker Books, 1998.

Bland, Dave. *The College Press NIV Commentary: Proverbs, Ecclesiastes & Song of Songs,* . Joplin: College Press Pub. Co., 2002.

Blenkinsopp, Joseph. *Isaiah 56-66: A New Translation with Introduction and Commentary.* New York: Anchor Bible, 2003.

Blomberg, Craig. *The New American Commentary: Matthew.* Nashville, TN: Broadman & Holman Publishers, 1992.

Boa, Kenneth, and William Kruidenier. *Holman New Testament Commentary: Romans.* Nashville: Broadman & Holman, 2000.

—. *Holman New Testament Commentary: Romans, Vol. 6.* Nashville, TN: Broadman & Holman, 2000.

Boisen, Sean, Mark Keaton, Jeremy Thompson, and David Witthoff. *Bible Sense Lexicon.* Bellingham: Lexham Press, June 25, 2014.

Boles, Kenneth L. *The College Press NIV commentary: Galatians & Ephesians*. Joplin, MO: College Press, 1993.

Borchert, Gerald L. *The New American Commentary: John 1-11* . Nashville, TN: Broadman & Holman Publishers, 2001.

Borchert, Gerald L. *The New American Commentary vol. 25B, John 12–21*. Nashville: Broadman & Holman Publishers, 2002.

Boyd, Gregory A, and Paul R Eddy. *Across the Spectrum [Secon Edition]*. Grand Rapids: Baker Academic, 2002, 2009.

Brand, Chad, Charles Draper, and England Archie. *Holman Illustrated Bible Dictionary: Revised, Updated and Expanded*. Nashville, TN: Holman, 2003.

Bratcher, Robert G., and Howard Hatton. *A Handbook on the Revelation to John*. New York: United Bible Societies, 1993.

Breneman, Mervin. *The New American Commentary, vol. 10, Ezra, Nehemiah, Esther*. Nashville: Broadman & Holman Publishers, 1993.

Briley, Terry R. *The College Press NIV Commentary: Isaiah*. Joplin, MO: ollege Press Pub, 2000.

Brisco, Thomas V. *Holman Bible Atlas, Holman Reference*. Nashville, TN: Broadman & Holman Publishers, 1998.

Bromiley, Geoffrey W. *The International Standard Bible Encyclopedia (Vol. 1-4)*. Grand Rapids, MI: William B. Eerdmans Publishing Co., 1986.

Bromiley, Geoffry W., and Gerhard Friedrich. *Theological Dictionary of the New Testament, ed. Gerhard Kittel, vol. 4*. Grand Rapids, MI: Eerdmans, 1964-.

Brooks, James A. *The New American Commentary: Mark (Volume 23)*. Nashville: Broadman & Holman Publishers, 1992.

Bruce, F. F. *The New International Commentary on the New Testament: The Epistle to the Hebrews (Revised)*. Grand Rapids, MI: William B. Eermans Publishing Company, 1990.

Buter, Trent C. *Holman New Testament Commentary: Luke*. Nashville, TN: Broadman & Holman Publishers, 2000.

Butler, Trent C. *Holman New Testament Commentary: Luke.* Nashville, TN: Broadman & Holman Publishers, 2000.

Butler, Trent C. *Holman Old Testament Commentary - Hosea, Joel, Amos, Obadiah, Jonah, Micah* . Nashville: Broadman & Holman Publishers, 2005.

Caba, Tedl et al.,. *The Apologetics Study Bible: Real Questions, Straight Answers, Stronger Faith.* Nashville: Holman Bible Publishers, 2007.

Calloway, Brent A. *THE BOOK OF JAMES: CPH CHRISTIAN LIVING COMMENTARY.* Cambridge: Chriwstian Publishing House, 2015.

Carpenter, Eugene E., and Philip W Comfort. *The Holman Treasury of Key Bible Words: 200 Greek and 200 Hebrew Words Defined and Explained.* Nashville: Broadman & Holman Publishers, 2000.

Carson, D. A, and Douglas J Moo. *An Introduction to the New Testament.* Grand Rapids, MI: Zondervan, 2005.

Carson, D. A. *New Bible Commentary: 21st Century Edition. 4th ed.* Downers Grove: Inter-Varisity Press, 1994.

Clinton, Tim, and George Ohlschlager. *Competent Christian Counseling; Volume One: Foundations and Practice of Compassionate Soul Care.* Colorado Springs, CO: WaterBrook Press, 2008.

Cole, R. Dennis. *THE NEW AMERICAN COMMENTARY: Volume 3b Numbers.* Nashville: Broadman & Holman Publishers, 2000.

Comfort, Philip. *Encounterring the Manuscripts: An Introduction to New Testament Paleography and Textual Criticism.* Nashville: Broadman & Holman, 2005.

Comfort, Philip W. *New Testament Text and Translation Commentary.* Carol Stream: Tyndale House Publishers, 2008.

Comfort, Philip, and David Barret. *The Text of the Earliest New Testament Greek Manuscripts.* Wheaton: Tyndale House Publishers, 2001.

Cooper, Lamar Eugene. *The New American Commentary, Ezekiel, vol. 17.* Nashville, TN: Broadman & Holman Publishers, 1994.

Cooper, Rodney. *Holman New Testament Commentary: Mark.* Nashville: Broadman & Holman Publishers, 2000.

Cottrell, Peter, and Maxwell Turner. *Linguistics and Biblical Interpretation.* Downers Grove: InterVarsity Press, 1989.

Cruse, C. F. *Eusebius' Eccliatical History.* Peabody, MA: Hendrickson, 1998.

Davis, Christopher A. *THE COLLEGE PRESS NIV COMMENTARY: Revelation.* Joplin: College Press Publishing Co., 2000.

Dockery, David S, and George H. Guthrie. *The Holman Guide to Interpreting the Bible.* Nashville: Broadman & Holman Publishers, 2004.

Dockery, David S. *HOLMAN CONCISE BIBLE COMMENTARY Simple, straightforward commentary on every book of the Bible.* Nashville: Broadman & Holman, 1998.

Dockery, David S., and Trent C. Church, Christopher L. Butler. *Holman Bible Handbook .* Nashville, TN: Holman Bible Publishers, 1992.

Easley, Kendell H. *Holman New Testament Commentary, vol. 12, Revelation.* (Nashville, TN: Broadman & Holman Publishers, 1998.

Easton, M. G. *Easton's Bible Dictionary.* Oak Harbor, WA: Logos Research Systems, 1996, c1897.

Edwards, Tyron. *A Dictionary of Thoughts.* Detroit: F. B. Dickerson Company, 1908.

Ellingworth, Paul. *The Epistle to the Hebrews: A Commentary on the Greek Text.* Grand Rapids, MI: W.B. Eerdmans, 1993.

Elliott, Charles. *Delineation Of Roman Catholicism: Drawn From The Authentic And Acknowledged Standards Of the Church Of Rome, Volume II.* New York: George Lane, 1941.

Elwell, Walter A. *Baker Encyclopedia of the Bible.* Grand Rapids: Baker Book House, 1988.

—. *Evangelical Dictionary of Theology (Second Edition)*. Grand Rapids: Baker Academic, 2001.

Elwell, Walter A, and Philip Wesley Comfort. *Tyndale Bible Dictionary*. Wheaton, Ill: Tyndale House Publishers, 2001.

Enns, Paul P. *The Moody Handbook of Theology*. Chicago: Moody Press, 1997.

Erickson, Millard J. "Biblical Inerrancy: the last twenty-five years." *Journal of the Evangelical Theological Society*, 1982: 387-394.

—. *Introducing Christian Doctrine*. Grand Rapids: Baker Book House, 1992.

Erickson, Millard J. *The Concise Dictionary of Christian Theology*. Wheaton: Crossway Books, 2001.

Erickson, Milliard J. *Christian Theology (Third Edition)*. Grand Rapids, MI: Baker Academic, 2013.

Ferguson, Everett. *Backgrounds of Early Christianity*. Grand Rapids, MI: Wm. B. Eerdmans, 2003.

—. *Baptism in the Early Church: History, Theology, and Liturgy in the First Five Centuries* . Grand Rapids, MI: Eerdmans, 2009.

Freedman, David Noel, Allen C. Myers, and Astrid B. Beck. *Eerdmans Dictionary of the Bible* . Grand Rapids, Mich.: W.B. Eerdmans , 2000.

Friberg, Timothy, Barbara Friberg, and Neva F. Miller. *Analytical Lexicon of the Greek New Testament*. Grand Rapids: Baker Books, 2000.

—. *Analytical Lexicon of the Greek New Testament, Baker's Greek New Testament Library*. Grand Rapids, MI: Baker Books, 2000.

Galli, Mark, and Ted Olsen. *131 Christians Everyone Should Know* . Nashville, TN : Broadman & Holman Publishers, 2000.

Gangel, Kenneth O. *Holman New Testament Commentary: Acts*. Nashville, TN: Broadman & Holman Publishers, 1998.

Gangel, Kenneth O. *Holman New Testament Commentary, vol. 4, John* . Nashville, TN: Broadman & Holman Publishers, 2000.

—. *Holman Old Testament Commentary: Daniel.* Nashville: Broadman & Holman Publishers, 2001.

Garland, David E. *1 Corinthians, Baker Exegetical Commentary on the New Testament.* Grand Rapids, MI: : Baker Academic, 2003.

Garrett, Duane A. *Proverbs, Ecclesiastes, Song of Songs, The New American Commentary, vol. 14.* Nashville: Broadman & Holman Publishers, 1993.

—. *The New American Commentary: Vol. 14 (Proverbs, Ecclesiastes, Song of Songs).* Nashville: Broadman & Holman Publishers, 1993.

Geisler, Norman L. *Systematic Theology in One Volume.* Minneapolis, MN: Bethany House, 2011.

Geisler, Norman L, and William E Nix. *A General Introduction to the Bible.* Chicago: Moody Press, 1996.

George, Timothy. *The New American Commentary: Galatians* . Nashville, TN: Broadman & Holman Publishers, 2001.

Green, Joel B, Scot McKnight, and Howard Marshall. *Dictionary of Jesus and the Gospels.* Downers Grove, IL: InterVarsity Press, 1992.

Greenlee, J Harold. *Introduction to New Testament Textual Criticism.* Peabody: Hendrickson, 1995.

Grudem, Wayne. *Making Sense of the Bible: One of Seven Parts from Grudem's Systematic Theology (Making Sense of Series).* Grand Rapids: Zondervan, 2011.

Gruden, Wayne. *Are Miraculous Gifts for Today?: 4 Views (Counterpoints: Bible and Theology).* Grand Rapids: Zondervan, 2011.

Guralnik, David B. *Webster's New World Dictionary, 2d college ed.* New York, NY: Simon and Schuster, 1984.

Guthrie, Donald. *Introduction to the New Testament (Revised and Expanded)*. Downers Grove, IL: InterVarsity Press, 1990.

Guthrie, George H. *The NIV Application Commentary: Hebrews*. Grand Rapids, MI: Zondervan, 1998.

Harris, Robert Laird, Gleason Leonard Archer, and Bruce K Waltke. *Theological Wordbook of the Old Testament*. Chicago: Moody Press, 1999, c1980.

Hastings, James, John A Selbie, and John C Lambert. *A Dictionary of Christ and the Gospels*. New York, NY: Charles Scribner's Sons, 1907.

Hendriksen, William. *Baker New Testament Commentary: Matthew*. Grand Rapids: Baker Book House, 1973.

Hill, Jonathan. *Zondervan Handbook to the History of Christianity*. Oxford: Lion, 2006.

Hoerth, Alfred. *Archaeology and the Old Testament*. Grand Rapids: Baker, 1998.

Holmes, Michael W. *The Apostolic Fathers: Greek Texts and English Translations*. Grand Rapids: Baker Academics, 2007.

House, Paul R. *The New American Commentary: 2 Kings* . Nashville: Broadman & Holman Publishers, 2001.

Johnson, W. Ronald. *How Would They Hear if We Do Not Listen?* Nashville: Broadman & Holman Publishers, 1994.

Keener, Craig S. *The IVP Bible Background Commentary: New Testament*. Downer Groves, IL: InterVarsity Press, 1993.

Keil, Carl Friedrich, and Franz Delitzsch. *Commentary on the Old Testament*. Peabody, MA: Hendrickson, 2002.

Kistemaker, Simon J. *Baker New Testament Commentary: Hebrews*. Grand Rapids: Baker Books, 1984.

Kistemaker, Simon J, and Hendriksen William. *New Testament Commentary: Exposition of the Gospel According to Luke*. Grand Rapids: Baker Book House, 1953-2001.

Kistemaker, Simon J, and William Hendriksen. *New Testament Commentary: Exposition of Paul's Epistle to the Romans* . Grand Rapids, MI : Baker Book House , 1953-2001.

—. *New Testament Commentary: vol. 15, Exposition of Hebrews.* Grand Rapids: Baker Book House, 1953-2001.

—. *New Testament Commentary: vol. 19, Exposition of the Second Epistle to the Corinthians.* Grand Rapids, MI:: Baker Book House, 1953-2001.

Kistemaker, Simon J., and William Hendriksen. *Exposition of the First Epistle to the Corinthians, vol. 18, New Testament Commentary.* Grand Rapids, MI: Baker Book House, 1953–2001.

Kittel, Gerhard, Gerhard Friedrich, and Geoffrey William Bromiley. *Theological Dictionary of the New Testament.* Grand Rapids: Eerdmans, 1995, c1985.

Knight, George W. *The Layman's Bible Handbook.* Uhrichsville: Barbour Publishing, 2003.

Kollar, Charles Allen. *Solution-Focused Pastoral Counseling: An Effective Short-Term Approach for Getting People Back on Track.* Grand Rapids: Zondervan, 1997.

Lange, J. P. *Commentary of the Holy Scriptures: Revelation.* New York: Scribner's, 1872.

Larson, Knute. *Holman New Testament Commentary, vol. 9, I & II Thessalonians, I & II Timothy, Titus, Philemon.* Nashville, TN: Broadman & Holman Publishers, 2000.

Lea, Thomas D, and David Allen Black. *The New Testament: Its Background Message. 2d ed.* Nashville, TN: B & H Academic, 2003.

Lea, Thomas D. *Holman New Testament Commentary: Hebrews, James.* Nashville, TN: Broadman & Holman Publishers, 1999.

—. *Holman New Testament Commentary: Vol. 10, Hebrews, James.* Nashville, TN: Broadman & Holman Publishers, 1999.

Lea, Thomas D., and Hayne P. Griffin. *The New American Commentary, vol. 34, 1, 2 Timothy, Titus.* Nashville: Broadman & Holman Publishers, 1992.

Lightfoot, Neil R. *How We Got the Bible.* Grand Rapids, MI: Baker Books, 1963, 1988, 2003.

Lukaszewski, Albert L., Mark Dubis, and Ted J Blakley. *The Lexham Syntactic Greek New Testament.* Bellingham: Logos Bible Software, 2013.

MacArthur, John. *Counseling: How to Counsel Biblically.* Nashville, TN: Thomas Nelson, Inc., 2005.

Macarthur, John. *Fool's Gold: Discerning Truth in an Age of Error.* Wheaton: Crossway Books, 2005.

MacArthur, John. *Pastoral Ministry: How to Shepherd Biblically.* Nashville: Thomas Nelson, 2005.

—. *The MacArthur Bible Commentary.* Nashville: Thomas Nelson, 2005.

Marshall, Alfred. *THE NASB-NIV INTERLINEAR GREEK-ENGLISH NEW TESTAMENT.* Grand Rapids: Zondervan, 1993.

Martin, D Michael. *The New American Commentary 33 1, 2 Thessalonians .* Nashville, TN: Broadman & Holman, 2001, c1995 .

Martin, Glen S. *Holman Old Testament Commentary: Numbers.* Nashville: Broadman & Holman Publishers, 2002.

Mathews, K. A. *The New American Commentary vol. 1A, Genesis 1-11:26 .* Nashville: Broadman & Holman Publishers, 2001.

Matthews, K. A. *The New American Commentary Vol. 1B, Genesis 11:27-50:26.* Nashville: Broadman and Holman Publishers, 2001.

McMinn, Mark R. *Psychology, Theology, and Spirituality in Christian Counseling (AACC Library).* Carol Stream, IL: Tyndale House Publishers, 2010.

McRaney, William. *The Art of Personal Evangelism.* Nashville: Broadman & Holman, 2003.

Melick, Richard R. *The New American Commentary: Philippians, Colossians, Philemon, electronic ed., Logos Library System*. Nashville: Broadman & Holman Publishers, 2001.

—. *The New American Commentary: vol. 32, Philippians, Colissians, Philemon*. Nashville, TN : Broadman & Holman Publishers, 2001.

Metzger, Bruce M. *The Text of the New Testament: Its Transmission, Corruption, and Transmission*. New York: Oxford University Press, 1964, 1968, 1992.

Metzger, Bruce M. *A Textual Commentary on the Greek New Testament*. New York: United Bible Society, 1994.

Microsoft. *Encarta ® World English Dictionary*. Redmond: Microsoft Corporation, 1998-2010.

Miller, Stephen R. *The New American Commentary: Volume 18 Daniel*. Nashville: Broadman & Holman Publishers, 1994.

Mirriam-Webster, Inc. *Mirriam-Webster's Collegiate Dictionary. Eleventh Edition*. Springfield: Mirriam-Webster, Inc., 2003.

Morris, Leon. *The Gospel According to Matthew*. Grand Rapids, MI: Inter-Varsity Press, 1992.

—. *Tyndale New Testament Commentaries: Revelation*. Grand Rapids: William Eerdmans Publishing Company, 1987.

Mounce, Robert H. *Romans: The New American Commentary 27*. Nashville: Broadman & Holman, 2001, c1995.

Mounce, Robert H. *The New American Commentary: Vol. 27 Romans*. Nashville, TN: Broadman & Holman Publishers, 2001.

Mounce, Robert. *Robert Mounce, The New International Commentary of the New Testament: The Book of Revelation*. Grand Rapids: William Eerdmans Publishing Company, 1977.

Mounce, William D. *Mounce's Complete Expository Dictionary of Old & New Testament Words*. Grand Rapids, MI: Zondervan, 2006.

Mounce, William D. *Basics of Biblical Greek Grammar*. Grand
   Rapids: Zonervan, 2009.

Myers, Allen C. *The Eerdmans Bible Dictionary* . Grand Rapids,
   Mich: Eerdmans, 1987.

Niessen, Richard. "The virginity of the `almah in Isaiah 7:14."
   Bibliotheca Sacra 137 , 1980: 133-50.

Osborne, Grant R. *BAKER EXEGETICAL COMMENTARY ON THE
   NEW TESTAMET: REVELATION*. Grand Rapids, MI: Baker
   Academic, 2002.

Oswalt, John N. *The NIV Application Commentary: Isaiah*. Grand
   Rapids, MI: Zondervan, 2003.

Outlaw, W. Stanley. *The Book of Hebrews* . Nashville, TN: Randall
   House, 2005.

Pink, Arthur Walkington. *An Exposition of Hebrews*. Swengel, PA:
   Bible Truth Depot, 1954.

Polhill, John B. *The New American Commentary 26: Acts*.
   Nashville: Broadman & Holman Publishers, 2001.

Pratt Jr, Richard L. *Holman New Testament Commentary: I & II
   Corinthians, vol. 7*. Nashville: Broadman & Holman
   Publishers, 2000.

Ramsey, Boniface (Editor). *Manichean Debate (Works of Saint
   Augustine)*. New City Press: Hyde Park, 2006.

Richards, E. Randolph. *Paul And First-Century Letter Writing:
   Secretaries, Composition and Collection*. Downers Grove:
   InterVarsity Press, 2004.

Richardson, Kurt. *The New American Commentary Vol. 36 James*.
   Nashville: Broadman & Holman Publishers, 1997.

Roberts, Alexander, James Donaldson, and A. Cleveland Coxe.
   *THE ANTE-NICENE FATHERS 1: The Apostolic Fathers with
   Justin Martyr and Irenaeus*. Buffalo: The Christian Literature
   Company, 1885.

Robertson, A. T. *An Introduction to the Textual Criticism of the
   New Testament*. London: Hodder & Stoughton, 1925.

Robertson, Paul E. "Theology of the Healthy Church." *The Theological Educator: A Journal of Theology and Ministry*, Spring 1998: 45-52.

Robinson, Darrell W. *Total Church Life: How to be a First Century Chrurch*. Nashville, TN: Briadman and Holman, 1997.

Rooker, Mark F. *The New American Commentary, vol. 3A, Leviticus*. Nashville: Broadman & Holman Publishers, 2000.

—. *Holman Old Testament Commentary: Ezekiel*. Nashville: Broadman & Holman Publishers, 2005.

—. *Leviticus: The New American Commentary*. Nashville: Broadman & Holman, 2001.

Schreiner, Thomas R. *The New American Commentary: 1, 2 Peter, Jude*. Nashville: Broadman & Holman, 2003.

Scott, Julius J. Jr. *Jewish Backgrounds of the New Testament*. Grand Rapids, MI: Baker Academic, 1995.

Smith, Gary. *The New American Commentary: Isaiah 1-39, Vol. 15a*. Nashville, TN: B & H Publishing Group, 2007.

—. *The New American Commentary: Isaiah 40-66, Vol. 15b*. Nashville, TN: B&H Publishing, 2009.

Souter, Alexander. *The Text and Canon of the New Testament*. New York: Charles Scribner's Sons, 1913.

Sproul, R. C. *What Is Faith?* Lake Mary: Reformation Trust, 2010.

Stein, Robert H. *A Basic Guide to Interpreting the Bible: Playing by the Rules*. Grand Rapids: Baker Books, 1994.

—. *The New American Commentary: Luke*. Nashville, TN: Broadman & Holman , 2001, c1992.

Stott, John. *The Letters of John (Tyndale New Testament Commentaries)*. Downers Grove: IVP Academic, 2009.

Stuart, Douglas K. *The New American Commentary: An Exegetical Theological Exposition of Holy Scripture EXODUS*. Nashville: Broadman & Holman, 2006.

Swanson, James. *A Dictionary of Biblical Languages - Greek*. Washington: Logos Research Systems, 1997.

Swindoll, Charles R, and Roy B. Zuck. *Understanding Christian Theology.* Nashville, TN: Thomas Nelson Publishers, 2003.

Taylor, Richard A, and Ray E Clendenen. *The New American Commentary: Haggai, Malachi, , vol. 21A .* Nashville, TN: Broadman & Holman Publishers, 2007.

Terry, Milton S. *Biblical Hermeneutics: A Treatise on the Interpretation of the Old and New Testaments.* Grand Rapids: Zondervan, 1883.

Thomas, Robert L. *New American Standard Hebrew-Aramaic and Greek Dictionaries: Updated Edition.* Anaheim: Foundation Publications, Inc., 1998, 1981.

—. *Revelation 1-7: An Exegetical Commentary .* Chicago, IL: Moody Publishers, 1992.

Towns, Elmer L. *Concise Bible Dictrines: Clear, Simple, and Easy-to-Understand Explanations of Bible Doctrines.* Chattanooga: AMG Publishers, 2006.

—. *Theology for Today.* Belmont: Wadsworth Group, 2002.

Tuck, Robert. *A Handbook of Biblical Difficulties: Or Reasonable Solutions of Perplexing Things in Sacred Scriptures (Reprint).* New York: Bible House, 2012.

Vine, W E. *Vine's Expository Dictionary of Old and New Testament Words.* Nashville: Thomas Nelson, 1996.

Walls, David, and Max Anders. *Holman New Testament Commentary: I & II Peter, I, II & III John, Jude.* Nashville: Broadman & Holman Publishers, 1996.

Walton, John H. *Zondervan Illustrated Bible Backgrounds Commentary (Old Testament) Volume 1: Genesis, Exodus, Leviticus, Numbers, Deuteronomy.* Grand Rapids, MI: Zondervan, 2009.

Walton, John H. "Isaiah 7:14: what's in a name?" *Journal of the Evangelical Theological Society 30,* 1987: 289-306.

—. *Zondervan Illustrated Bible Backgrounds Commentary (Old Testament) Volume 3: 1 & 2 Kings, 1 & 2 Chronicles, Ezra, Nehemiah, Esthe.* Grand Rapids, MI: Zondervan, 2009.

—. *Zondervan Illustrated Bible Backgrounds Commentary (Old Testament) Volume 5: The Minor Prophets, Job, Psalms, Proverbs, Ecclesiastes, Song of Songs.* Grand Rapids, M: Zondervan, 2009.

Walvoord, John F. *Daniel: The Key to Prophetic Revelation.* Chicago, IL: Moody Publishers, 1971, reprint 1989.

Walvoord, John. *The Revelation of Jesus Christ.* Chicago: Moody Press, 1996.

Watson, Richard. *A Biblical and Theological Dictionary: Explanatory of the History, Manners and Customs of the Jews.* New York: Waugh and T. Mason, 1832.

Weatherly, Jon A. *THE COLLEGE PRESS NIV COMMENTARY: 1 & 2 Thessalonians.* Joplin: College Press Publishing Company, 1996.

Weber, Stuart K. *Holman New Testament Commentary, vol. 1, Matthew.* Nashville, TN: Broadman & Holman Publishers, 2000.

Wegner, Paul D. *A Student's Guide to Textual Criticism of the Bible: Its History Methods & Results.* Downers Grove: InterVarsity Press, 2006.

Westcott, B. F., and Hort F. J. A. *The New Testament in the Original Greek, Vol. 2: Introduction, Appendix.* London: Macmillan and Co., 1882.

Whiston, William. *The Works of Josephus.* Peabody, MA: Hendrickson, 1987.

Whitney, Donald S. *Spiritual Disciplines for the Christian Life with Bonus Content (Pilgrimage Growth Guide).* Colorado Springs, CO: Navpress, 1991.

Wilkins, Michael, and Craig A. Evans. *The Gospels and Acts (The Holman Apologetics Commentary on the Bible).* Nashville: B & H Publishing Group, 2013.

Wolf, Herbert M. "Solution to the Immanuel Prophecy in Isaiah 7:14-8:22." *Journal of Biblical Literature 91* , 1972: 449-56.

Wood, D R W. *New Bible Dictionary (Third Edition)*. Downers Grove: InterVarsity Press, 1996.

Wright, N. T. *Hebrews for Everyone*. London: Westminster John Knox Press, 2003.

Zodhiates, Spiros. *The Complete Word Study Dictionary: New Testament*. Chattanooga: AMG Publishers, 2000, c1992, c1993.

Zuck, Roy B. *Basic Bible Interpretation: A Prafctical Guide to Discovering Biblical Truth*. Colorado Springs: David C. Cook, 1991.

www.ingramcontent.com/pod-product-compliance
Lightning Source LLC
LaVergne TN
LVHW011346080426
835511LV00005B/149